Frontier Military Series
XXII

Tom Custer in civilian dress Circa. 1871.
Courtesy Little Bighorn National Monument.

Tom Custer

Ride to Glory

by
CARL F. DAY

THE ARTHUR H. CLARK COMPANY
Spokane, Washington
2002

Copyright 2002 by
CARL F. DAY

Arthur H. Clark Company
P.O. Box 14707
Spokane, WA 99214

LIBRARY OF CONGRESS CATALOG CARD NUMBER 2001042470
ISBN-0-87062-310-9

Library of Congress Cataloging-in-Publication Data

Day, Carl F.
    Tom Custer : ride to glory / by Carl F. Day.
        p. cm.— (Frontier military series ; 22)
    Includes bibliographical references and index.
    ISBN 0-87062-310-9 (alk. paper)
        1. Custer, Thomas Ward, 1845–1876. 2. United States. Army. Ohio Infantry Regiment,
    21st (1861–1865) 3. Ohio—History—Civil War, 1861–1865—Regimental histories. 4.
    United States—History—Civil War, 1861–1865—Regimental histories. 5. United
    States—History—Civil War, 1861–1865—Campaigns. 6. Soldiers—United
    States—Biography. 7. Brothers—United States—Biography. 8. Custer, George Arm-
    strong, 1839–1876. 9. Little Bighorn, Battle of the, Mont., 1876. I. Title. II. Series.

E525.5 21st .D39 2001
973.7'471—dc21
                                                                    2001042470

Contents

Illustrations

Maps

Acknowledgements

Many people contributed to the writing of this book, and it is necessary for me to thank them for their help, time, and infinite patience.

First and foremost I must thank my family. My wife, Jean, and my two sons, John and Nick. My wife's faith in me allowed me to quit work, go back to school, and get my degrees. Without her support I never would have written a single word. John and Nick wound up being dragged across the United States looking for little scraps of paper that would eventually become this book. I am sure there were many times when they wondered when this madness, and boredom, would end. To their amazement they got an education that few children actually get to have. They saw a book come together from beginning to end and all the miles in between —not to mention the endless parade of historical sights, many in the middle of absolute nowhere. It was hardly the delight of my nurse wife and two teenage boys. Thank you for humoring an old man.

I would like to thank my mother and father who sadly will never read this book. They did not finish the eighth grade, and I can say that I never saw them read a book in my entire life. But their lack of knowledge spurred them to make sure that I would read. They bought me countless books that opened up the world of history, one of which was a child's book on Custer. Little did they know . . .

I would also like to thank Reverend Raleigh Gordon who led me to my Savior, and taught me how to love books. In fact he probably planted the desire to in me to someday write my own. He also taught me the value of family—a lesson that it took me some time to learn, but that was my own fault.

My quest for knowledge brought me to the classroom of Professor Patrick Riddleberger of Southern Illinois University at Edwardsville. Dr. Riddleberger became not only my mentor, but one of the best friends I have ever had. His belief and encouragement made me work all the harder. I would never have finished school without his help, and I certainly would have never written this book. I have learned many things from my good friend, and I thank God that I was so blessed to meet him and have him in my life.

Father Vincent Heier of the Archdiocese of St. Louis was also very instrumental in my work, and my life. Father Heier made his vast library of Custer books available to me and introduced me to a multitude of people who also contributed to this work. He is my good friend and another person pivotal to the writing of this book.

Through Father Heier I was introduced to Joan Croy of Monroe, Michigan, who has always encouraged me and done a lot of foot work for me. What a great lady.

Professor Greg Urwin of Temple University provided me with a great deal of encouragement and numerous items from his research that I found invaluable in my work. One of my regrets in life is that I have never been able to be a student in his classroom.

I would also like to thank Gary Gilbert for his help in proofreading the facts of the manuscript. If any errors are present they are my fault, not Gary's. His knowledge of the people and time period is astounding.

Speaking of proofreading, I must also thank Maureen

Rund and Sharon Capps. Maureen was one of my students who could have a great career as an editor. Sharon takes the blame for hiring me into the Alton School District and now teaches next door to me. Both Maureen and Sharon took the time to read through my manuscript and point out my numerous errors. Thank you very much.

Thanks are also due to the staff of the Monroe County Library, Monroe County Historical Society, Harrison County Historical Society(Ohio), Little Big Horn National Battlefield, the Museum of the Confederacy in Richmond, Virginia, Appomattox Court House National Battlefield, Chris Calkins of Petersburg National Battlefield, and Stones River National Battlefield.

To those who I have accidentally overlooked, I apologize. I can only plead a poor memory. Thanks to everyone, and God bless you all.

Introduction

There are few names in American History so recognized as Custer. The fame, or infamy, of George Armstrong Custer is as hotly debated now as it was during his lifetime. His overwhelming notoriety all but overshadows everyone in his circle of family, friends, and enemies. One of those obscured by Custer's presence is his younger brother, Thomas Ward Custer. Tom Custer was a hero in his own right. He is the first man in our history to receive two Medals of Honor for heroism on the battlefield. And yet this is the first book to document his life.

Tom's story has been told in several magazine articles and he receives mention in any Custer biography worth salt. Yet he remains in the background—aloof, and deemed by many to be but a carbon copy of his more famous and flamboyant older brother. His story was not as well documented. Many of the articles that exist have the facts of his life in error. Even the government that he served to his death perpetuates falsehoods concerning his military service. The government citations noting his winning of the two medals are in error by maintaining the wrong dates of his actions. His tombstone at Fort Leavenworth cemetery lists the wrong units for his military service.

I can understand why no one has taken it upon themselves to write a proper biography of Tom. Finding the necessary information has taken me the better part of ten years and thousands of miles of driving. The search for Tom Custer became a quest. Every dead end became a challenge that dared me to continue. Did I find everything? I hope that I didn't. I know there are more things out there and maybe someday I'll discover them, or if not me, then someone else. The search for knowledge should never end.

What I found was a tale of great bravery. More than that I found a story of love and devotion. The life of Tom Custer is very much a family story, and that, for me, is the most intriguing. The interaction between the principal character is wonderful. In today's world of fractured families this narrative is a beacon of hope. Yes, the Custers played hard and loved hard, but their passion for each other and life in general is inspiring. Many of us could learn something from these people.

Tom was very much his own man. Yes, he did live in the shadow of his older brother, but that was a place with which he was quite comfortable. He was not jealous or envious of brother Armstrong, as Tom called him, except perhaps for his brother's relationship with his wife, Libbie. Much of Tom's life was spent trying to find a suitable companion, but sadly this never happened.

This is a story of love, honor, and devotion—qualities we desperately need today. This is the story of a man who went "above and beyond the call of duty."

CHAPTER ONE

"Where Am I To Sleep?"

For Captain Thomas Ward Custer, younger brother of flamboyant and controversial Lieutenant Colonel George Armstrong Custer, the malodorous scent of death was overpowering. Only an hour before, Tom and the other members of the attacking force made up of five companies of the United States Seventh Cavalry could smell victory in the air. Within the half hour, though, that sweet odor soured, and was transformed into an omnipresent stench which permeated their senses. The hope of victory disintegrated and, man by man, death reached out and savagely wrenched life away from each embattled trooper.

The oppressive heat and dust intensified the death throes of the hundreds of men and horses who battled on top of the sun swept hill in southeastern Montana Territory. The battle raised a dust cloud so thick that it coated soldiers and braves alike. It coated the trooper's hair and settled on their clothes. It became mixed with the beads of sweat which ran down their foreheads and into their eyes causing a painful momentary blindness which the soldiers tried to relieve by frantically rubbing their eyes. The dust collected in the mouths of all the combatants, exacerbating their already parched throats. The cool, clear water of the Little Big Horn River, only a few hundred yards away, might as well have been on the moon. To the men of the Seventh Cavalry, death was the only relief possible.

From his hilltop vantage point above the Little Big Horn, Tom surveyed the scene around him. No matter which direction he looked, all he could see were dead and dying troopers. He drifted in and out of consciousness, overcome by the heat and the pain of a broken arm.[1] The Indian warriors had completely routed the five companies of cavalrymen, and were in the process of annihilating them. Cries of the dying troopers and victorious braves filled the air. One by one, pockets of resisting soldiers were overrun by the determined Sioux and Cheyenne warriors. For Tom Custer, eternity was only a few breaths away.

Firing from the beleaguered troopers' position on the hilltop gradually died off, and the Indian braves rushed among the dead and dying to count coup. Suddenly, a "dead" trooper raised on one elbow, and glared at his tormentors. The braves shrank back from the soldier, whom they believed had returned from the dead. Tom Custer raised his revolver and tried to level it at his foes. A Lakota warrior, braver than the rest, rushed forward and tore the gun from Tom's hand. He placed the barrel against Tom's forehead and shot him through the head. Other warriors ran to him and struck his lifeless body with their coup sticks.[2]

In his last seconds of life, a million memories flooded Tom's mind. He remembered lying beside the creek that ran in front of his boyhood home in Wood County, Ohio. He dreamt of quenching his thirst with water from the well from his first home in New Rumley, Ohio. He saw his mother's face, and heard her comforting voice speaking to him. She reached out, and lovingly stroked his hair. She leaned over and blew out the candle beside him. Tom closed his eyes and went to his dreamless sleep.

---

[1]Hardorff, *The Custer Battle Casualties*, p. 23.
[2]Miller, *Custer's Fall*, p. 154.

On 15 March 1845, the United States of America was sixty-eight years old. A few days earlier, James K. Polk of Tennessee recited the oath of office and became the eleventh president of the growing republic. In Illinois, a young lawyer named Abraham Lincoln made preparations to run for the Congress of the United States. Congress found itself embroiled in border disputes with both Great Britain and Mexico—over the boundary of the Oregon Territory in the north, and the boundary between the Republic of Texas and Mexico in the south. Legislation had been introduced to admit Texas into the Union, and if granted, the probability of war with Mexico was very likely.

The presumption that the Divine Plan called for the United States to conquer the North American continent was all pervasive. Any talk of war, with either Great Britain or Mexico, met with an enthusiastic response from the public. The spirit of Manifest Destiny, a newly coined phrase, was, however, imbued with its own fatal flaw. Within fifteen years regional sectionalism, exacerbated by the belief in Manifest Destiny, would plunge the United States into a violent civil war.

On that March day in the village of New Rumley, Ohio, Emanuel and Maria Custer celebrated the birth of another child. The proud parents named him Thomas, after Maria's maternal grandfather. Tom's middle name, Ward, was Maria's maiden name.[3] Emanuel tenderly placed the newborn infant in the same crib that had held his elder brothers. One by one, the curious children silently crept into the room to gaze at their sleeping sibling.

The Custer family history has been recounted many times, most often inaccurately. Marguerite Merington erroneously traced the family origin to the Cusiters of the Orkney Islands, off the coast of Scotland.[4] Others have written that the first

---

[3]Bell, *Ancestry of Maria Ward Kirkpatrick Custer*.
[4]Merington, *The Custer Story*, p. 3.

Custer was a Hessian officer who elected to stay in America after the Revolution.[5] Another enduring myth says that Sarah Ball Custer, wife of Paul Custer, was the sister of Mary Ball Washington, mother of George Washington.[6]

The ancestors of Tom Custer came from Kaldenkirchen, Germany. The family name originated from the German word Kuster, which means "one in charge of the sacristy where the sacramental vessels and vestments are kept."[7] The name acquired its many subsequent variations because of regional dialects and inconsistent spellings.[8]

Paulus Kuster, the first Custer to immigrate to America, settled near Philadelphia, Pennsylvania.[9] Successive generations lived in eastern Pennsylvania until Paulus's great, great grandson John moved his family to Cresaptown, Maryland, a modest hamlet situated on the Potomac River. Tom's father, Emanuel, was born in that small village on 19 December 1806.

The lure of available land opening up in Ohio prompted Jacob Custer, Emanuel's uncle, to move to Harrison County, Ohio, in 1813. Jacob chose a ridge along the stage route from New Philadelphia to Steubenville as the location for his new home. Along with a surveyor, he laid out the plat of a town that he christened New Rumley, after an earlier settlement.[10] He built a modest house, and began work as the village blacksmith. In 1824, seventeen–year–old Emanuel relocated to New Rumley to work in his uncle's shop, where he became an accomplished blacksmith.[11] The work was strenuous, but very satisfying to young Emanuel, who enjoyed the forge, and the camaraderie of his uncle. Uncle Jacob, however, longed for a

---

[5]Whittaker, *Life of General George Armstrong Custer*, p. 3.
[6]Custer, *Custer Genealogies*, Appendix XXIII.
[7]Custer, "The Kusters and Doors of Kaldenkirchen, Germany, and Germantown, Pennsylvania," p. 24.
[8]Custer, *Custer Genealogies*, Appendix XXIII
[9]Ibid.   [10]Ibid., p. 1.
[11]Wallace, *Custer's Ohio Boyhood*, p. 5.

different lifestyle. One day he walked into the shop and announced to his nephew that he was quitting. Jacob explained that the life of a farmer appealed to him more. He turned his house and shop over to Emanuel and began his new life.[12]

Emanuel soon knew everyone in the small community, and he became known as a man who loved a practical joke, either upon himself or on anyone else. He matured into a man of firm convictions in both his politics and his religious beliefs. He was a fervent Jacksonian Democrat, as well as a founding member of the New Rumley Methodist Church.

The youthful blacksmith was also popular with the young women of New Rumley. Emanuel became especially good friends with Matilda Viers, the daughter of the local Justice of the Peace. Their friendship ripened into love, and they married on 7 August 1828. Their first child, a daughter named Hannah, was born in 1830, but she died shortly after birth. The following year saw the birth of a son named Brice. Two years later another son, John, was born to the happy couple. But tragedy again turned their happiness to sorrow as Matilda's health failed, and after a short illness, she died in 1835. Emanuel found himself with two small children to raise as well as a blacksmith shop to operate. The village of New Rumley now possessed within its boundaries a widower and a widow.

The widow was Maria Ward Kirkpatrick, the daughter of James Ward, the local tavern owner. Maria was born on 31 March 1807, near Burgettstown, Pennsylvania. The Ward family moved to New Rumley in 1816. The town was on the stage line and James Ward, sensing a good opportunity, opened up a part of his large, two-story home as a tavern.[13] Maria met Israel Kirkpatrick, and after a period of courtship, married him on 13 January 1823, a year before Emanuel Custer arrived in New Rumley. Maria bore three children:

---

[12]Ibid., p. 7.   [13]Ambrose, *Crazy Horse and Custer*, pp. 87–88.

David in 1823, Lydia Ann in 1826, and John in 1833. Maria's happiness was shattered when Israel fell ill and died in 1835.[14]

Frontier life was hard enough for a man and woman, but it could be brutal upon partial families. Emanuel and Maria sought each other out, not only because of their common sorrow, but through mutual necessity. After a while they found their feelings of sadness and words of consolation replaced by emotions and expressions of love. Emanuel and Maria married on 23 February 1836. Emanuel moved his children up the street to Maria's larger house, and they started their lives anew.

Their happiness was short–lived, however, as three-year-old John Custer became ill and died. Later that same year, Maria bore Emanuel a son, James, but he also died. Two years later another son, Samuel, died in infancy. The small graveyard behind the church rapidly filled with Emanuel and Maria's hopes and dreams.

Maria became pregnant again in 1839 and, on 5 December, she delivered a healthy baby boy they named George Armstrong. A fourth son, Nevin, was born in 1842. He was followed by Thomas Ward in 1845, Boston in 1848, and Margaret Emma in 1852. The family was so harmonious that "outsiders knew no difference between full or half brothers and sisters, and they themselves almost resented the question."[15] In later years, it required a conscious effort on the part of General Custer to remember, with accuracy, the exact parentage of his brothers and sisters.

Young Tom grew up in a house saturated with love and laughter. Mother Custer gathered her little ones about her and sang to them. Father Custer romped and played just as hard as any of the children. Father and children chased each other at top speed through the house and into the yard, yelling and screaming the whole time. They raced up and down the stairs

---

[14]Wallace, *Custer's Ohio Boyhood*, p. 6.   [15]Ibid., p. 9.

in riotous games of tag. At times the furniture suffered, but nothing ever detracted from the pursuit of the intended victim. Objects were strategically placed in the most unsuspecting places, to be encountered by both father and children.[16]

It was a war of love between the children and father, with Mother Custer standing by to make sure the games did not get too far out of hand. In later years, Maria said she was never as contented as when all of her family was gathered in at dusk. She reached out and caressed the little heads as they ran by her in the midst of their frolic.[17]

At night, the children slept in the half–attic of the house. Procuring and maintaining a spot in the communal bed was tenuous at best. One night, Tom found himself ejected from the bed by one of his sleeping siblings. The space that he had occupied quickly disappeared among the snoring inhabitants of the bed. Try as he might, he could not find a way back into the bed. Tired and dejected, Tom went to the top of the stairs and despondently cried out to his mother, "Where am I to sleep?"[18] This tale was told and retold with great relish by the family. Anytime in later years, if anyone was inadvertently overlooked, Tom's mournful exclamation was dutifully repeated by one and all.

In spite of Emanuel's joy at home, the day to day drudgery of the blacksmith shop caused him to begin to dream. Farming beckoned to him as it had to his Uncle Jacob. Emanuel secured title to the former Kirkpatrick homestead in 1848, and in 1849 he sold the property and purchased eighty acres of land a few miles from New Rumley.[19]

The move to the farm was a great change for the family. They exchanged their large, comfortable, two-story house for a simple log cabin. Only Emanuel and the older boys had

---

[16]Custer, *Tenting On The Plains*, p. 1.

[17]Monaghan, *Custer*, pp. 4–5.

[18]Elizabeth B. Custer, "A Beau Sabreur," p. 224.

[19]Custer, *The Custer Family*, p. 6.

Tom Custer in his early teens.
*Monroe County Historical
Commission.*

labored in the blacksmith shop, but on the farm everybody had
to work. Four-year-old Tom was too young to work around the
farm at first so he stayed near the house where Mother Custer
could watch him, and where he would be out of the way. He
attempted to help around the house by playing with baby
Boston, while Mother Custer cooked the family meals. When
not helping his mother, Tom played in the yard chasing the
chickens, and being chased by the rooster. He ran as fast as he
could and flung himself into the haystacks to hide, hoping to
scare anyone who ventured near. As he grew older, he joined
the older boys in their labors. All of the boys had chores to perform, according to their ages and abilities. Emanuel soon
learned that the boys would use any pretext to slow their work.
When working in the fields, Emanuel placed his malingering
sons at five yard intervals to insure the progress of their work.[20]

---

[20]Wallace, *Custer's Ohio Boyhood,* p. 49

From an early age, Tom admired his daring older brother George, called Autie by the family. Nothing frightened Autie, and he would meet any challenge. All of the Custers possessed a great love for horses, and Autie rode as soon as he could hold on. His favorite trick was to ride standing up on the horse's bare back. After a few falls, Tom also mastered his brother's equestrian abilities.[21]

In the fall of 1851, young Tom walked the mile and a half to Creal School, the local one–room school house. It occupied the top of a flat ridge near an apple orchard. Tom burst with excitement at the prospect of attending school with his older brothers. His enthusiasm, however, quickly faded away. The rigid discipline of the schoolmaster proved too much for the younger Custer. Tom became second only to Autie in the amount of mischief devised. In one activity, Tom even excelled his brother. As brother Nevin later recalled, "Tom was always gettin' licked."[22] Autie had a certain refinement that Tom lacked, and Tom paid the price on a regular basis for that shortcoming.

Tom completed his first year of school when Autie went to live with their half-sister, Lydia Ann, in Monroe, Michigan, in 1852. This was the first of several times that the boys were separated. Even though Tom and Autie spent considerable time apart, nothing could erase the bond between them. The summer passed slowly for Tom, and the farm work seemed more arduous with Autie absent. Seven-year-old Boston filled in as best he could, doing all of the smaller chores. The days and weeks passed, and the heat of summer gave way to the cool of autumn.

The end of harvest signaled the beginning of another school year. Tom's schooling continued at the same tempestuous pace that he had set the year before. Yet in spite of his rowdiness, Tom was well–liked by his classmates. While the older

[21]Custer, "General Custer as His Brother Remembers Him."
[22]Ibid.

boys occasionally bullied the younger boys, Tom was always their friend. In the fall he climbed the nearby apple trees, and shook down apples for the smaller children. He helped them get their coats on in the winter, and took them sledding on his homemade bobsled. He arranged them from the tallest to the shortest on his sled, then climbed in front to steer. Off they went down the steep incline to squeals of delight from the children. They flew at breakneck speed down the hill, ending up buried in a snow bank at the bottom. Such energetic play raised havoc with Tom's clothing, so he always kept a spare pair of trousers in his desk, to be worn over his good clothes to protect them from harm. But of all sports, Tom most excelled at a game called town ball, an early form of baseball, and his hitting prowess was the envy of all the other boys.[23]

Tom also succumbed to the usual schoolboy vices. He was particularly fond of tobacco, which he chewed constantly. His fondness for tobacco led to one of his more memorable beatings at school. The time from first bell to last seemed an eternity to the tobacco-loving Tom. After much thought, he arrived at a scheme which would enable him to satisfy his craving. The next morning, Tom left for school before the other boys and, upon arriving, set to work boring a hole in the floor under his desk. When school began, he kept his foot over the hole, and his face hidden behind a book so the teacher could not see him chewing his tobacco. When he needed to spit, he moved his foot and leaned over the hole. This continued for some time, but eventually the teacher became aware of what was going on, and Tom received the appropriate corporal punishment.[24]

Sometime later, the boys devised another prank, and when the schoolmaster left the classroom on a necessary errand, they quickly locked the door. The irate teacher

---

[23]Harrison, *The Story of the Dining Fork*, p. 304
[24]Ibid.

pounded on the door, but to no avail. No amount of pleading or threatening would move the Custer boys to open the door. The teacher tried to gain entrance through a window, but Tom was prepared for him. The teacher beat a hasty retreat when confronted by a shovel that Tom had been heating in the stove. At length, the teacher gained entry, and Tom received another application of the rod.[25]

Sometime later, Tom tried another variation of locking the teacher out of the classroom. Once again, the teacher left the room and Tom used one of the benches to bar the door. Tom anchored the bench against the door with a heated poker that he used to bore a hole into the floor. Tom then locked all of the windows, save one. He then lowered the children out of the window, and closed it. The children howled with delight as the schoolmaster attempted to gain access to his school. Fun was fun, and Tom eventually hoisted one of the boys back in through the window and reopened the school.[26]

Autie returned from sister Lydia's in early 1855, and the brothers resumed their camaraderie. In the evenings they hitched up the horse to the sled and rode into town to pick up their friends. They brought the crowd back to the Custer farmhouse, and enjoyed a great party. When the hour grew late, Tom and Autie hitched up the team and drove everyone home. Strangely enough the young girls always seemed to be the last ones delivered to their doorsteps.[27]

In 1857, Autie received an appointment to the United States Military Academy at West Point, New York. Tom watched in envy as Autie's train left the station. Tom returned to the farm dreaming of the day when he too would board a train and find adventure.

Tom eagerly anticipated Autie's letters home describing

---

[25]Ibid.
[26]Ibid.
[27]Ronsheim, *Life of General Custer,* appendix.

his new world. The family treated each new missive as a wondrous occurrence, scrutinizing every word. Tom relished Autie's recounting of his escapades at West Point. But Tom was bewildered when Autie wrote to sister Lydia complaining about Emanuel's apparent lack of parental concern about Tom's tobacco habit.[28]

Tom's immediate future held another surprise. Emanuel decided their meager farm was too small to give them anything but a subsistence level of income, and in the spring of 1860, the Custers moved to Wood County in the northwest corner of Ohio. Emanuel purchased forty acres of land along Tontogony Creek that adjoined forty acres owned by his stepson, David Kirkpatrick.[29] Here, Tom, his father, and his brothers toiled to make their living off of the land. Local tradition has it that the area of the farm was a favorite campground of the local Indians. Their oral tradition also told of a shooting star that fell from the sky, and landed on the site of the Custer farm.[30]

As the boys labored in the fields, Mother Custer thoughtfully gazed at them from the house. She later wrote:

> Many times I have thought there were things that my children needed [and] it caused me tears. Yet I consoled myself that I had done my best in making home comfortable. . . . I was not fortunate enough to have wealth to make home beautiful . . . so I tried to fill the empty spaces with little acts of kindness . . . It is sweet to toil for those we love.[31]

Father Custer viewed his offspring in a similar manner. He tried to teach them good Democratic politics, and instill within them his religious convictions. He spanked them as children, and scolded them as young men. Above all, he wanted his "boys to be foremost, soldiers of the Lord."[32]

---

[28]Merington, *The Custer Story,* p. 9

[29]Wallace, *Custer's Ohio Boyhood,* p. 54

[30]Private Collection, Bowling Green, Ohio.

[31]Merington, *The Custer Story,* p. 6

[32]Ibid., p. 4

CHAPTER TWO

The Civil War:
The Western Theater

On 4 March 1861, Abraham Lincoln recited the oath of office and became the 16th President of the United States. In the face of the Republican victory, the state houses of the South reverberated with angry voices, threatening secession. So bitter was the election that sectional dissension had torn the Democratic Party into two factions, each nominating a candidate. Lincoln, the Republican candidate, had been so undesirable to the South that his name had not even appeared on the ballot in those states. Within a few weeks of the election South Carolina voted for secession, and by Inauguration Day six other states seceded, with others threatening to follow.

Emanuel Custer lectured his boys while they planted their crops that stormy spring. He knew in his heart that if the Democrats had held together, instead of fragmenting into factions, the election might have been much different. Tom and his brothers listened, masking their smiles, as their father's discourses went on and on. The boys often used their father's fervor for politics to avoid work. Any query or remark from the cunning youngsters would bring on a political diatribe which would carry on throughout their work time.

Simultaneously, hundreds of miles to the east along the Hudson River, brother Autie, whom Tom now referred to as

Armstrong, found himself consumed by the crisis. His letters home held the family captivated as Emanuel read them aloud. "I fear that there will be much trouble. Several of the Southern states and perhaps all of them will withdraw from the Union in a few days, and it is probable that war will be the result."[1] The probability of hostilities brought somber meditation upon the family. Tom grew envious of Armstrong, who would surely become involved if the crisis erupted into violence.

The next few weeks passed in hushed apprehension while the spring planting continued. At night the family assembled and Emanuel read to them from the newspapers, which reported the seizure of several Federal forts in the South by troops of the newly formed Confederate States of America. Fort Sumter in Charleston harbor, South Carolina, seemed of singular importance as the newspapers speculated about its ability to forestall its capture. For the next few days the eyes of the nation rested upon that solitary structure. In the early morning hours of 12 April 1861, Confederate artillery opened fire upon the fort, and the Civil War began.

"The excitement here is intense, we can scarcely study."[2] Tom excitedly read these words of Armstrong's latest letter home. Tom had been anticipating his older brother's imminent visit, but events now made that visit impossible.[3] After reading the letter the boys mentioned the Presidential proclamation calling for troops to put down the rebellion. Tom and Nevin pointed out that a regiment, the Twenty-first Ohio Volunteer Infantry, was being recruited and enrolling men for three months service. But in spite of the fact that many of their friends and neighbors were volunteering for military service, the Custer boys showed no such

---

[1] Letter, George A. Custer to Lydia Reed, 10 November 1860 Elizabeth B. Custer Collection (Hereafter E.B.C. Collection.) Little Big Horn National Battlefield.
[2] Letter, George A. Custer to Lydia Reed, 26 April 1861. E.B.C. Collection.
[3] Letter, George A. Custer to Lydia Reed, 31 May 1861. E.B.C. Collection.

inclination.[4] The regiment formed and went away with hopes for a swift victory.

On 21 July 1861 the first major land battle of the Civil War exploded at a sleepy village called Manassas Junction, Virginia. Armstrong had joined the Federal army only a few days earlier as a second lieutenant of cavalry, just in time to witness the rout of the Federal army. His role that day was one of a spectator, as he observed the rout of the Federal troops. A few weeks later another Federal force was defeated at Wilson's Creek, Missouri. These early defeats did not weaken the North's determination, nor did it bring about the political solutions sought by the South. Instead, these battles reaffirmed the gloomy predictions that the war would be long and bloody.

The initial hesitation that the Custer boys had shown about the war dissipated after the Federal reversals in the summer of 1861. The boys began to harass their parents daily in the hopes of their being permitted to enlist. Tom had no strong feelings about slavery or patriotism. He knew that, like the other boys, he loathed farming with its infinite days of tedious labor. He did not know much about the army, but he did know that it promised excitement and adventure. In the metaphor of the time, he longed to "see the elephant." It was a way for a boy to demonstrate his personal bravery, and by doing so become a man.

At first Emanuel and Maria protested against any more of their sons enlisting in the Union army. They pointed out that Autie was already representing the family, and one son was enough. Their logic, however, made no impact upon the boys, who assailed them all the more. Eventually, Emanuel and Maria succumbed and said one of the boys could enlist. Tom, Nevin, and Boston then fell to quarreling with each other over who would go. Father Custer settled the argument by

---

[4] Custer, "His Brother Remembers Him."

announcing that since Tom and Boston were underage, and could not join, Nevin would be the one to volunteer. They grudgingly accepted their parent's decision, and Nevin cheerfully rode to town and enlisted. A few days later Nevin left with his regiment to report to the state camp at Columbus.

Less than a week later, however, Tom and Boston looked up from their work in the fields to see Nevin sauntering up the lane toward the house. The boys stopped their chores and dashed to the house. Seated at the dinner table, Nevin angrily related to the family how at camp near Columbus an attack of rheumatism caused his discharge from the army. Nevin's rage spread to Tom and Boston, and the three brothers vented their anger against, "the whole United States; North, South and in between."[5]

Later, Tom and Boston realized that with Nevin home it might now be feasible for one of them to join the army. The two of them began again the daily barrage of verbal assaults upon their parents. Emanuel repeatedly pointed out to the two boys they were not old enough to enlist—with Tom being only sixteen and Boston a youth of thirteen. The boys' ceaseless arguments eventually broke down Emanuel's and Maria's defenses and they finally gave Tom their permission.

Emanuel informed his son of the location of the nearest recruiting officer, and Tom saddled the horse and raced down the dusty road to offer himself for military service. The enlistment officer scrutinized the young man before him and asked his name and age. Tom dutifully gave his name and stated his age as eighteen years. The soldier shuffled a few papers and looked up sternly at the applicant. The recruiter announced that he had it on good authority that Tom was only sixteen years old. The officer counseled Tom to go home and come back in two years, if the war was still going on.

Tom returned home in a fury. He angrily recounted the

---

[5]Ibid.

events of the morning to the family. He raved on and on, incensed at his misfortune. Emanuel kept silent during Tom's harangue; a smile ever widening upon his face. Finally, he could not contain himself any longer and exposed his culpability as the informer.[6]

The truth did not alleviate Tom's outrage, or his embarrassment. The hapless parents once again were exposed to daily assaults by their offspring. Not many days passed before they again gave Tom their permission to enlist. Father Custer assured Tom he would not interfere this time. On Monday morning 2 September 1861, Tom rode the few miles to Gilead, Ohio, to enroll. He presented himself to Captain Caton of the Twenty-first Ohio Volunteer Infantry.[7] Tom filled out the enlistment paper stating he was 5'7" tall, with blue eyes and sandy colored hair. He listed his age as eighteen.[8] This time no one questioned him, and he completed his enlistment papers.

Tom returned home that evening and announced to the family he was now Private Custer, Company H of the Twenty-first Ohio Volunteer Infantry. Nevin sneered and informed his younger brother he too would find himself sent home, as soon as the truth about his age came out.[9]

On Thursday, 19 September 1861, the Twenty-first Ohio Volunteer Infantry was formally inducted into the Federal army at Findlay, Ohio. Captain E. Morgan Wood of the Fifteenth United States Infantry officiated at the ceremony. The need for men was so acute that no medical exams were conducted. The men received their uniforms, and were offered advances for more clothing, which some happily took, but Tom, needing no such allowance, refused.[10]

---

[6]Custer, "A Beau Sabreur," p. 224.
[7]Captain S.S. Canfield, *History of the 21st Regiment Ohio Volunteer Infantry*, p. 10.
[8]Thomas Ward Custer Military Service Records, National Archives, Washington, D.C. (Hereafter TWC Service Records, N.A.)
[9]Custer, "His Brother Remembers Him.
[10]Muster Roll of the 21st Ohio Volunteer Infantry.

Tom and the rest of the Tontogony boys bivouacked for the next few days at Camp Vance near Findlay. They finally left camp and boarded a train for Camp Dennison near Cincinnati. The old engine raced along at about three or four miles per hour. To amuse themselves the boisterous boys took turns running alongside the engine. At Cory, Tom and the rest boarded another train which went considerably faster. The train carried the boys across the Ohio countryside passing fields and towns where happy citizens lined the tracks waving and shouting words of encouragement.[11]

At Camp Dennison the Twenty-first were issued arms and equipment, Army life began in earnest. Reveille was at 6 A.M., followed by several hours of company drill. The regiment broke for lunch at noon, and repeated several more hours of drill in the afternoon. The regiment staged a dress parade at 4:30 P.M. followed by supper at 6 P.M. The day ended at 8:30 P.M., when the bugler sounded Tattoo.[12]

At night, Tom slept in a Sibley tent, a large cone shaped shelter, opened at the top, which could hold from twelve to twenty men. The men slept in a circular fashion with their feet at the center. A Massachusetts soldier later wrote that to enter such a tent and "encounter the night's accumulation of nauseating exhalations from the bodies of twelve men was an experience no soldier has ever been known to recall with great enthusiasm."[13]

Tom soon discovered, in spite of the busy routine, camp life could become tedious. Tom and the others soon found diversions to break the boredom. To a young boy away from his family for the first time, temptation sometimes became too great. Already an avowed tobacco user, Tom found the newer distractions also appealing. Alcohol, a curse to both

[11]Letter, Liberty Warner to My dear ones at home, Mid-October 1861. Liberty Warner Papers, Center for Archival Collections, Bowling Green University, Bowling Green, Ohio.

[12]Canfield, *History of the 21st Ohio*, p. 11.   [13]Robertson, *Tenting Tonight*, p. 28.

TWC shortly after joining his brother's command in Virginia. *Courtesy Little Bighorn Battlefield National Monument.*

armies, became a new pleasure for Tom. The monotony of camp life was also alleviated by card playing and gambling, for which Tom acquired a weakness he never outgrew.

There were also other diversions to occupy Tom's day. The camp was inundated with local people trying to separate the young men from their money. Vendors of every size and description invaded the camps daily selling wares of every type. Most popular were the pie vendors who found themselves the targets of a the mischievous natures of the young recruits. Stealing pies quickly became a most delectable past time for Tom and the other boys.[14]

The days of inactivity came to a close when Tom and the

[14]Letter, Liberty Warner to My dear ones at home, Mid October 1861. Liberty Warner Papers, Center for Archival Collections, Bowling Green University, Bowling Green, Ohio.

Twenty-first joined other regiments and moved into Kentucky on 2 October 1861. Kentucky, one of four slave-holding border states, proclaimed itself neutral. The Governor rejected calls for troops from both the Federal and Confederate Governments. Sectional sentiments, however, ran deep throughout the state, and the promise of neutrality was, at length, impossible. Confederate forces moved into Kentucky in early September, and Kentucky's pro-Union legislature asked for Federal troops to help repel the invaders.

Kentucky was critical to the Union's strategy. The possibility of the interruption of trade and the threat of invasion made control of Kentucky paramount to both North and South. Kentucky bordered those states that made up the heartland of the Union. If the Confederates could control Kentucky they could launch raids or major invasions into Illinois, Indiana, or Ohio. They could also interfere with trade from east to west, for whoever governed Kentucky controlled the Ohio River.

The regiment marched southeast from Lexington, passing through the rich farmlands of the Blue Grass country. On the roads Tom saw scores of slaves whose owners had run away as the Federal troops approached. The slaves were delirious with joy at their apparent liberation.[15] The regiment proceeded to Hazel Green, Kentucky, where the troops were attacked by a new antagonist. Tom and many others of the regiment found themselves stricken with diarrhea. Another problem arose from the growing numbers of pistols which led to numerous accidental shootings. The commander of the regiment, Lieutenant Colonel James Neibling, eventually ordered all pistols confiscated.[16]

While in camp, Tom and the other men received their new tents. Tom shared his tent with Ike Valkenberg, and the two boys quickly set it up and dug a small moat around it to

---

[15]Canfield, *History of the 21st Ohio*, p. 12.
[16]Ibid., p. 22.

divert whatever rain water that might come their way. Tom and Ike covered their floor with fresh straw, stoked up their small stove, and laid back to enjoy the peace of their new home. They feasted upon hard tack, pickled pork, coffee, rice, and occasionally potatoes.[17]

A few days later at Ivy Mountain, Kentucky, Tom experienced his first combat. Confederate troops held positions on the slopes of a hill, blocking the Union advance. The Twenty-first moved into position in the rear of the rebels and charged, forcing the confederates to withdraw. The regiment led the pursuit of the retreating Confederates who fled through Pound Gap into Virginia.

For the next few weeks, the regiment marched across eastern Kentucky. From Ivy Mountain the men advanced to the village of Piketon, where they remained until 16 November, replenishing their supplies. With their provisions restored, the regiment marched east to Prestonburgh. From there they advanced northward to Louisa, on the western border with Virginia. Tom soon learned it was prudent to carry only those articles that were absolutely necessary. He tolerated the marching and counter-marching well, as did most of the men. There was one, however, who could not endure, and during this march the regiment experienced its first self-inflicted casualty. A private, who could take no more, calmly dropped out of the line of march and shot himself in the head.[18] They buried their unfortunate comrade, and continued their march from Louisa to Catlettsburg on the Ohio River. Here they boarded steam boats and proceeded down river to Louisville.

After arriving in Louisville, Tom's regiment settled back into camp life, and daily drilling resumed. Camp life also brought a second attack of sickness when almost one quarter

---

[17]Letter, Liberty Warner to Dear Brother, January 10, 1862. Liberty Warner Papers, Center for Archival Collections, Bowling Green University, Bowling Green, Ohio.
[18]Ibid., p. 29.

of the men fell ill with the measles. A change in divisional command at this time brought the regiment under Brigadier General Don Carlos Buell.[19]

The day to day tedium of winter camp life at Louisville ended in mid-February 1862, with news of the fall of forts Henry and Donelson in western Tennessee to the Federal forces under Brigadier General Ulysses S. Grant. Tom and his companions broke camp, and made ready to join in the invasion of Tennessee. Experiencing little opposition, the regiment entered Nashville on 22 February. Two weeks later the regiment went into camp at Shelbyville, Tennessee. Tom and the others experienced an enthusiastic reception when they entered the town. Union sentiment ran very deep and the population turned out in force to welcome them. Tom found the town festooned with flags and the populace cheering wildly.

Their time in camp was brief, and they were soon back on the march. The Twenty-first joined other regiments and advanced into Alabama. After a march of twenty miles in two days, they were within twenty-five miles of Huntsville. While in camp outside Fayette, the regiment learned of the bloody battle of Shiloh. The regiment continued their advance and finally reached Huntsville on 11 April to find the town already occupied by Federal troops.

While northern Alabama and Georgia were only lightly defended by Confederate forces, much resistance was encountered from the local populace. Partisan guerrillas, aided by loyal Confederate citizens, began a campaign of terror against the Federal troops. Snipers were everywhere, and Union stragglers found themselves in constant peril. Repeated warnings against acts of terrorism produced no positive results. The violence escalated to new heights when Colonel John Turchin of the Nineteenth Illinois Infantry turned his men loose upon the town of Athens, Georgia.

---

[19]Ibid., p. 35.

Colonel Turchin closed his eyes while his men raped and pillaged for an hour.[20]

A few days later, on 23 April, Tom's unit received orders to escort Confederate prisoners north to Columbia, Tennessee. The Confederates had at first been distrustful of their Union captors. They had been anticipating all manner of abuse and mistreatment during their captivity. To their great relief they found that Tom and the men of Company H were sympathetic to their misfortunes. Tom and the rest did all they could to ease the fears of their prisoners and make their captivity as tolerable as possible. When they reached Columbia, both sides expressed the hope they would all meet again under better circumstances, in a country at peace.[21]

With their mission completed, Tom's company returned to regimental headquarters at Nashville. The regiment, now under the divisional command of Brigadier General James Negley, spent the summer marching and counter-marching throughout central Tennessee. While in camp at Shelbyville, men from the Second, Twenty-first, and Thirty-third Ohio Infantry volunteered to go behind Confederate lines, capture a locomotive, and move north, destroying as many bridges and as much rail road track as possible. Unfortunately, the Confederates reacted much quicker than anticipated, capturing many of the raiders.

A new strategic situation developed in September, leaving Nashville behind enemy lines. Confederate General Braxton Bragg moved his forces into Tennessee, and by late September, advanced his soldiers into central Kentucky. Bragg had hoped to capitalize on anti-Union sentiment in Kentucky and bring the state into the Confederate fold. He launched a two pronged advance with himself and General Edmund Kirby Smith in command of two armies. The Confederates moved rapidly through Tennessee into central Kentucky. Smith's

---

[20]Street, *The Struggle for Tennessee*, p. 14.   [21]Canfield, *History of the 21st Ohio*, p. 47.

army captured Lexington and the state capital of Frankfort. Believing Kentucky in their grasp, Bragg and Smith installed a new pro-Confederate legislature and governor.

Hard on their heels came Major General Buell and his Army of the Ohio. Buell had received a terse note from President Lincoln referring to his apparent lack of speed and determination in chasing his adversary. Buell moved his men into Kentucky, and was able to disrupt the inauguration of the new governor. Union artillery rained shells upon the proceedings which were, by necessity, abruptly halted.

Buell's attack on Frankfort was a diversion intending to confuse the Confederate high command. The bait was swallowed and Bragg split his command into two wings. Kirby Smith's army, augmented with one division from Bragg's army, moved to meet the Federals threatening Frankfort. Bragg, with the rest of the army, moved toward Perryville where, unknown to him, the bulk of Buell's army was waiting.

The Federal garrison at Nashville, now many miles behind enemy lines, was cut off from the rest of the Union forces for almost eight weeks. During this time foraging parties scoured the countryside for food and provisions.[22] On 17 November Federal troops returned and relieved the beleaguered garrison.

Bragg's army, defeated at the battle of Perryville, Kentucky, on 8 October, fell back into central Tennessee and took up positions around Murfreesboro. While at Murfreesboro the fierce acrimony viewing between Bragg and his generals erupted. The situation became so volatile that Confederate President Jefferson Davis personally traveled to Tennessee to settle the dispute between his quarreling generals.[23]

In the meantime, Tom's regiment had been refitting and replenishing their supplies for the expected advance, but under a different commanding general. Buell was relieved of command and replaced by Major General William Rosecrans. The

[22]Adams, *The Diary of Jacob Adams*, p. 640.   [23]McDonough, *Stones River*, p. 37.

change in command was accompanied by a flurry of activity as preparations for the offensive began. On the day after Christmas, Tom's regiment received orders to move in the advance of the army in the direction of Murfreesboro. By 29 December, the Twenty-first bivouacked within three miles of the town. The next day, the regiment was ordered into line with Brigadier General Philip H. Sheridan's men to their right and Brigadier General Alexander McCook's men to their left.[24]

Tom and his company spent the day of 30 December moving into their positions in the line of battle. The Federals took up positions on the north bank of Stones River. General McCook's troops were placed on the Union right, General George Thomas, divisional commander of the Twenty-first, commanded the center, and General Thomas Crittenden's men held the left flank. The Twenty-first, under Colonel John F. Miller, moved to the center of the Union line of battle. Temporary camps were laid out and the men began to forage for food and fuel. It had rained sporadically for the last few days and the men tried to construct as much shelter as possible. By late afternoon the men were settled in and busily cooking supper.[25]

Daylight was fast disappearing, and the evening star could be seen when one of the Federal bands began to play "Yankee Doodle." This was followed by "Hail Columbia" and other tunes popular in the Union army. During a lull, a Confederate band across the "no man's land" began to play a medley of their favorite songs. The bands of both armies then took turns serenading the other. The men of both armies stopped their work and listened, applauding when their own band's music ended. Darkness had descended when one Federal band began to play "Home Sweet Home." The bands of both armies hushed. After a few measures a Confederate band joined in, then another and another until the bands of both armies were playing in unison. When the last note sounded

---

[24]Canfield, *History of the 21st Ohio*, p. 73.   [25]Ibid.

the armies hushed in reflective silence, lost in the dreams of home and loved ones far away.[26]

The battle of Stones River began just after 6 A.M. on 31 December 1862. General McCook's men were hit hard and driven back. Tom and his companions moved by brigades into positions facing a cornfield. The beating of drums became steadily louder and rebel battle flags came into view on the horizon. Tom watched the gray lines move closer and closer. The command to fire rang out and the Union lines exploded in a sheet of flame and smoke. The acrid odor of gunpowder permeated the cold, damp air. The Confederate lines dressed to the right, filled in the gaps in their lines, and continued moving inexorably forward.

Tom reloaded his Springfield rifle and fired repeatedly at the gray clad men moving ever closer. The order to fix bayonets was given and Tom affixed the steel blade to his rifle. Tom and his companions discharged a final volley at the oncoming Confederates and made ready to charge. At the last minute the rebel troops broke and fled back into their lines.[27]

The Twenty-first continued to stubbornly hold their ground until it became apparent that Sheridan's men on their right were being steadily forced back step by step. Soon the men of the Twenty-first were being struck on their right flank by hostile fire. Lieutenant Colonel Neibling ordered the men to fall back in order to re-establish contact with the retreating Union lines. They took up new positions to the right of the Murfreesboro and Nashville Turnpike, near the Chicago Board of Trade artillery battery. The fighting finally abated, and nightfall mercifully ended the day's hostilities.

A cold rain began to fall. Tom and the rest of the tired Union troops tried to build makeshift shelters to ward off the icy rain and wind. Between the lines lay the freezing wounded of both armies. Their cries for help continued

[26]McDonough, *Stones River*, p. 152   [27]Canfield, *History of the 21st Ohio*, p. 76.

throughout the night. Many men remembered this as one of the longest nights of their lives.[28]

New Year's Day of 1863 passed uneventfully for Tom and the Twenty-first. The regiment had been pulled out of line and reassigned to guard the supply train. While on this duty, the men were reminded that Lincoln's Emancipation Proclamation went into effect today. The feelings of the men varied on the subject of slavery. The rest of the day was spent speculating if the battle would begin again tomorrow, and debating the merits of the Proclamation.[29] The issue of slavery divided the regiment as it had the nation. The viewpoints held by the men mirrored the national sentiments with part of the command staunch Democrats and the rest ardent Republicans. The Democrats held slavery an issue to be determined by the individual states. The Republicans believed slavery was a moral evil and followed the lead of the abolitionists who felt it should be outlawed. The regiment's leaders were also divided, as some officers would return slaves to their owners, while others would help them escape.

The next morning dawned overcast and cold. Expectations were high throughout the army that the Confederates were planning to renew the hostilities. But the morning passed as did the early afternoon with little or no firing along the lines. Tom drew his ration of flour and prepared to cook his meager supper when orders were given for the regiment to fall in and prepare for battle.

The Twenty-first took up positions on the Union left, north of the railroad line on the west bank of the Stones River. They were in support of a Union division on the heights east of the river. Tom could hear the sounds of the battle moving closer and closer. He could see the rear of the Union division, and he observed the growing numbers of stragglers heading toward the river bank. Finally, he saw the

---

[28]McDonough, *Stones River*, p. 152.   [29]Street, *Struggle for Tennessee*, p. 49.

entire division break ranks and run for the safety of the west bank. The regiments on the west bank opened and allowed the blue clad fugitives to pass through their lines. This done, the order to move forward was given. The Twenty-first moved down the hill to McFadden ford and crossed the frigid river. Tom's woolen clothing absorbed the ice cold water. Gaining the east bank the Twenty-first quickly redressed their lines and prepared to move forward.[30]

Advancing toward them was the division of Confederate General John C. Breckenridge. The gray lines extended for half a mile; sixteen regiments of men, battle flags snapping in the cold, damp breeze. They were targeted by massed batteries of Federal artillery who raked them with solid shot. Great gaps were torn in the rebel infantry. Over 100 rounds per minute struck the oncoming rebel lines.[31] The rifles of the Twenty-first then joined the Union artillery, firing volley after volley into the embattled Confederate troops.

Units from other Union brigades joined the Twenty-first on the east side of the river. General Rosecrans ordered a general advance against Breckenridge's troops and the Confederates were forced to withdraw. A soldier in the Sixty-fourth Ohio began to sing the *Doxology*, "Praise God from whom all blessings flow . . ." The simple hymn was taken up by his comrades, then by the regiment; finally it spread along the entire Union line.[32] For Tom and his companions the battle of Stones River was over. The Twenty-first Ohio lost 24 men killed, 109 wounded, and 26 missing. The Confederate army retreated, leaving the Federals the task of burying the dead of both armies.

The next weeks found the Federal troops in camp at Murfreesboro, caring for the wounded and replenishing their supplies. During this period, Tom received orders reassigning him to other duties. A General Order dated 20 April

---

[30]Adams, *Diary of Jacob Adams*, p. 642.
[31]Street, *Struggle for Tennessee*, p. 154.   [32]Linderman, *Embattled Courage*, p. 10.

1863, assigned Private Thomas Custer to be an escort for Brigadier General James Negley.[33] Escort duty was a perilous assignment. Tom carried messages from the general to his various commanders. To accomplish this he rode through unfamiliar, and often hostile, terrain at all times of the day and night. He went forward to the scenes of battle to determine the strength of the attack. Tom became the eyes and ears of the general and his reports would often influence the decisions made by General Negley. Years later, after the battle of the Little Big Horn, General Negley communicated with the Custer family. He remembered Tom fondly and said he was a splendid soldier, "so full of courage and fidelity."[34]

Tom served as an escort for General Negley until November 1863. During the battle of Missionary Ridge, 25 November 1863, he functioned as an escort for Major General Ulysses S. Grant. He later served in the same capacity for General George Thomas.[35]

On 1 January 1864, Tom re-enlisted in the army. He received a one hundred dollar bounty and the rank of corporal. He was assigned for duty as escort for Brigadier General James Palmer. In such capacity he served during the campaign into Georgia, which culminated with the capture of Atlanta on 2 September 1864.

Meanwhile, in the eastern theater of the war, Armstrong had been catapulted through the ranks. On 29 June 1863, Captain George A. Custer was promoted to Brigadier General of Volunteers, just in time for the battle of Gettysburg. General Custer repeatedly distinguished himself on the fields of battle and by the fall of 1864, commanded the Third Cavalry Division of the Army of the Potomac. With such rank and stature he now made the necessary application to have his brother transferred to his command.

---

[33]T.W.Custer, Service Records, N.A.   [34]Elizabeth B. Custer, "A Beau Sabreur," p. 225.
[35]T.W.C. Service Records, N.A.

In order for Tom to be transferred, a position had to be secured. Even though he was now a general, and becoming quite renowned through the Northern newspapers, Custer still did not have the political connections required to obtain Tom's commission. Custer sought out those men under his command who did possess the necessary political clout.

Custer approached Lieutenant Colonel Russell A. Alger of the Sixth Michigan Cavalry. The battle of Gettysburg was hardly over when Custer began to apply pressure on Alger. He seldom allowed an opportunity to pass without his pressing Alger with his desire to have Tom transferred to Alger's command. Alger, however, would have none of it. He repeatedly refused Custer's entreaties. Alger reminded Custer of the many men in his command who were deserving of the promotion Custer desired for his brother. Custer's demands became more determined and heated. Alger replied he could not, would not, authorize Tom's transfer at the expense of men in his own command, that he would rather resign his command rather than have an outsider promoted into his regiment. Custer angrily told him he would come to regret his decision.[36]

The rank, as second lieutenant in Company B of the Sixth Michigan Cavalry, was eventually procured by Colonel James Harvey Kidd.[37] Having secured the commission, General Custer wrote to the Adjutant General, Brigadier General E. D. Lawrence, requesting Tom's discharge and reassignment.[38] He next wrote to Major General George Thomas, commander of the Army of the Cumberland, requesting his aid in Tom's transfer. On 23 October, at Gaylesville, Alabama, Tom was mustered out of the Twenty-first Ohio Infantry for reassignment.[39]

---

[36]*Evening Post,* Grand Rapids, Michigan, 12 February 1892.

[37]Letter, George A. Custer to James H. Kidd, 3 October 1864. Michigan Historical Collection, Bently Historical Library, University of Michigan.

[38]Letter, George A. Custer to Brigadier General E.D. Lawrence, Adjutant General U.S. Army. T.W.C. Service Records, N.A.

[39]T.W.C. Service Records, N.A.

CHAPTER THREE

Valor, Above and Beyond

Tom traveled home for a few days before reporting to his brother's command in Virginia. Mother Custer made some new shirts for Tom, while brother Boston and sister Margaret sat spellbound, listening to his thrilling narratives of the war. The pleasant days passed quickly, and Tom was again on his way.

Tom knew the Civil War experience in the East had been very different from the war in the West. Poor generalship, coupled with misguided strategy, plagued the eastern Federal armies. Time after time, Confederate General Robert E. Lee's Army of Northern Virginia had outwitted and defeated its more numerous foes. Lee received his first serious check in July 1863, at the battle of Gettysburg, but even that Union victory was not flawless.

In disgust, Lincoln turned to one of the few successful Union commanders in the field, Ulysses S. Grant. Lincoln ordered Grant to Washington and placed him in command of all Union forces. Grant and Lincoln secluded themselves and discussed the war and Grant's plans for the conduct of the war. Grant understood that Lee had limited resources in men and material. Most importantly, Grant realized that in order to defeat the Confederacy, their armies and their ability to wage war must be destroyed. Lincoln liked what he heard, and vowed to support Grant in all his endeavors.

Tom and his companions poured over all the newspapers

they could get their hands on detailing Grant's spring offensive in May 1864. Lee and Grant hammered each other savagely. Lee managed to hang on, but while other Union commanders had retreated, Grant advanced. Only by a forced march did Lee beat Grant to Spotsylvania Court House, where another bloodbath ensued. Lee realized Grant was trying to place the Federal army between the Army of Northern Virginia and the Confederate capital of Richmond, not with the intention of capturing the city, but to force Lee to continue fighting. By the end of the first month, the Army of the Potomac had sustained over 40,000 casualties. The war of attrition had begun.

In spite of the damage inflicted upon the rebel army, Lee was able to thwart Grant's maneuvers at every turn. With casualties mounting and success still eluding him, Grant tried an even bolder stratagem. On 12 June the Federal army, now east of Richmond, crossed the James River to capture the important railhead of Petersburg, just thirty miles south of the Confederate capital. The troops, however, did not move rapidly enough and Lee's army was able to repel the half-hearted Union attack.

Lee realized once his ability to maneuver was gone, so would be all hope of victory. Petersburg soon became surrounded with a miles of siege lines, and Grant's strangle hold on the Army of Northern Virginia grew tighter every day. In desperation, Lee sent General Jubal Early and 14,000 men on an invasion through the Shenandoah Valley, into Maryland, and to the very gates of Washington. But success was transitory, and the offensive dissolved into retreat forcing Early to fall back to the Shenandoah.

This was the third time the Confederates used the Shenandoah as an passageway for attack. Grant decided to make the necessary preparations to permanently close that strategic avenue forever. For this task, Grant selected a young officer he had brought with him from the west to command the heretofore ineffectual Federal cavalry. Major General Philip H. Sheridan took command of a combined force of infantry and cavalry, with orders to destroy everything in the Valley which could be used to sustain the Confederate war effort. Most importantly, Sheridan was to find and destroy the remnants of Early's force.

Tom eagerly studied the progress of Sheridan's campaign of terror in the Valley. He read how the campaign narrowly averted catastrophe on 19 October at Cedar Creek, Virginia. Sheridan's men were attacked by Early's troops and driven from the battlefield in disarray. Sheridan arrived in time to avert a full scale disaster, and rallied his demoralized soldiers. He quickly regrouped and rejuvenated his troops, counter attacked, and won a major victory.

Tom arrived at the regimental headquarters of the Sixth Michigan Cavalry at Cedar Creek on 8 November. Special Order 102 assigned him to the staff of the commanding general as an aide-de-camp.[1] Tom traveled to division headquarters, located a few miles south of Winchester. Upon arrival he reported to General Custer, who received him and explained to the young officer his duties. When the formal interview ended, the two threw off their accouterments of war and embraced.

A few days later, Tom wrote to his family, informing them of his safe arrival. Sister Margaret wrote to tell him that Mother Custer mailed those items he requested, along with the finished shirts. Tom also asked for some of his pictures to be sent, but owing to a lack of funds, this was not done. Margaret closed with her love, and said she would send Tom, Autie, and Libbie some apples from home.[2]

Libbie was the young bride of Armstrong. Elizabeth Bacon and Armstrong married on 9 February 1864, in their home town of Monroe, Michigan. Tom first met Libbie a few days before

---

[1]T.W.C. Service Records, N.A.

[2]Letter, Margaret Custer to Thomas W. Custer, 16 November 1864. Lawrence Frost Collection, Monroe County Historical Society, Monroe, Michigan. (Hereafter M.C.H.S.)

Brother Armstrong,
Tom, and Libbie.
*Courtesy Little
Bighorn Battlefield
National Monument.*

the wedding. He had procured a furlough to be present at the
happy occasion. Tom and Armstrong met by chance on their
trip home, and could not resist an attempt to try to "put one
over" on Emanuel. "Let's fool Pop," an excited Armstrong stut-
tered. "I'll introduce you as Major Drew, my aide." Upon their
arrival, they quickly informed their mother of the intended
deception. Armstrong introduced "Major Drew" to Emanuel,
but two and half years of military service could not disguise the
son from his father, and the merriment continued.[3]

Libbie happily accepted Tom into her home. Her own
brother died when she was young, and Tom became a substitute sibling. She showered upon him the affection of a big sister, and watched over him as a surrogate mother. She later

---

[3]Monaghan, *Custer,* p. 176.

wrote, "We could not help spoiling him owing to his charm and our deep affection."[4] Libbie, in her letters and writings, usually referred to Tom as "Our Brother," never as Armstrong's brother or as her brother-in-law. Their relationship grew with mutual affection and endured throughout their lives.

Libbie, one of the few wives living in camp, soon learned that life with two Custers carried with it no small degree of danger. The boys were both incorrigible practical jokers who showed no mercy. Tom's sister, Margaret, gave Libbie her sympathy. "Does Tom like to pinch you?" she asked. "He left a big blue mark on me last time."[5] Margaret also noted that with Tom there, Libbie would now have help against Armstrong. Play was an integral part of any Custer relationship. When the three were alone, their house filled with laughter at the pranks and never ending scuffles.

Tom's relationship with Armstrong was equally as intense. The two boys had always been very close, and the playful times they experienced as children began again. But in one matter the relationship was now drastically different. Armstrong was Tom's commanding officer and in all military matters their relationship was very strict. In reporting, Tom always deferred to his superior officer. He snapped to attention and addressed the General as "Sir." Even Libbie was taken aback at their military demeanor.

The first time Libbie saw Tom in his role as the general's aide, she assumed he was in some military difficulty, and she prepared to interrupt the proceedings and plead the young officer's cause. It took a few minutes before she realized Tom was in no trouble, and when his report was concluded the two brothers resumed their friendly banter. Libbie later noted it took some time before she became accustomed to the duality of the brothers' relationship.[6] In private, Tom referred to his

[4]Frost, *General Custer's Libbie*, p. 122.

[5]Letter, Margaret Custer to Elizabeth Custer, 2 December 1864. Lawrence Frost Collection, M.C.H.S., Monroe, Michigan.

[6]Frost, *General Custer's Libbie*, p. 122.

commanding general as the "Old galoot," or "Old sorrel top that you are so fond of," but abruptly changed in mid-sentence when the tone of the conversation transformed to one of a military formality. Occasionally, Tom appealed to Libbie to intercede with Armstrong, to try and stop his being blamed for "every darned thing just because I happen to be his brother."[7]

Nepotism was not unheard of in the Federal armies. General Philip Sheridan's brother, Michael, served on his staff. Even President Lincoln's son, Robert, occupied a position on the staff of General Grant. General Custer might be a practicing believer in nepotism, but never of favoritism. Being General Custer's brother was not easy, and Tom was repeatedly selected for the most arduous of tasks. Libbie recorded that:

> If after a tumultuous day, the General and his staff threw themselves down around the camp fire to sleep and were awakened by news that required one of them to saddle and start off for night duty, Tom was the one selected. If I protested the General would state he must never show preference.[8]

The rest of the General's staff also noticed Tom's treatment, and agreed with Libbie's appraisal stating, "If anyone thinks it is a soft thing to be a commanding officer's brother, he misses his guess."[9] Years later, a friend asked Armstrong what he thought of Tom. Without any hesitation he replied, "If you want to know what I think of him, all I can say is, Tom ought to be the General and I the Captain."[10]

The winter of 1864-65 in Winchester became a happy time for the trio. During the day, Tom and Libbie rode through the winter landscape of the Shenandoah. At night the Custer headquarters rang out with laughter, as the staff enjoyed many pleasurable hours telling tales and playing endless

---

[7]Custer, *Civil War Memories*, p. 127.
[8]Custer, "A Beau Sabreur," p. 226.
[9]Ibid.
[10]Ibid., p. 237.

hands of a card game called "smut."[11] The realities of war, however, soon intruded.

In mid December, General Sheridan ordered the railroads near Gainesville and Charlottesville, across the Blue Ridge Mountains, to be destroyed and sent the bulk of his cavalry to accomplish that task. He directed General Custer to move his command up the Shenandoah Valley to Staunton in order to serve as a diversion. Sheridan hoped to confuse General Early with Custer's movements and cause him to concentrate his attention upon Custer, allowing the destruction of the railroads without interruption.

Libbie waved goodbye as Tom and the rest of the command moved out at 7 A.M. on 19 December. The troopers moved south along the Valley Turnpike arriving at the hamlet of Lacey Springs late in the afternoon of 20 December. The cavalrymen set up camp and cooked their meals, huddling close to the fires to ward off the wintry winds. Snow began to fall and very quickly the entire area was blanketed.

Tom, Armstrong, and the rest of the staff commandeered a large farm house to serve as headquarters. After inspecting the camp, and positioning a larger than normal number of sentries, the staff retired. Tom, however, remained on duty, sharing an anxious night with other officers. They were aware that Confederate scouts had been watching the column since it left Winchester. So great was the apprehension that orders were given to have the command up at 4 A.M., and in the saddle by 6:30 A.M.[12]

The command awoke as ordered, shook off the snow, and cooked a hasty breakfast. Suddenly, gunfire erupted from the pickets and the men scrambled to grab their weapons. The Confederate cavalry, under General Custer's West Point classmate Tom Rosser, poured into the camp before any alarm could be

---

[11]Letter, Elizabeth B. Custer to Judge Daniel Bacon, 20 November 1864. Marguerite Merington Collection, New York Public Library. (Hereafter, Merrington Collection.)

[12]Urwin, *Custer Victorious*, pp.221–222.

sounded. The gray clad horsemen rode through the rows of tents, firing left and right at the startled bluecoats. Union officers shouted commands, and the surprised bluecoats fell into line and moved forward to repel the invaders. Confusion reigned, with the bullets flying fast and furiously from every direction.

General Custer jumped from bed at the sound of the first shots and dashed to the window. He was startled to see Confederate cavalrymen filling the yard of the farmhouse. He hurried to his trunk and pulled from it a captured Confederate officer's coat and hat. He quickly donned the rebel apparel, raced down the stairs, and walked out onto the porch of the farmhouse. The rebels, presuming he was an officer, paid no undue attention to him while he calmly walked to a horse, mounted, and rode off. Once away from the rebels, Armstrong discarded his gray coat and drew his pistol. He led his men forward against the Confederates in his shirt sleeves and stocking feet.[13] The Union counterattack drove the Confederates from the camp, but they left behind over fifty of their comrades.

Tom and the other aides inspected the camp and made dispositions for the dead and wounded. The General decided they had made a sufficient demonstration, and the command prepared to return to their winter quarters in Winchester. As the troopers began their march down the Valley Turnpike, the weather grew colder and the wind-driven snow lashed both horses and riders. Upon their arrival at Winchester the Second Ohio reported forty-five men suffering from "frozen feet."[14]

Tom and Armstrong spent the evening of their return to Winchester near the fireplace, telling tales of their recent adventure. Tom laughingly related to Libbie the story of an old man whose house he had tried to commandeer for use as headquarters. The old farmer listened patiently to Tom's request, but recoiled in horror at the notion of what Tom asked. The farmer went inside to explain to his wife what the

---

[13]Ibid.   [14]Ibid., p. 224.

Yankee wanted. He had not been inside very long when he came back out, shaking his head back and forth. The farmer looked up at Tom and very emphatically stated, "The old lady is agin' it!"[15] With that the old farmer walked away, leaving the bemused Tom to find another house.

Tom and Armstrong thought the old man's sobriquet was so appropriate they christened Libbie "the old lady." From that time on whenever Libbie reproached the two brothers, they would turn to each other and complain, "The old lady is agin' it," and burst into laughter.

With the Christmas season upon them, the Custers applied for leave, but all requests for leaves were refused. Instead, Libbie's family came to Winchester and spent the holidays. Leave was finally granted on 15 January 1865, and Tom, Armstrong, and Libbie traveled to Washington D.C., Baltimore, New York, and finally home to Monroe.[16]

While the Custers were enjoying their holiday, the wheels of war continued to turn. General Grant formulated his plans for the upcoming spring offensive. He ordered Sheridan to prepare to move up the Valley and destroy the Virginia Central Railroad, the James River Canal, and capture Lynchburg. With those goals accomplished, Sheridan was to move south into North Carolina, and join forces with General William T. Sherman.[17] Sheridan did not like the last section of Grant's orders. He felt confident the spring offensive would bear the fruits of victory, and he wanted to be in on the kill.

In preparation for the spring offensive, Sheridan made an administrative change in command. He had grown increasingly unhappy with his Chief of Cavalry, General Alfred Torbert, and he replaced him on 27 February with Wesley Merritt. Merritt completed the preparations for the imminent offensive and issued the necessary orders to the command.

---

[15]Ambrose, *Crazy Horse and Custer*, p. 200.
[16]Frost, *General Custer's Libbie*, p. 124.   [17]Sheridan, *Personal Memoirs*, p. 112.

The column contained two divisions of cavalry under Generals Custer and Thomas Devin, totaling 10,000 officers and men. In support were two sections of artillery, eight ambulances, sixteen ammunition wagons, a pontoon train with eight boats, and a small supply train carrying provisions.[18]

In preparation for the offensive, Tom carried seventy-five rounds of ammunition, five days rations, and thirty pounds of grain for his horse.[19] He also carried his blue great coat and poncho to ward off the elements.

Reveille sounded at 3 A.M. on 27 February, and by sunrise the troopers were moving south. The morning air grew warmer as the sun rose higher, and many men removed their heavy woolen coats. Rivulets of water grew from the banks of snow that lay across the gentle landscape of the Shenandoah Valley. As the hours passed, however, the sky filled with threatening clouds and a light rain began to fall. The troopers reached Woodstock late in the day and pitched camp. As the weary troopers began their evening meal the light drizzle of the early afternoon transformed into a steady downpour.

The next day the troopers continued their movement south along the Valley Turnpike. The rain continued and very quickly the roadway became a bottomless morass, into which both horses and wagons sank. The troopers worked incessantly to keep the column moving, alternately freeing horses and wagons from the mud. In two days of arduous marching the troopers traveled sixty miles.[20]

The first skirmish of the campaign occurred at Mount Crawford on 1 March. The Confederates tried to deny the Federals the crossing of the middle fork of the Shenandoah River. After a brisk but short action, the Confederates fell back and the Union advance continued.

---

[18]Ibid.
[19]Stephen Starr, *Union Cavalry in the Civil War* (Baton Rouge, Louisiana, 1985) p. 368.
[20]Urwin, *Custer Victorious*, p. 225.

The next morning the bluecoats entered Staunton. Confederate General Jubal Early had evacuated the town a few hours earlier, and moved his command to the east, toward Waynesboro and Rockfish Gap. General Sheridan ordered Custer to move his division in pursuit of Early, and if possible attack him. Tom and the other troopers moved out in a freezing rain. Sheridan rode out to review the troops as they passed. The men, however, were so spattered with mud that Sheridan could barely recognize his own officers as they passed by.[21]

Shortly after noon, General Early received a dispatch informing him of the Federal advance toward Waynesboro. Early sent an aide to General Gabriel Wharton, commander of the left flank, to prepare for the Federal troops moving upon his positions; but the messenger failed to find General Wharton.[22]

Early did not intend to give battle at Waynesboro. He hoped to be there only long enough to remove the military stores, and continue his retreat through Rockfish Gap.[23] To cover these moves, he placed Wharton's men on a ridge to the west of town. Wharton's division, down to only a thousand effectives, took up positions along the ridge with their backs to the rain swollen South River. Six pieces of artillery, placed along the heights, supported the troops. Wharton did not expect to see action, and so did not secure his left flank where a gap of one eighth of a mile existed between Wharton's left flank and the river.[24] At 3 P.M. the Federal cavalry came into view, and the startled Confederates hastily made preparations to receive their attack.

General Custer scanned the enemies' position and noticed Wharton's unsecured left flank. He ordered Colonel William Wells to move his command forward as dismounted skirmishers. Colonel Henry Capehart moved his Third Brigade and a battery of horse artillery forward and prepared

---

[21]Ibid.

[22]Jubal Early, *Jubal Early's Memoirs* (Baltimore, Maryland, 1989) p. 463.

[23]Ibid., p. 462.   [24]Urwin, *Custer Victorious*, p. 226.

to charge. General Custer ordered Colonel Alexander Pennington to dismount three regiments from the First Brigade, move them into the woods near the South River, and position themselves on the Confederate left flank.[25]

Colonel Wells' dismounted troopers moved forward in skirmish order and engaged the Confederate troops. With the Confederates' attention focused on their front, Custer ordered his bugler to sound "Charge!" The notes rang out through the cold, damp air and the trap was sprung. The Confederates were completely surprised and in a few minutes the Federals were in the rear of Wharton's infantry. All resistance along the Confederate line disintegrated, and their retreat dissolved into a complete rout.

Tom placed himself in front of Colonel Capehart's brigade and led the charge over the breastworks. The remaining Confederate infantry scattered in every direction. The artillerymen stayed with their guns until the last moment, before joining the retreat.[26] For his part in the battle, Tom received his first commendation for bravery.[27]

From his command post, General Early watched his command crumble in the face of the Union attack. Tom and the other troopers raced through the streets of Waynesboro to cut off the Confederate's avenue of escape. Early and his staff barely outdistanced the advancing Federal cavalrymen. The battle of Waynesboro destroyed Early's command. The Confederates lost all of their artillery, 200 wagons loaded with supplies, seventeen battle flags, and 1,600 men.[28]

The next day the Federals continued their advance through Rockfish Gap, and arrived in Charlottesville in the afternoon of 3 March. The city leaders met General Custer and Tom just outside the city, and surrendered the town. That night the blue coats slept in the halls of the University of Virginia, glad to be out of the ever present rain.

---

[25]Ibid., pp. 227–228.   [26]Ibid., p. 229.
[27]T.W.C. Service Records, N.A.   [28]Urwin, *Custer Victorious*, p. 230.

Tom's next few days were filled with activity, overseeing the destruction of the all the rail lines and bridges entering the city. Sections of the James River Canal were also destroyed by Custer's cavalrymen. This pattern of destruction continued as the command moved across central Virginia. The troopers skirmished the entire distance of their march, but no effective resistance could be mounted against them. When they reached the Union lines at White House Landing on 18 March, General Sheridan wrote:

> The hardships of this march far exceeded those of any previous campaigns by the cavalry. Almost incessant rains had drenched us for sixteen days and nights, and the swollen streams and well nigh bottomless roads east of Staunton presented grave difficulties on every hand, but surmounting them all, we destroyed the enemy's means of subsistence. . . All were filled with the comforting reflection that our work in the Shenandoah Valley had been thoroughly done, and everyone was buoyed up by the cheering thought that we should soon take part in the final struggle of the war.[29]

The cavalry arrived back in time to participate in Grant's spring offensive. The stalemate around Petersburg was entering its tenth month, and Grant was determined to bring it to a conclusion. Across the "no man's land," Lee also contemplated an end to the siege of his army.

Lee met with General John Gordon and asked him to study the Union lines and find a weak spot. Gordon returned later with his recommendation. He explained to Lee that the Union position at Fort Stedman, due east of Petersburg, was the most advantageous target. The distance between the lines was short, and an attack, if successful, might pull the Union troops from their extreme left to bolster the line. This would give the Army of Northern Virginia an avenue of escape, and make it possible for Lee to move south and effect a link up with Joseph Johnston's Confederate Army in the Carolinas.

---

[29]Sheridan, *Personal Memoirs*, p. 123.

The Confederates attacked Fort Stedman before dawn on 29 March. Their surprise was complete, and they captured several hundred yards of the Union entrenchments. Union troops, however, counter-attacked and, yard by yard, recovered the lost ground. The Confederates in the captured Union positions found themselves unable to return to their lines. They resisted as long as their ammunition held out, but finally surrendered. The Confederates lost 1,600 men killed and wounded, with another 1,900 taken prisoner. Lee's bold gamble had failed.

Lee's assault on Fort Stedman coincided with Grant's own spring offensive. Grant met with Sheridan and outlined his role in the coming offensive. Grant spread a map of the Petersburg environs before Sheridan and placed a finger upon a cross roads named Five Forks. Five Forks was west of the Confederate right flank and near the Southside Railroad line, Lee's last link with the ever shrinking Confederacy. Grant pointed out to Sheridan that a Federal presence at Five Forks would compel the rebels to come out of their siege lines to defend the railroad. Once the siege lines weakened, the Army of the Potomac could strike and smash through. Sheridan would then proceed south along the Danville rail line and move into North Carolina, placing his command behind the army of Joe Johnston. Sheridan listened intently, but Grant could sense he was not pleased. Grant assured Sheridan the proposed movement to North Carolina would never happen, that the maneuver to Five Forks would end the war.[30]

On 27 March a contingent of Federal infantry under Major General Edward O.C. Ord transferred across the James River to the south bank. They moved behind the Federal lines to the left flank, and relieved those troops in the trenches so they could, in turn, shift to the left and be ready for the movement to Five Forks.[31] Orders issued to Major

---

[0]Ulysses S. Grant, *Personal Memoirs of U.S. Grant* (New York, 1982) pp. 530–531.
[31]Chirstopher Calkins, *The Battle of Five Forks* (Lynchburg, Virginia, 1985) pp. 3–5.

General Gouverneur K. Warren, commander of the Fifth Corps, directed him to move along Vaughan Road and place his men behind the Confederate flank. The Federal's left flank would be secured by Sheridan's Cavalry Corps, which would move through Dinwiddie Court House to Five Forks and, if possible, demolish the Southside Railroad line.[32]

Two days later, on the day Lee attacked Fort Stedman, the Union cavalry began its movement to the west. Custer's Third Cavalry Division received orders to escort the wagon train. This task was nearly impossible, as the incessant rains turned the Virginia countryside into one vast bog. The roads were hopelessly congested with wagons sunk up to their axles in the mud. The disgusted troopers measured their progress in feet, as the seemingly bottomless roads sought to devour both wagons and men. The troopers tried in vain to corduroy the roads to expedite the wagon's progress. The Second Ohio watched one company of engineers cut pine trees and lay them in the road, then cover them with planks and fence rails. When the first wagon tried to drive over the makeshift roadway, it submerged in almost two feet of mud and water. One cavalryman's horse fell while on the road and, if not for the quickness of his friends, the trooper would have drowned.[33]

Lee's spies could not fail to notice such large troop movements. Lee ordered the Confederate cavalry to move to the extreme right flank. Three brigades of General George Pickett's infantry moved by rail to Sutherland Station, where they disembarked and moved overland toward Five Forks and Dinwiddie Court House.[34]

Pickett's infantry reached Five Forks late in the afternoon of 30 March. The cavalry, under Generals Tom Rosser and W.F. "Rooney" Lee, had still not arrived owing to the exceedingly inferior condition of the roads. Pickett ordered his sen-

---

[32] Jerry Korn, *Pursuit to Appomattox* (Alexandria, Virginia, 1987) p. 79.
[33] Starr, *Union Cavalry*, pp. 432–433.
[34] Douglas Southall Freeman, *Lee's Lieutenants*, Vol. III, (New York, 1943) p. 657.

tries posted farther than normal in advance of his camp, where they stumbled upon scouts of the Federal cavalry. Pickett decided he could advance no further without the cavalry, and commanded his men to bivouac for the night, which was miserable night. It began to rain again and many of the men had not brought sufficient provisions with them.[35]

Tom and brother Armstrong spent the day and evening in much the same fashion as their gray clad counterparts. The wagons were stuck in mud all day. As soon as one was free, two more would sink. There was no time for cooking, and that night the two brothers slept upon the wet ground. Armstrong and Tom made pallets out of branches and covered them with their ponchos. When Armstrong awoke the next morning he found himself lying in two inches of water.[36]

The Confederate cavalry arrived at Pickett's encampment at daylight on 31 March. Pickett conferred with his commanders and ordered the cavalry to move forward and locate the Federals. The gray horsemen prepared a hasty breakfast of corn, stolen from the grain supply intended for the horses.[37] After eating they moved out toward Dinwiddie Court House. They had gone only a short distance when they ran into the Federal pickets, and gunfire erupted.

It took more time for Pickett's infantry to join the battle, but by early afternoon Confederate pressure upon Sheridan's troopers was telling. Sheridan's First and Second Cavalry divisions, pressed hard by Pickett's men, fell back. By late afternoon the situation for the Federals was critical. Sheridan dispatched a courier to Custer with orders for him to move at once to Dinwiddie Court House with two brigades of his cavalry. Sheridan also sent aides to his division commanders with orders to contest every inch of

[35]Ibid., p. 659.
[36]Letter, George A. Custer to Elizabeth B. Custer, 30 March 1865. Merington Collection.
[37]Freeman, *Lee's Lieutenants*, p. 661.

ground. After the orders were issued Sheridan rode north from Dinwiddie Court House scout for a defensive position that Custer's men could hold, and behind which the rest of his command could consolidate.[38]

Custer received Sheridan's message and ordered Colonel Wells' brigade to remain with the wagons while he took Capehart's and Pennington's brigades forward to the sound of the guns. Tom and his impatient brother had been chafing all afternoon to get to the very audible battle, and they raced ahead of their brigades. They arrived at Dinwiddie Court House at around 4 P.M. Sheridan quickly explained the situation and gave orders to Custer for the disposition of his troopers.[39]

Armstrong and Tom rode forward to ascertain for themselves the state of affairs. Seeing the dangerous situation the Federal troops were in, Armstrong, Tom, and other staff members raced along the front of the Union lines, shouting encouragement to the beleaguered troopers. The bullets flew thick and fast at the racing soldiers, killing one of the aides. But the dramatic performance achieved its desired effect, and the embattled troopers continued fighting.[40]

The brigades of Pennington and Capehart arrived and moved into their positions in the new line of battle north of Dinwiddie Court House. Pennington's men dismounted and took their place in front of and slightly to the right of Capehart's men. To support the new positions, Sheridan rushed forward a battery of artillery.[41] The two brigades dug in, and the Federal troops fell back to the new positions. The brunt of the rebel attack fell upon Pennington's men, who grudgingly gave ground before Pickett's infantry. The troopers fell back and regrouped on a ridge where they hastily erected barricades made from fence rails. This new position proved stronger. The gray infantry attacked twice more, but were

---

[38]Sheridan, *Personal Memoirs*, pp. 151–152.   [39]Starr, *Union Cavalry*, p. 236.
[40]Ibid.   [41]Calkins, *Five Forks*, p. 44.

repulsed each time. Sensing the ebb of the Confederate's strength, Custer's men counter-attacked and drove the Rebels back into their own lines.[42]

Lengthening shadows heralded the end of the day. The Federals had fought a desperate battle, and by sheer determination, held their ground in the face of overwhelmingly superior numbers. Armstrong and Tom moved among the fatigued troopers, inspecting their positions, giving orders for picket duty, and ensuring the distribution of ammunition and supplies.

General Grant, wishing to ascertain Sheridan's progress, sent his aide, Colonel Horace Porter, to see Sheridan. Sheridan told Porter that he had "one of the loveliest days in his experience, fighting infantry and cavalry, with only cavalry."[43] Sheridan felt that if reinforced by infantry, his position would be much improved. He was very animated in his talk, walking back and forth, smashing his fist into his hand to drive home his point. He believed he could hold Dinwiddie Court House and felt just as strongly about the enemies' precarious position. "This force is in more danger than I am," he said. "If I am cut off from the Army of the Potomac, it is cut off from Lee's army, and not a man in it ought ever to be allowed to get back to Lee."[44]

Porter returned to Grant and reported his observations and discussions with Sheridan. Grant issued orders transferring the Fifth Corps, under Major General Warren, to Sheridan's command. Warren received Grant's orders and issued the necessary commands to start his men moving west.

Rebel scouts soon detected Warren's movement and rushed back to inform Pickett. The Confederate general believed he could not withstand a combined force of Federal cavalry and infantry. Pickett issued orders for his troops to fall back and prepare positions at the cross roads of Five Forks. He also notified General Lee of his dilemma. Lee, in

---

[42]Ibid., p. 45.   [43]Porter, *Campaigning With Grant*, p. 432.
[44]Ibid.

turn, instructed the commander at Burgess' Mill on the Confederate right flank to maintain contact with Pickett's left flank, and assist in repelling the Federal infantry.[45]

Arriving at Five Forks, Pickett deployed his men. He sent W.H.F. Lee's cavalry to the right of the Confederate line. He sent Tom Rosser's cavalry to the left and placed his infantry in the middle. He strategically placed his six pieces of artillery at intervals along the Confederate entrenchments.

The next morning, 1 April, the Federals discovered that the Confederates had retreated during the night. Sheridan immediately set into motion his plan of attack. He ordered Warren to move his infantry and attack the Confederate left flank, severing Pickett's command from the rest of the Confederate army. The Federal cavalry moved forward, driving the Confederate pickets and scouts from their front.[46]

Unknown to Pickett the Confederate infantry at Burgess' Mill, already defeated by the Federal infantry the day before at the battle of White Oak Road, found it impossible to maintain contact with Pickett's left flank. Sheridan urged Warren on, before Pickett realized that his left flank was unsecured, and he was cut off from the rest of the Confederate army. Because of the poor conditions of the roads and confusion among the Federals, Pickett reached Five Forks unmolested, but oblivious to the perilous situation he was now facing.[47]

With the troop dispositions made, and no Federals in sight, a lull fell over Five Forks. Tom Rosser rode up and invited General Pickett to partake of some fish he had caught. General Fitz Lee arrived and was also invited to the shad bake. No one had eaten properly in almost two days, and the famished generals gratefully accepted Rosser's offer. The generals rode away from headquarters without informing anyone of where they were going. Just as Fitz Lee was leaving, a courier brought news of the defeat

---

[45]Freeman, *Lee's Lieutenants*, pp. 660–665.   [46]Sheridan, *Personal Memoirs*, p. 159.
[47]Ibid., pp. 156–157.

of the Confederate infantry the day before at White Oak Road. Fitz Lee dispatched an aide to Burgess' Mill to confirm the report, and he too left for the shad bake. With the three generals truant, the command dissolved upon "Rooney" Lee, but he did not know of the shad bake, nor was he made aware of yesterday's defeat. The recipe for catastrophe was now complete.[48]

Meanwhile, at Union headquarters, Sheridan was in a rage. The day was slipping away and Warren had still not attacked Pickett's left flank. The Union cavalry had driven in all of the forward elements of the Confederate command and the trap had to be shut soon. Finally, at 4 P.M. Warren's men were in position and the attack began. The delay, however, proved injurious to Warren who was relieved from command by the impatient Sheridan.

With Warren's men attacking, the Federal cavalry moved forward. General Custer and Tom led the charge against the rebel fortifications. The Federals were raked by rifle fire and double charges of grapeshot and canister from the Confederate artillery. The first attack failed to carry the rebel works and the cavalrymen fell back. General Custer rode to the front of the Second Ohio and yelled encouragement, "We are going to take those works, and we will not come back again until we get them!"[49]

Armstrong and Tom led the next charge. As they crossed the fields, the rebel line became ominously hushed. Instinctively several members of the command threw themselves to the ground as the entire Confederate line exploded. The bullets whizzed through the air and rent the earth all around Tom. Armstrong seized his personal battle flag, and he and Tom raced toward the rebel lines.[50]

Meanwhile, Sheridan ordered the regimental bands forward and they began playing as the cavalry charged. Before

[48]Freeman, *Lee's Lieutenants*, pp. 660–667.   [49]Urwin, *Custer Victorious*, p. 241.
[50]Ibid.

the Confederates could reload and fire again, their lines were breached in a dozen places by the Union cavalrymen. All Confederate resistance seemed to disintegrate at once. The Confederate cavalry held their ground, but eventually gave way under pressure of the Federal cavalry. The brigades of Wells and Capehart moved around the shattered Confederate right flank, and continued until they linked up with Warren's infantry moving around the Confederate left.

Meanwhile, the shad bake was proceeding well with good food and stimulating conversation. The picnicking generals were oblivious to the events unfolding around them. A freak atmospheric phenomenon obliterated any sounds of the raging battle just a few hundred yards away. Pickett, apprehensive because of the ominous silence, decided to send a messenger to headquarters to check on the Federals' movements. Pickett watched a courier ride off toward Five Forks and, to his astonishment, saw the aide captured by Union soldiers not a hundred yards away. Suddenly, Union soldiers seemed to be everywhere, and the Confederate generals narrowly avoided capture.[51]

In the space of an hour, Pickett's entire force was shattered. The Federals captured over 5,000 men, along with thirteen battle flags, and the six pieces of artillery.[52] Those fortunate enough to escape ran in all directions.

When word of the Union victory reached Grant, he gave orders for a general attack on the Petersburg entrenchments at 4 A.M. The assault proceeded and the Union infantry breached the fortifications at several points. The Confederates battled tenaciously to hold on to the remainder of their lines, but several hundred yards were lost to the jubilant Union infantry.

The din of the Federal attack woke General Lee from his restless sleep. When he received the news of the successful Federal assaults upon Petersburg, he gave orders to his com-

---

[51]Freeman, *Lee's Lieutenants*, pp. 669–670.
[52]Humphreys, *The Virginia Campaigns*, p. 353.

manders that the rest of the siege lines must be held at all costs. He also wrote a message to President Jefferson Davis in Richmond stating it would be impossible to continue the defense of Petersburg. The army must evacuate without delay if it was to be saved.[53] Lee's army was spread in an arc that began north of Richmond, crossed the James Peninsula and river, in front of Petersburg and to Burgess' Mill on the extreme right. Lee studied his map and chose Amelia Court House as the point of convergence for the retreating army. He issued orders, apprising the various commanders as to their routes of retreat and of their order of march. Lee's commands were communicated to his commanders and the evacuation of Richmond and Petersburg began.

It was apparent to the Union commanders the Confederate forces were attempting to flee. Grant, anticipating such a maneuver, had prepared for it by placing Sheridan on the Confederate's right flank. Sheridan's cavalry launched a vigorous pursuit of the retreating rebels.

Tom took his place behind his commanding general, his red necktie dancing in the cool morning breeze. Orders reverberated through the various commands down the road. Buglers sounded the advance and Tom spurred his horse forward. They followed the infantry of the Fifth Corps, now commanded by Charles Griffen, up Ford's Road. They had not gone far when shots rang out from the woods in front of them. Members of W.H.F. Lee's cavalry suddenly appeared in the road, and a brief fire fight ensued. Federal skirmishers quickly cleared the woods of the rebel snipers, and the advance continued. It was not long, however, before the gray cavalry appeared again to give battle. This time the rebels could not be shaken off. They retreated just out of range and took up new positions. The fighting continued for miles, causing both sides to lose formation. Finally, General Custer

---

[53]Edward Porter Alexander, *Fighting For The Confederacy*, pp. 514–515.

halted his men to regroup.[54] Lee's men, however, had gained the necessary time. Daylight was fading fast and Custer ordered the troopers to halt and bivouac for the night.

The dawn of 3 April found Tom and the rest of the troopers continuing north in their pursuit of the Confederates. They had not gone far when they came to Namozine Creek. The bridge had been destroyed by the retreating rebels, and the creek itself was now a raging torrent, fed by the heavy spring rains. Suddenly, shots rang out from the opposite bank. The rebels occupied positions in the woods, determined to deny the Federals the crossing. General Custer ordered skirmishers to advance to the river's edge and engage the rebels on the opposite bank. Simultaneously, other men dismounted and moved down stream to ford the creek and attack the enemy's flank. The Confederates fought with resolve, but were forced from their positions by the Federals on their flank. The rebels retreated and melted into the woods.[55]

As the Federal advance continued, the Confederate commanders conferred over what to do next. General W.H.F. Lee met General Rufus Barringer at the intersection of Green Road and Cousin's Road. They agreed that a last ditch action must be attempted in order to save the rest of the army. General Lee ordered General Barringer to fortify positions at the crossroad and hold back the Federals at all cost.[56]

General Barringer turned his attention to the disposition of his men, three regiments of cavalry. He placed his brigades parallel to Cousin's Road, facing Namozine Road. The First North Carolina took up positions on the Confederate left flank. The Second North Carolina held the center of the line, and the Fifth North Carolina anchored the right flank.

---

[54]Christopher Calkins, "We Had A Spirited Fight At Namozine Presbyterian Church, April 3, 1865." *Blue and Gray,* August 1990.

[55]U.S. War Dept., *The War of the Rebellion,* Series 1 volume XLVI.

[56]Clark, *Histories,* p. 650.

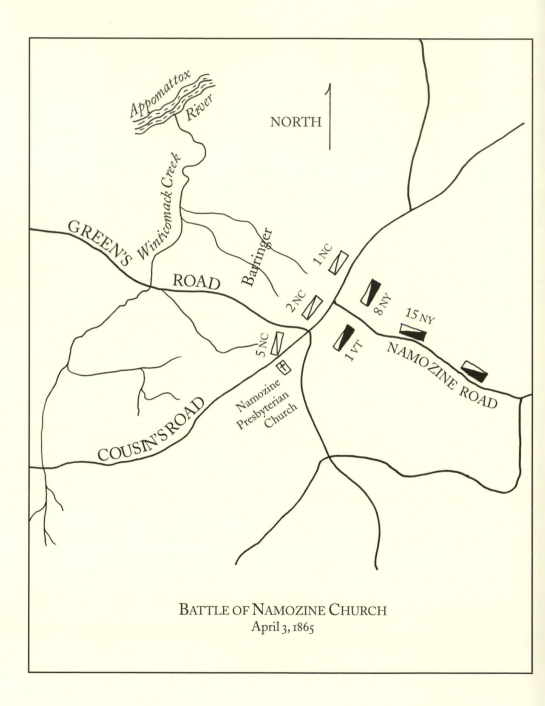

Appomattox River

Winticomack Creek

NORTH

GREEN'S

Barringer

1 NC

ROAD

2 NC

8 NY

15 NY

5 NC

1 VT

NAMOZINE ROAD

Namozine
Presbyterian
Church

COUSIN'S ROAD

BATTLE OF NAMOZINE CHURCH
April 3, 1865

Namozine Presbyterian Church scene of the Battle, 3 April 1865.
Carl F. Day Collection.

Namozine Presbyterian Church occupied the small clearing
in their front. Beyond the church clearing lay the woods,
unbroken except for Namozine Road. In their rear lay Green's
Road which crossed Winticomack Creek first, and the Appomattox River second. A single battery unlimbered to the left
of Green's Road, guarding the Confederate's possible line of
retreat. Less than 800 men filled the Confederate lines.[57]

Colonel Wells' brigade led the Federal advance up
Namozine Road toward the church. As they entered the
church's clearing they saw the entrenched Confederates. Wells
ordered his men into line and prepared to charge. The Eighth
New York led the charge against the rebel skirmishers posted
in the woods around the church, and quickly drove them back

[57]Christopher Calkins, "We Had a Spirited Fight," April 3, 1865."

to their entrenchments. The First Vermont joined the New Yorkers and the two regiments again moved forward.[58]

General Barringer ordered the Second North Carolina to mount and charge the oncoming Federals. Though determined, they could not stop the Federal juggernaut. Barringer turned to the Fifth North Carolina and ordered them to mount, but the Federals were too fast and stampeded their horses.[59]

Tom rode to the front of Wells' brigade and joined in the charge. He raced his horse across the open ground and leaped the improvised rebel barricade. Shots flew from every direction, as the Confederates fell back in confusion. Directly in front of him, Tom saw a Confederate color bearer. He struck his horse's flanks with his spurs and raced forward. Tom seized the flag of the Second North Carolina cavalry from the standard bearer, and ordered the men around him to drop their weapons and surrender. He took his prisoners, three officers and eleven enlisted men, to the rear.[60] He also requisitioned another horse; his had been shot in the charge. For his bravery, and the capture of the rebel battle flag, Tom won his first Medal of Honor.

The capture of a battle flag was an old custom. Such flags denoted individual persons, or units, on the field of battle. The flag symbolized the honor of the regiment and it was a privilege to bear it, albeit very dangerous. In combat, with the field full of noise and smoke, the soldiers watched their regimental flag and if it advanced or retreated they followed. The names of the battles that the regiment participated in were sometimes stitched onto the flag. The loss of a regimental flag was a disgrace to the command.

While Tom carried his trophy to the rear, the action continued. General Barringer tried to slow the Federal advance, but all resistance was futile. His brigade all but ceased to

---

[58]Ibid.   [59]Ibid.

[60]Letter, Thomas W. Custer to Brevet Major General David Hunter, date unknown. TWC
    Service Records, N.A.

exist. When the Army of Northern Virginia surrendered at Appomattox Court House, only twenty-three men of Barringer's brigade were present.[61]

The next morning Armstrong sat down and wrote a few lines to Libbie to inform her of the previous day's activities.

> You have already heard how God has blessed us with victory. The Third Division had the advance yesterday and was on the extreme left of our army. With my three brigades of cavalry I fought and whipped six brigades of infantry and two divisions of cavalry capturing nine caissons, one piece of artillery, and one battle flag. Tom in the most gallant manner led the charge of the Second Brigade and captured the battle flag of the Second North Carolina Cavalry, also the color bearer. He also captured two officers and twelve men. None of our men were near him. His horse was shot. He also had a horse shot two days ago in the fight in which Boehm was wounded. Tom is always in the advance. He will go to Washington with his captured flag when the trophies are sent there. He will receive thirty days leave and a Medal of Honor.[62]

Colonel Wells' brigade captured 350 men, 100 horses, and one cannon. The Federals lost only three men killed and fifteen wounded. General Custer ordered Wells' brigade to follow Fitz Lee's retreating troops down Cousin's Road to Deep Creek bridge. Colonel Capehart's brigade received orders to pursue Rooney Lee's men. By 1 P.M., the Federals reached Deep Creek bridge, capturing numerous prisoners during the pursuit.

Back at the crossroads, the small white church now served as a field hospital. General Sheridan arrived and wrote General Grant a note recounting the day's action. "Resistance made was feeble. They threw their artillery shells along the side of the road and then set fire to the fence rails and woods. We have captured 200-300 men and 1 battle flag."[63]

Tom and the Union cavalry spent the next two days pursu-

---

[61]Clark, *North Carolina Regiments*, pp. 652–653.   [62]Custer, *Civil War Memories*, p. 137.
[63]Tremain, *Last Hours of Sheridan's Cavalry*, p. 115.

ing the retreating Confederates, but with little success. Lee, meanwhile, lost a full day waiting for much needed supplies at Amelia Court House. His men used the day to scatter and forage for what food they could find. The delay, no matter how badly needed, proved fatal for the Army of Northern Virginia.

The morning of 6 April found the Confederates again marching west. General James Longstreet's men took the advance with the troops of Generals Anderson and Ewell following. Behind them came all the remaining vehicles of the army. General John Gordon's Corps made up the rear guard.[64] The Confederates arrived at Rice's Station at sunrise. General Lee ordered the wagons to cross Sayler's Creek at Perkinson's Mill, near its mouth at the Appomattox River. The infantry crossed two miles up river, on the road to Rice's Station.[65]

Tom and the rest of the Federals were up before sunrise and by 6 A.M. were on the move. Tom was hungry, but the Federal advance was moving so fast that they had outdistanced the supply wagons. He also knew the rebels were close, and felt sure they would soon be in sight. His capture of the battle flag had whetted his appetite for another. If the opportunity presented itself again, he had no doubts about his intentions.[66]

The Federals advanced only a few hundred yards when they came upon a barricade in the road. A small rear guard detachment fired at the oncoming bluecoats. The Federals charged twice, but could not dislodge the rebels. A third charge finally cleared the road and the advance continued.[67]

The Federals advanced only a few hundred yards when shots again rang out from the thickets in their front. They had struck the rear of General Gordon's Corps, and a fierce fire fight ensued, which continued for fourteen miles. The roads, made difficult by the unrelenting spring rains, were

[64]Freeman, *Lee's Lieutenants*, p. 699.   [65]Humphreys, *Virginia Campaigns*, p. 377.
[66]Elizabeth B. Custer, "A Beau Sabreur," p. 299
[67]Tremain, *Sheridan's Cavalry*, p. 153.

torturous to both sides. But the Federals had cut loose from their wagons, while the Confederates could not. As the Confederates approached Sayler's Creek, confusion among the Confederate generals resulted in the infantry and wagons moving in the wrong direction, and the gaps between the wagons and infantry grew ever wider.

Generals Ewell and Anderson halted their commands and evacuated the road, allowing the slower moving wagons to pass through. The two generals, however, did not notify headquarters of their actions. Now an even larger void existed between the retreating Confederate Corps. Before long the Federals came into view.

Anderson brought his men into line at the cross roads, approximately one mile south of General Ewell's line. General Bushrod Johnson's division took up positions on the right flank, and General George Pickett's division on the left. The men tore down the fences and erected barricades in the soft mud. In their front, the open fields filled with Federal cavalry.

As the Confederates hurried to meet the Federals another disaster befell them. Tom and Armstrong sighted a Confederate battery unlimbering and preparing to fire. Armstrong barked out an order and the troopers charged before the rebels could fire. The attack resulted in the capture of nine cannons, 800 men, and 300 wagons.[68]

Elated with their success, the Federals continued and soon found themselves facing the entrenched Confederates of Anderson's command. General Custer wheeled his command into line and prepared to charge. The Federal bands came into the clearing and added their music to the roar of the battle.

Colonel Capehart's brigade, in the advance, moved forward on command. Tom raced to the front of the troopers, riding alongside of Colonel Capehart. With the Federal bands blaring

---

[68]Urwin, *Custer Victorious*, p. 245.

Only known photograph
showing Tom's battle
scars taken shortly after
the end of the war.
Don Horn Collection.

and the cannons booming, the bugles of the brigade could barely
be heard sounding "Charge!" Tom laid his spurs to his horse and
streaked forward toward the barricades. The rebel line disappeared in smoke as their rifles erupted in unison. Tom's horse
leaped the barricade and he found himself surrounded by the
enemy. He discharged his pistol to the left and right, as the Confederate line shattered and fled from the thundering onslaught.

Tom observed the Confederates attempting to form
another battle line. His eyes came to rest on the red and white
banner waving in their midst; the stars and bars of the dying
Confederacy. Without a moments hesitation he urged his
horse forward and charged the color bearer. Colonel Capehart recorded the scene for Libbie Custer.

> I saw your brother capture his second flag. It was in a charge made by
> my brigade at Sailor's Creek, Virginia, against General Ewell's
> Corps. Having crossed the line of temporary works in the flank of the
> road, we were confronted by a supporting line. It was from the sec-

ond line that he wrested the colors, single-handed, and only a few paces to my right. As he approached the colors he received a shot in the face which knocked him back on his horse, but in a moment he was upright in his saddle. Reaching out his right arm, he grasped the flag while the color bearer reeled. The bullet from Tom's revolver must have pierced his heart. As he was falling Captain Custer wrenched the standard from his grasp and bore it away in triumph.[69]

The Confederate color bearer shot Tom in the face. There has been confusion over the extent of the wound. Tom and Armstrong both state in letters that Tom was shot through the right cheek, with the bullet exiting under the right ear. In his application for reinstatement in the army, Tom wrote he, "received a severe wound through my right cheek. . ."[70] Tom's medical records continue the confusion. His medical report of 9 April listed his injury as a gunshot wound to the face and neck.[71] Two days later Tom reported to the medical officer at City Point, Virginia, where his wound was listed as being restricted to the face. A photograph that appears to have been taken shortly after the event clearly shows what appears to be a scar, or some minor soft tissue damage to his right lower jaw extending to a point just below the right ear.[72] It seems clear from the photographic evidence Tom's wound was not as severe as he and Armstrong stated. Had the bullet entered the mouth, or the soft tissue of the throat, it would have probably struck one of the major vessels and Tom would have bled to death. The wound looked much worse than it was, and because of the blood rich tissue bled quite a bit, quickly covering Tom's face and neck with bright red blood. But the joy at having a second banner overshadowed any wound. General Edward Whittaker, General Custer's chief of staff, later wrote, "Tom, on that day, fought like a lion."[73]

---

[69]Elizabeth B. Custer, "A Beau Sabreur," p. 227. [70]T.W.C. Service Records, N.A.
[71]T.W.C. Service Records, N.A.
[72]Don Horn, *Little Big Horn Associates Newsletter,* Vol. XXIV, April 1995.
[73]Ibid.

Tom held his captured trophy aloft, turned his horse around, and headed back into the Federal lines. An officer of the Third New Jersey cavalry saw Tom with his captured banner flapping in the wind, and realized the danger in which the young lieutenant had placed himself. He anxiously shouted at Tom, "For God's sake, Tom, furl that flag or they'll fire on you!"[74]

Tom, intoxicated with his success, ignored the plea and continued, determined to find his brother. He soon saw Armstrong's personal battle flag and rode toward it. Brother Armstrong looked up to see Tom riding toward him, covered with blood. Only seconds before, one of his other aides had been shot in the face and had fallen from the saddle lifeless.

"Armstrong, the damned rebels have shot me, but I've got my flag," roared Tom as he rode up. Tom handed the flag to an aide and made ready to return to the battle. Armstrong shouted to him to report to the surgeon. Tom, intoxicated with the savagery of the battle, ignored the order. The general placed his wounded brother under arrest, and ordered him to the rear under guard.[75] For Tom, the Civil War was over.

The next day Armstrong wrote to Libbie recounting the previous day's action and praising Tom.

> ...The battle flags were taken after very hard fighting. Tom led the charge before the enemy's breastworks and was the first man to leap his horse over the breastworks behind which the enemy were strongly posted. Tom seized the Rebel colors and the color bearer shot him through the face and neck. He shot the color bearer. This is the second flag that he has captured within the week. He must be very careful as his wound is near the main artery. Tom's conduct was gallant in the extreme and is spoken of by all in the highest admiration. He will go to Washington with his flags to present them to the War Department. Caution him against violating any regulation or orders concerning wounded officers while in the capital. He must go to Dr. Bliss's hospital. He must be very careful of

---

[74]Ibid., p. 228.   [75]Ibid.

himself. His wound is much like the mortal wound Sergeant Michow received at Trevillian. Won't Father Custer and Father Bacon be delighted to hear of Tom's gallantry? . . .[76]

The battle of Sayler's Creek resulted in the capture of one quarter of the Army of Northern Virginia. General Lee, looking down from a nearby hilltop, exclaimed, "My God! Has the army dissolved?"[77] The retreat continued, with the Confederates desperately trying to outdistance the Federals who were like ravenous wolves scenting a wounded animal.

Lee's army could no longer elude the fate that awaited it. On the morning of 9 April, they found themselves surrounded by the Federals. With all hope of further resistance or retreat completely gone, Lee surrendered the Army of Northern Virginia to General Grant at Appomattox Court House, Virginia.

Tom was not at the surrender at Appomattox. The regimental surgeon attended to his wound and ordered Tom to report to the Cavalry hospital at City Point. The morning after the battle of Sayler's Creek, Tom, his orderly, and other wounded officers began their trip to the rear. Tom arrived at Burksville in the late morning of 9 April and took a room in the local hotel. A few of the men went in search of forage for their mounts, and returned with a "liberated" silver mounted carriage. Tom and the other officers rode in style from Burksville to Wilson's Station, where they gave their barouch to a surgeon and boarded the train for City Point.[78] Tom arrived at the Cavalry Hospital at City Point on 11 April. Tom later left the hospital without authorization, and went on to Washington D. C.[79]

The jubilance of the Confederate surrender was short lived. On 14 April, Good Friday, President Lincoln attended Ford's Theater. During the performance, John Wilkes Booth entered the Presidential box, and murdered the President.

---

[76]Custer, *Civil War Memories*, pp. 137–138.   [77]Freeman, *Lee's Lieutenants*, p. 711.
[78]Chester, *Recollections of the War of the Rebellion*, p. 167.
[79]T.W.C. Service Records, N.A.

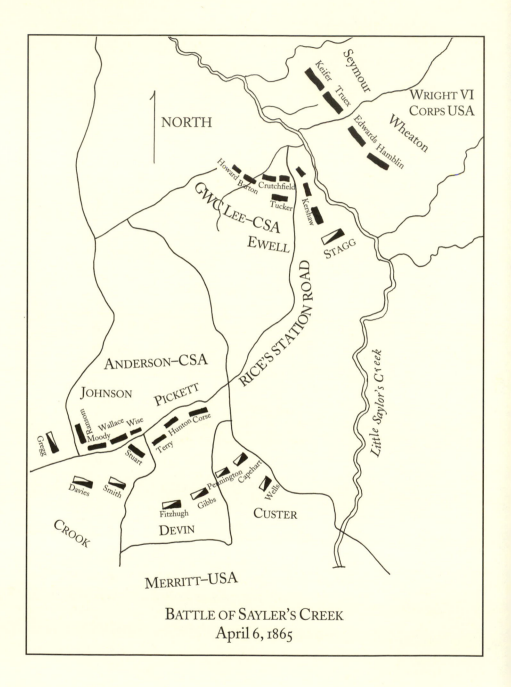

NORTH

Seymour

Keifer

Truex

WRIGHT VI
CORPS USA

Wheaton

Edwards Hamblin

Howard Barton

Crutchfield

GWC LEE–CSA

Tucker

EWELL

Kershaw

STAGG

RICE'S STATION ROAD

Little Saylor's Creek

ANDERSON–CSA

JOHNSON

PICKETT

Ransom

Wallace Wise

Gregg

Moody

Hunton Corse

Stuart

Terry

Davies

Smith

Pennington Capehart

Fitzhugh

Gibbs

Wells

CUSTER

CROOK

DEVIN

MERRITT–USA

BATTLE OF SAYLER'S CREEK
April 6, 1865

A reporter acquaintance of Tom's, from the *New York Times*, remarked to his friends that Tom Custer had been in town that night. He continued, saying how he regretted Tom was not in Ford's Theater, as he would certainly have prevented the assassination and apprehended the assailant.[80] But Tom was seeking his amusement elsewhere on that fateful evening.

On 24 April in a ceremony at the office of the Secretary of War Edwin M. Stanton, Tom, along with others, received the first of his Medals of Honor. Mr. Stanton thanked the men for their bravery:

> In the name of the people of the United States, of the President and of this department, I return to General Sheridan, to your companions in arms, and to yourselves thanks—Thanks for the loyal patriotism and valor which have brought such trophies into the archives of the department; thanks for your devotion to your country's cause. It is with profound grief that I cannot return to you the thanks of the late President, who since you won these spoils has gone from the pinnacle of honor and glory in this world to the right hand of God, where, if it be permitted mortals to look upon what is passing in the world beneath, now sees transpiring in this chamber.[81]

In another ceremony on 22 May, Tom received his second Medal of Honor, making him the first man in American military history and the only Federal soldier in the Civil War to win two medals. Armstrong filled with pride at his younger brother's accomplishments. In a letter to a family friend Armstrong wrote:

> You might think that Tom lacks caution, judgement. On the contrary he possesses both in an unusual degree. His excellent judgment tells him when to press the enemy, and when to be moderate. Of all my staff officers he is quickest in perceiving at a glance the exact state of things. This trait frequently excites comment. When at first he joined me I was anxious concerning his conduct. But now I am as proud of him as can be, as soldier, brother. He has quit the

---

[80]Merington, *The Custer Story*, p. 151.
[81]Millbrook, *Michigan Medal of Honor Winnters*, pp. 21–22.

use of tobacco, is moderate in drink, is respected and admired by
officers and all who come in contact with him.[82]

Further honors fell upon the young officer. For his gallant
actions in the Battle of Waynesboro, Tom received the brevet
rank of first lieutenant. He was breveted captain for his part
in the action at Namozine Church, and major for his participation at Sayler's Creek. Brevet rank was an honorary rank
that carried no change in pay or work. Advancements in the
army were slow and brevets filled the void. Officers were
addressed by their unofficial brevet ranks, and could wear the
insignias denoting their brevets.

Tom took advantage of his 30 day furlough to go home
and visit his family. Rebecca Richmond, Libbie's cousin, met
Tom during his time at home and she was struck by his growing personality. "He is going to be so much like Armstrong.
Under his air of abandon and carelessness he has great
thoughtfulness and ambition . . . He feels his lack of schooling and would make a devoted student could he once overcome the natural reluctance to entering school at his age."[83]

Tom arrived back in Washington in time for the presenta-
tion of his second medal, and the great parade planned for the
armies of the Republic. The city was resplendent with flags and
banners everywhere. On the morning of 23 May the units of the
Army of the Potomac lined up and marched triumphantly
through the streets of the city. Sheridan's cavalry brigades led
the parade, with the Third Cavalry Division in the lead.

Tom's medals shone brightly in the sunlight, and his face
still bore the powder burn across his right cheek. He and the
others basked in the adoration of the grateful populace of
Washington as they cheered the passing soldiers.

---

[82]Merington, *The Custer Story*, p. 157.
[83]Lawrence A. Frost, *General Custer's Libbie* (Seattle, Washington, 1876), p. 136.

CHAPTER FOUR

Texas and Home

The last notes of martial music following the defeat of the Confederacy were still reverberating when Tom received orders to prepare to depart on a military expedition to Louisiana and Texas. A situation had developed necessitating the presence of Federal troops in those states. Several units of the former Confederate Army, under the immediate command of General Edmund Kirby Smith, refused to surrender to the Federal Government. These armed bands moved through central Texas avoiding surrender, and possibly hoping to escape into Mexico. General Grant instructed General Sheridan

> Your duty is to restore Texas, and that part of Louisiana held by the enemy, to the Union in the shortest practical time, in a way most effectual for securing permanent peace . . . If Smith holds out . . . he and his men are to be treated as outlaws.[1]

Grant also ordered Sheridan to place troops at the Rio Grande River, along the boundary with Mexico. Mexico had incurred a sizeable debt to France, and had failed to make restitution. France used that excuse, and the fact that the United States was embroiled in civil war, to invade Mexico. The French installed a puppet dictator, Maximilian, on the throne and set about wrenching its money from the Mexican citizens. The United States protested the French military

---

[1]Sheridan, *Personal Memoirs,* p. 208

action. As long as the Civil War continued, however, there was little the United States could do but protest.

But with the Civil War over, there was much the United States could accomplish. Sheridan received orders to advance into Texas with his command. He divided his force into two wings with General Wesley Merritt advancing to San Antonio and General Custer to Houston. With these forces, and the promise of more if necessary, Sheridan was to bring the recalcitrant rebels to heel, curb the lawless elements, and pose a military threat to the French.

Tom, Armstrong, and Libbie boarded a Baltimore and Ohio train in Washington and traveled to Louisville, Kentucky. Discharged soldiers on their way home crowded the train, and space was at a premium. Tom and the rest of the staff became separated from their general. Tom, though, devised a way to remedy this situation. At the next stop, Tom requisitioned one of Libbie's bags and exited the train. At the call for "All aboard!" Tom demanded entrance to Libbie's car, with the excuse that he was Libbie's escort. The conductor, satisfied with the tangible proof of Tom's statement, granted him entrance into the crowded car. Tom's ruse worked so well the rest of the staff began to appear in Libbie's car, all carrying her belongings. There was one problem though, Tom lost one of Libbie's bags when he got off at one of the train's stops, and the necessary items had to be repurchased.[2] The train trip ended in Louisville where, after many more farewells were said, the trio boarded the steam boat *Ruth* for the trip downriver to New Orleans.[3]

They found the river boat almost as crowded as the train. Once again sleeping arrangements proved to be a challenge. Soldiers slept in every available space, contorted into every possible position. Tom fended for himself as best he could, but one night he became particularly incensed after overhearing a

[2]Custer, *Tenting On The Plains*, pp. 35–36.   [3]Ibid., p. 50.

conversation between two civilians. The two men sat down in front of Tom, and began complaining about all the soldiers taking up space on the boat. Their conversation turned to the profits they had accumulated during the war. Tom turned to his friend sitting next to him and began to expound upon the virtues of his army greatcoat, now placed on the seat next to the two prosperous farmers. Tom went on to relate how he could never be parted from his coat even though he had used it to cover another comrade inflicted with smallpox. The eaves-dropping farmers quickly left. The next morning, Armstrong and Libbie found Tom stretched out comfortably upon the seat having enjoyed a splendid night's rest.[4]

The trip continued lazily down the river, and the Custer boys grew bored. To amuse themselves they lapsed into their childhood habits of practical jokes. Libbie had always enjoyed being the object of the majority of the jokes perpe-trated by her husband and brother-in-law. She proved to be a most gullible victim, who would believe almost anything she was told. Armed with this knowledge, the two pranksters bided their time.

The river boat docked periodically, replenishing wood to fire the ship's boilers. During one such stop, a black laborer fell into the Mississippi. The crew attempted to rescue him, but without success. Tom witnessed the incident and after-wards related it to Libbie, embellishing the tale as best he could. Libbie listened, horrified at the terrible accident. Tom and Armstrong continued the scheme by telling Libbie the tragedy was compounded daily. They convinced her the many calls made by the crew were all in response to other men falling off of the boat. They continued their subterfuge by running out of the cabin when such shouts were heard coming from the crew. They dutifully reported to Libbie the crew member had been either saved or lost. "The Old Lady,"

---

[4]Ibid., pp. 49–50.

as Tom and Armstrong referred to Libbie, believed the two pranksters completely. She was now ready for the next phase of the ruse.

The boat made one of its many scheduled stops for refueling. Tom and Armstrong raced up the steps to find Libbie. "Come, Libbie, hurry up! Hurry up! You'll miss the fun if you don't scrabble." Tom told Libbie the crew was about to bury a poor unfortunate who had fallen overboard. Libbie quickly raced with her conniving loved ones to the scene of the "burial." She watched as the boat was tied to bulwarks on the shore. She heard the deck hands speak of burying the "dead man." As she watched and listened it dawned on her that the "dead man" was the crew's vernacular for tying up the boat. She now fully realized Tom and Armstrong had tricked her. She turned and began beating her conniving husband, much to Tom's delight.[5]

To break the monotony, they got off of the boat at its various stops and visited the shops of the little towns they encountered. By the time they reached New Orleans on 18 June, they were penniless and had to purchase the fare on credit to Alexandria, Louisiana.[6] Lack of money made only a small impact on the trio. Tom and Armstrong were accustomed to being short on funds, owing to the irregularity of pay in the army. The captain of the river boat knew of their predicament, and graciously invited Armstrong and Libbie to be guests at his table. Some time later, the captain extended his invitation for dinner to Tom, who feigned surprise and indignation at the captain's proposal. Tom shoved his hand into his pocket and rattled his few pennies against his pocket knife to show he was not quite the pauper the others were. Armstrong witnessed Tom's performance unfold, and left the room to keep from bursting out in laughter. Tom finally accepted the captain's offer, leaving the bewildered

---

[5]Ibid., pp. 52–53.
[6]Monaghan, *Custer*, p. 255.

man to believe Tom was the only soldier on the boat with any money at all.[7]

The trip up the Red River continued uneventfully. Tom and Armstrong amused themselves by firing at the alligators resting on the sandbars and riverbanks. The two marksmen devised a game, keeping track of the animals they shot.[8]

Upon their arrival at Alexandria, Tom and Armstrong found their new command in turmoil. The troops were angry that instead of being mustered out of the service, as many others had been, they had been ordered south. These men signed up to fight the war, and now the war was over and they wanted to go home. Unaccustomed to such behavior from his men, General Custer tried to instill them with the *esprit de corps* which had existed in the Third Cavalry Division, but without success. He tried sterner measures, but only succeeded in making the men hate him and the rest of his officers all the more. Tom found it prudent to begin wearing his side arm.

While in Alexandria, Tom embarked upon a program of self-education. He purchased a set of school books while in New Orleans and began to apply himself in earnest. It became his habit to study at every possible moment, encountering all those disciplines so carefully avoided at the Creal School in Ohio.[9]

The days in Alexandria passed quickly. In the early morning hours of 8 August the command set out for Texas. The troops moved out at 3:00 A.M. in order to avoid the heat of the day. They moved through large forests of pine trees, which eventually gave way to the flat land and cotton fields of east Texas. At the end of the day, Tom and the rest spent considerable time removing from themselves the primary beasts of the land, ticks. The journey took nineteen days of hard

---

[7]Custer, *Testing On The Plains*, pp. 69-70.

[8]Frost, *General Custer's Libbie*, p. 137.

[9]Letter, George Armstrong Custer to Emanuel Custer, July 9, 1865. E.B.C. Collection.

marching. Armstrong hoped the discipline of the march would build the moral character of the command.

The march into Texas was a grueling ordeal. The oppressive heat and humidity made the privations suffered by the soldiers most acute. Tom endured the incessant attacks by hordes of insects as best he could. Mosquitoes, chiggers, scorpions, and venomous snakes waited for the soldiers at every turn. Fifteen miles a day was all the command could tolerate. The soldiers made camp in the early afternoon to avoid the most intense hours of the afternoon sun. During this time, Tom experienced his first bout of malaria.[10]

After two weeks of arduous marching, they finally arrived at the site of their base camp at Hempstead, Texas. Here the climate was a little better; at least a decent drink of water could be found. The locals seemed to be more friendly, perhaps owing to the fact the war had not touched this part of the country.

Friendly farmers often invited Tom and Armstrong to accompany them on their hunting excursions, and the two brothers found a new aspect to hunting. The Texans used large packs of dogs, which they controlled by blowing on a hollowed out cow's horn. The gracious Texans gave Tom and Armstrong gifts of dogs so they too could join in the fun. The two brothers immediately acquired horns of their own and set about mastering the different calls. Libbie reveled in the sight of the two men straining to make the necessary sounds. Their faces turned blood red, their eyes bulged, but no amount of ridicule could turn them from achieving their desired goals. Finally, after days of noisy torment, the two mastered their new "musical" instruments. They leaped into their saddles, put their horns to their lips, and rode off blasting their calls into the air. The dogs responded by racing after them, adding to the chorus with their barking and howling.[11]

---

[10]Custer, *Tenting On The Plains*, p. 144.
[11]Ibid., p. 162.

Deer was a favorite object of their hunting trips. During one excursion, Tom took up a position on the opposite side of the woods from Armstrong. The dogs were sent into the woods to drive the deer out and into Tom's sights. Tom quietly waited, listening to the dogs' barking coming closer and closer. Suddenly an animal burst from the woods! Tom quickly sighted his rifle on the creature and fired. He rushed forward to claim his prize, but found to his dismay he had killed one of Armstrong's dogs, as well as the deer. Later, when anyone questioned Tom's marksmanship, Armstrong would respond, "Oh Tom's a good shot, a sure aim—he's sure to hit something!"[12] A few days later, Armstrong strategically placed an article near Tom's bed which told of an eastern newspaper editor who had gone hunting for the first time in two years. The editor managed to bag a farmer at a distance of 66 yards. Such articles continued to appear in Tom's room for years following the accident.

While they camped at Hempstead, another family member arrived. Emanuel Custer came to Texas to see his family. He joined his sons in their hunting and riding. Once again open warfare erupted between the father and sons. Armstrong wrote to Libbie's father, Judge Daniel Bacon, that the weather agreed with Father Custer. The boys could not remember seeing their father look so robust. Armstrong further added that Tom was always working on improving his personal habits, and was continuing his studies.[13]

Now reunited with his sons, Emanuel began again to attempt to exercise his parental control. His Methodist aversion to card playing and drinking came out strongly. Tom tried to convince his father there was nothing wrong with a harmless game of cards. The two boys connived to get their father to join them in a game. Emanuel reluctantly agreed

---

[12]Ibid., pp. 163–164.
[13]Merington, *Custer Story*, p. 175.

and sat down to play. After a few practice hands to instruct Emanuel on the rules of the game, the boys began play in earnest. Emanuel won the first game, then the second, and the third. Suddenly, however, Emanuel's luck began to change. No matter how hard he tried, he found he could not win another game. He finally realized his mischievous sons had placed him in front of a mirror so they could see his cards. He quickly and loudly terminated the game. Enraged, he vowed that he would return to Monroe as "the same good old Methodist that left it."[14]

The pranks were unending. Like his sons, Emanuel was an excellent rider. It was the habit of his sons for one of them approach him on one side and engage him in conversation. The other rode up along the other side and slapped Emanuel's horse, causing it to jump and gallop off. The brothers roared with laughter as Emanuel struggled to maintain his balance on the rampaging horse. Emanuel, though, could not be dislodged from his saddle, so the boys devised another plan. Once again they quietly came up behind their father, one grabbed Emanuel's coat and brought it up over his head, while the other struck his horse.[15]

In November, the command received orders to move to a new camp near Austin, Texas. Tom and the others took up residence in a school for blind students. The weather alternated between warmth and cold, and they were at a loss to judge which season was upon them. A norther blew in one Sunday and the temperature plummeted. Tom went out to find firewood and returned with a few twigs. After some effort the fire was started and they all huddled about it. Tom produced a scorpion which he threw upon the fire. The boys remarked upon the agility of the creature. The windows rattled with the onslaught of the wind. Emanuel took up his position nearest the fire, so the smoke from his pipe would be

---

[14]Custer, *Tenting On The Plains,* p. 246.   [15]Ibid., pp. 179–180.

drawn up the chimney, so as not to offend Libbie who disliked the scent of his tobacco. Libbie noticed her husband and Tom were extremely close to the fire, obviously feigning a chill. Armstrong abruptly got up and went to his desk, where he seemed to busy himself writing. After a few moments he came back to the fire, and leaned over his father to deposit some waste paper into the hearth. Suddenly the fire exploded and Emanuel leaped up from his place and scurried to safety. Tom and Armstrong convulsed in laughter at the sight of their father retreating from their explosive surprise. At anytime a firecracker might be tossed into the fire, or be attached to Emanuel's chair.[16]

The time in Austin was pleasant, and the local citizens quickly warmed to the soldiers. The soldiers quickly restored law and order to the area, and confrontations between the army and the civilians were minimal at best. South of the border, Mexican citizens began to take matters into their own hands. Hatred of the French and Maximilian erupted into violence, with bands of revolutionaries roaming the countryside. The French found themselves surrounded and in a very tenuous situation. It was clear that unless the French dispatched more troops to Mexico, they were in danger of losing everything. But with the proximity of American troops in Texas, it was very unlikely France would commit to a stronger military presence. Very quickly the reasons for the cavalry's presence in Texas evaporated.

Soon the Christmas season was upon them. The Custers invited their staff members to share the festivities with them on Christmas Day. They gave a gay party, followed by a supper. They exchanged gifts and Tom received a Jew's-harp with a note attached begging him to "give the piano a rest." Tom had been endeavoring to teach himself the piano, which he "played" constantly, much to the consternation of everyone else.[17]

---

[16]Ibid., p. 239.   [17]Ibid., p. 247.

At the end of January 1866, Tom received orders directing him to report to Detroit, Michigan, to be mustered out of the service.[18] Unbeknownst to Tom, his regiment, the Sixth Michigan Cavalry, had been mustered out of the service on 24 November 1865. Tom had been paid up to the time of his January notification. The army now wanted its money back.

Armstrong was also relieved of his command, so the little group made ready to depart together. They traveled to Galveston and from there took a steamer to New Orleans. In New Orleans they boarded a river boat for the trip upstream. On the boat the boys once again found themselves with time on their hands.

The intended victim of their abuse was, of course, their father Emanuel. Their plan unfolded during supper. The family sat down at their table. Armstrong sat across from his father and Tom sat down next to him. They ordered their food, and just before it came, Armstrong embroiled Emanuel in a discussion of politics, intentionally taking a position guaranteed to incense his father. Emanuel could not contain himself and soon became lost in the argument with his son. Soon his food arrived. Emanuel, however, would not be swayed by the presence of his meal. He was so caught up in his argument he did not notice Tom reach in front of him, and steal his plate. Tom wolfed down the food and replaced the empty plate in front of Emanuel. Armstrong abruptly terminated the discussion and began eating. Emanuel looked at his plate and discovered his food had vanished.[19]

Emanuel never tired of his children's constant attacks upon him. He gave as good as he got, and reveled in all of the antics that his offspring devised. He bided his time and finally turned the tables on his mischievous children, with almost devastating results.

---

[18]T.W.C. Service Records, N.A.
[19]Custer, *Tenting On The Plains*, p. 287.

Tom and Emanuel shared a cabin together. Emanuel wisely slept with his purse under his pillow. Tom watched as Emanuel readied for bed and when his back was turned, stole his father's purse. After they had retired for the night, Emanuel noticed Tom passing an object through the transom. Emanuel jumped up and opened the door in time to see a fleeing form in the darkness. Emanuel ran to Armstrong's room and began to hammer upon the door, demanding the return of his money. Without warning he found himself drenched with water from above. Emanuel returned to his cabin to find Tom fast asleep.

The next morning, Emanuel confronted his sheepish offspring about the whereabouts of his purse. Armstrong listened to his father's tale and explained that he probably was beating on the wrong door and the lady inside had poured water on him in her own defense. Not to be outdone, Emanuel grabbed Armstrong's money. The two boys caught up with him and rescued their funds. Emanuel began to charge everything to his two sons, making them responsible for his bills.[20]

Later Emanuel caught sight of his purse in Armstrong's possession. He lunged forward and grabbed it. The two boys began to scuffle with him, and Emanuel shouted out that he was being robbed. A crowd quickly descended upon the two boys, and pulled them off of Emanuel. The crowd angrily talked of the swift and sure justice of the rope. After a few tense moments, Emanuel explained everything was a simple misunderstanding, and the crowd released the two "thieves."[21]

The happy travelers finally arrived home for a joyous reunion. Returning to civilian life after so many years in the army was somewhat unsettling for Tom and Armstrong. The

[20]Ibid., p. 296.
[21]Ibid.

Thomas Custer, pur-
ported to be Tom's
illegitimate son.
*Wood County
Genealogical Society.*

two story house again reverberated with the noisy antics of the
Custers. Emanuel, so long the butt of Tom and Armstrong's
jokes, now turned the tables on them. Father Custer was an
early riser and began to assail his slumbering offspring in a
stentorian voice to get them out of bed. The boys awoke to
find it was not quite six o'clock. They moaned and made every
effort to ignore the repeated demands and threats of their
father. With the boys ignoring his demands, Emanuel loosed
the dogs on his belligerent house guests. Tom and Armstrong
countered by demanding their privileges as guests to have hot
water delivered to their rooms, having their shoes shined, and
generally inquiring as to the qualities of the proprietor and his
ability to run a proper establishment.[22]

---

[22]Ibid., p. 297.

Maria took great delight in having her boisterous brood around her once again. The house had grown very quiet with her boys grown and gone in the service of their country. But now they were home, and everything was the way it used to be. Emanuel and the boys quarreled with each other constantly. Maria, Emanuel noticed, seemed to always take the boys' side in everything.

Tom used his time at home to take advantage of his new found fame. His military experiences, medals of honor, and his "red badge of courage" so conspicuously displayed upon his right cheek served him well. The young ladies of Monroe and back in Tontogany, where Nevin resided, welcomed his attentions. Tom pursued, and was pursued, by a number of eligible young ladies. With his stature as a war hero, his social calendar was always full. One particular woman especially alarmed Libbie. This older woman attempted to entangle Tom, who adroitly eluded her trap. Libbie knew that in all likelihood, Tom would live with them, or near them, for the rest of his life. She hoped that whoever Tom chose for his soul mate would also meet with her approval.[23]

There was, however, one young lady in Tom's life who may have apprehended him in a most compromising way. While visiting with Nevin in Tontogany, Tom encountered a former schoolmate, Miss Rebecca Minerd. Her family lived only a short distance from Nevin's farm, and she and Tom began to see each other socially. The following year, Rebecca gave birth to a son that she named Thomas Custer. It is very obvious the Minerd family regarded Tom as the baby's father. In a time when such activity carried a social stigma, Rebecca very conspicuously showed no hesitation of naming the child's father. It is unknown how Tom responded to Rebecca's delivery. The Custer family could not ignore the child that bore Tom's name, but publicly they said nothing.

---

[23]Ibid., p. 339.

Young Tom died in 1896 from tuberculosis. A picture of him reveals more than a passing resemblance to the Custer clan.[24]

This young man, however, does not appear to be the only child supposedly fathered by Tom. Northwestern Ohio is rife with stories of Tom's sexual escapades and progeny. Libbie in her writings makes allusions to Tom jumping from "flower to flower" during this summer.[25]

Armstrong, meanwhile, traveled to Washington hoping to reinstate both himself and Tom in the army. Tom received a personal endorsement from Phil Sheridan, who according to his chief of staff, endorsed very few.[26] A plethora of letters ensued between Tom, Armstrong, and official Washington. All aspects of Tom's military career were recounted and embellished for the purpose of procuring an active duty rank and station for him.

Armstrong's labor was finally rewarded, and Tom received a commission as second lieutenant in the First United States Infantry. Armstrong's letter home urged Tom to continue his studies, especially in the area of tactics.[27] Armstrong purchased a number of military books and sent them home to Tom, with the instructions they were to be studied thoroughly. There was talk that both Tom's and Armstrong's appointments had been curried through political favoritism. There were attempts to tie the two to the political star of President Andrew Johnson. It is clear, however, the appointments were made well before General Custer joined in President Johnson's ill-fated 1866 campaign through the Midwest.

George Custer received his commission as lieutenant colonel of the newly formed Seventh Cavalry to be assembled at Fort Riley, Kansas. The regiment's commander,

---

[24]Wood County Genealogical Society, Bowling Green, Ohio.

[25]Custer, *Tenting On The Plains*, p. 339.

[26]Letter, George Forsyth to George A. Custer, 9 January 1966. E.B.C. Collection.

[27]Merington, *The Custer Story*, pp. 177–178.

Colonel Andrew Jackson Smith, took no active part in its formation. For better or worse, the Seventh became indelibly stamped by the personality of George Armstrong Custer.

Tom was fortunate in securing his appointment with the First U.S. Infantry. Very few vacancies existed in the peacetime army, and applicants fought over every position. Tom obtained his commission over some who had been breveted major generals. Armstrong stated that "Custer's Luck" had played no small part in Tom's appointment.[28]

Tom's service with the First Infantry was brief. This interval was, however, not a happy time for him. Without Armstrong and Libbie around to provide a proper influence, he fell back into his old habits. Tom wrote a letter to Libbie in which he confessed that he had begun drinking again, blaming his distance from his family for his weakness. Tom, like any soldiers, fought a battle with alcohol for most of his life, alternately winning and losing.[29]

Tom traveled to Washington in October to clear up the matter of back pay. He felt he was due the pay for the time period between his regiment's muster out date and his notification of termination of service. The government, however, operated under the fact Tom had been paid for three months of service after he had been officially mustered out, and the Government wanted their money back.

In the meanwhile, Armstrong worked at effecting a transfer so Tom could rejoin the family at Fort Riley. This was accomplished without much trouble, and soon Tom found himself heading west.

---

[28]Ibid., p. 178.
[29]Letter, Thomas W. Custer to Elizabeth B. Custer, 1866. E.B.C. Collection.

CHAPTER FIVE

To The Plains of Kansas

At the conclusion of the Civil War the Great Plains beckoned to a war weary populace. The tide of western migration, interrupted by the war, now resumed on a massive scale. There were a number of reasons for the flood tide of settlers moving west. The Homestead Act of 1862 made it possible for every family to own land. Every male twenty-one years of age, or older, could apply for the free land. It was then up to the homesteader to live on the land and make improvements. At the end of five years, the land would be theirs, free and clear.

In addition to the enticement of free land, the growth of railroads also added to the preponderance of people migrating west. The great rail lines began to stretch west to bind the nation together. Civilization followed the railheads and with each new day east and west grew closer together.

Lastly, many veterans returning home found they could not adjust to a life of peace. Many Northern veterans discovered they had grown accustomed to the rough and tumble life of the army with all of its dangers. The family farm held no such challenges and offered only a life of tedium. Those who could not adjust felt the enticement of the West too powerful to ignore. They packed up their families and belongings and headed west in search of that missing piece of their souls.

Southern veterans found themselves in a greater predicament than their Northern counterparts. Many returned home to find their farms ravaged. Those not destroyed were held in abeyance by the government for failure to pay taxes. With no income and no money there was little recourse open to most families. Their lifestyle was gone forever and their resources were too meager to start over. Free land offered a chance for them to start over in a new land, and leave painful memories behind.

Tom Custer suffered from the same malady of many of his contemporaries. He had always disliked farming, and his soul longed for adventure. The Civil War provided him with a lifestyle which he found he could not give up. Monroe, Michigan, was agreeable, and Tom certainly savored the diversions of polite society, but it could not satiate his inner yearnings. Young women held his attention for a while. He enjoyed the element of danger; risk taking was his nature. He relished army life because it provided an outlet for his energy. He was a man, but he was living out a boy's fantasy. He was basically unencumbered by rules and responsibilities, except those thrust upon him by his older brother; but even those restrictions held promise of excitement. He could, with Armstrong's approval and company, break any rule that restrained him. While Armstrong entertained the hope of other financial ventures, the army was the only life that would allow him the freedom he desired to continue his lifestyle. In the end there was no question where they both belonged.

With the flood of settlers heading west, it was necessary for the Federal Government to provide protection for the emigrants. For this reason the army was enlarged. Two new regiments of cavalry and two of infantry were created and placed on the Plains to safeguard the great migration from the Native American tribes who stood in their way. The conclusion of one war would now be the opening chapter of the next.

Relations between the white settlers and Native American tribes of the West had, heretofore, been mostly uneventful with just a few outbreaks of violence. The inexorable westward movement of the whites had pushed the tribes of the East farther and farther west until they had been all but eradicated by the 1850s. It was hoped by some that the continued expansion into the West could be accomplished with greater attention to the plight of the Native Americans. The area was so vast that many believed it would take over a hundred years to fully invest the Plains. That time, it was hoped, would allow for the tribes to acclimate themselves to the white civilization. But with the passing of the Homestead Act, the growth of the railroads, and the ending of the Civil War, time was a commodity that neither the Native Americans or the whites had.

Tom arrived at Fort Riley, Kansas, on 16 November 1866, commissioned first lieutenant of troop A. Upon arrival, however, he found himself assigned duty as the Acting Regimental Quartermaster. As before, Tom made his home with Armstrong and Libbie, taking up residence in the bedroom at the top of the stairs. The Custers occupied half of a large double house facing the parade ground. Libbie was pleased with her new home and made every effort to adorn it and make it comfortable.

Tom was at the post barely two weeks when he came down with what Libbie described as breakbone fever, a form of inflammatory rheumatism. This attack was so severe that he was unable to perform any of his duties for nearly three months.[1]

As the officer corps assembled, a very pronounced attitude began to assert itself. Many of the officers had served during the Civil War and attained advanced rank. They were envious of any officer promoted before them. Professional jealousies and petty rivalries began to fester. Some officers resented being commanded by the flamboyant Custer. The officer corps began to polarize into two distinct camps, one

---

[1]T.W.C. Service Records, N.A.

favorable to Custer and the other against. In time this parti-
sanship would become intense.

The Custer Clan, as the pro-Custer officers came to be
called, included Tom, Captain Myles Keogh, Second Lieutenant William W. Cooke, Captain George Yates, Captain
Louis Hamilton, and Sergeant Major Myles Moylan. The
diversity of this group reflected the overall makeup of the
Seventh Cavalry. Irish born Captain Keogh had served in the
Papal army before immigrating to the United States and
serving in the Civil War. Canadian born Lieutenant William
Cooke crossed the border to fight in the Civil War. Also in
the Custer camp was Captain Louis Hamilton, the great
grandson of Alexander Hamilton.

The diversity of the officer corps and of the troopers
themselves reflected the change in American society. A large
number of the enlisted men were immigrants, some of whom
could not yet speak English. Their personal lives proved to be
as varied as their nationalities. The Seventh was made up of
former soldiers, thieves, husbands who had abandoned their
families, prospectors, failed businessmen, and those looking
for adventure. They enlisted for different reasons but, whatever the reason, their motivation was not as high minded as
those who had fought the Civil War. Warfare in the West
was not as clear cut in its aspirations as the Civil War had
been. On the plains the goals of Manifest Destiny were
obscured by racial fears and prejudices. The great western
migration of civilization collided head on with the culture of
the Plains Indians. Unfortunately, the soldiers found themselves in the middle, required to carry out orders that would
accomplish the settlement of the west at the expense of the
Native Americans. Many soldiers, Custer included,
empathized with the Indians. But they were duty bound to
carry out the mandates of their superiors, and of the population that they served.

The Seventh Cavalry was in Kansas to protect settlers and railroad workers from the Southern Cheyenne, Arapaho, and Kiowa. When spring came, work would begin on extending the railhead to the west. As the railhead moved westward, so did the settlement. The two were inexorably linked, as was the consequence—trouble with the tribes. It was feared the spring thaw would open the prairie to the hit-and-run tactics of the warriors.

Tom settled into his new surroundings with little trouble. He was back with Armstrong and Libbie, and that was the only thing that mattered. The frolicsome escapades commenced again. It had been the Custer boys' routine at home to steal up behind their mother, seize her, and carry her laughing through the house. Libbie now found herself the recipient of Tom and Armstrong's attentions.[2]

Tom enjoyed living at the extreme edge of civilization. It did, however, pose a few problems. His diet suffered from an acute lack of fresh vegetables and fruit. Fashion was an impossibility to achieve and maintain, although Libbie felt this more acutely than Tom or Armstrong. Packages from home, filled with those common things now considered delicacies, were always anxiously anticipated.

Armstrong's periodic trips east became buying sprees. He always returned with samples of the newest fashions. But his new clothes disappeared almost as soon as he arrived home. Tom rummaged through his brother's suitcases and appropriated anything that caught his eye. He appeared at the dinner table, attired in his new finery, and of course, said nothing about where he had acquired his new clothes. Armstrong knew this would happen, so many times he purchased two of everything.[3]

The trio took advantage of every opportunity to explore

---

[2]Custer. *Tenting On The Plains*, p. 389.
[3]Ibid., pp. 423–424.

their new environment. To announce their imminent departure, Tom and Armstrong began whooping and hollering as loudly as possible. The boys grabbed their Texas horns and began serenading the house. The dogs, in a frenzy, raced for the door. Once mounted, Tom, Armstrong, and Libbie galloped across the prairie, with the dogs racing to keep up, barking the entire time.

Under Tom and Armstrong's tutelage, Libbie's equestrian skills greatly improved. Her horse never faltered in keeping up with the others. Tom and Armstrong began to conspire to get Libbie to take her horse to the post race track, so they could time him properly. After much cajoling she did so, though, not without some fear and trepidation.[4]

Back under the influence of his family, Tom again became temperate. Other men were not so fortunate, and alcoholism became a considerable dilemma for the troops on the frontier. Courts-martial were frequent in the army posts across the West. Tom tried to help his fellow soldiers by admonishing those who drank too much, and by offering his encouragement and help in abandoning their addiction. As many reformed men do, Tom became an ardent opponent of all such degrading activity.

One night at mess, Tom overheard one officer chiding another officer for his attempts at a temperate life. Tom became incensed, leaped across the table, and manhandled the abusive officer. Armstrong said nothing, but gave a stern glance at the two struggling men, and they immediately separated. Libbie later berated her husband for his failure to interfere. "You're laughing, your own self, and you think Tom was right, even if you don't say a word and look so dreadfully commandery-officery at both of us!"[5]

The winter passed quietly at Fort Riley. But it was an omi-

[4]Ibid., pp. 391–392.
[5]Ibid., p. 397.

nous lull that exploded in late December. News arrived at the fort of the massacre of Captain William Fetterman and his command of 80 men near Fort Phil Kearny on the Bozeman Trail in Wyoming Territory. The Northern Plains erupted into warfare, with Fort Kearny in a virtual state of siege. This news, combined with the pressure from the railroads to provide protection, made a spring campaign against the tribes of the Southern Plains inevitable.

The commander of the army, Lieutenant General William T. Sherman, appointed Major General Philip H. Sheridan to command the Division of the Missouri. Major General Winfield S. Hancock took command of the Department of the Missouri. Hancock, nicknamed "Hancock the Superb" for his defense of Cemetery Ridge against Pickett's Charge at the battle of Gettysburg, received overall command of the troops in Kansas.

All of these officers, Lieutenant Colonel Custer included, brought to the Plains a great deal of bravery, determination, and military seasoning. Unfortunately, this experience would prove ineffectual in dealing with the warriors of the Plains. These officers were steeped in the military traditions of civilized warfare. Their adversaries on the Plains, however, knew nothing of military convention. Time and time again the army found itself confounded in its attempts to force a military solution. They made the miscalculation that, because the Plains Indians did not fight in the style to which the soldiers were accustomed, they were inferior and cowards, avoiding any real chance of confronting the military on its own terms.

Sheridan wanted the campaign to begin as soon as possible. The winter, however, had been exceptionally harsh. The spring, too, proved inhospitable with an interminable downpour of rain causing all the rivers and creeks to overflow their banks. This inclement weather continued throughout most of the summer months, making movement and resupply extremely difficult.[6]

General Hancock's command consisted of eight troops of cavalry, seven companies of infantry, and one battery of light artillery totaling 1400 men.[7] Hancock's orders were to seek out the hostile tribes, parley with them, and see if some peaceful solution could be found. The size of the expedition, however, fooled no one in its true purpose. The incidents of Indian depredations grew as the spring snows melted. The stage lines and isolated farms proved irresistible targets to the fast-moving bands of warriors.

As preparations for the upcoming campaign continued, Tom found that his participation was uncertain. He still suffered from inflammatory rheumatism, although he was much better. By 10 March, though, he was not sufficiently recovered to resume his duties. He was not strong enough to walk outside so letter writing, never his forte, became his outlet. He wrote long letters to his family back in Michigan, freely giving his advice to his nieces and nephews.[8]

General Hancock and his immediate command reached Fort Riley in the last week of March. Here four companies of the Seventh Cavalry joined the expedition. The command proceeded to Fort Harker, covering ninety miles in four days. From there they moved to Fort Larned, a distance of seventy more miles, arriving on 3 April. The chiefs sent word that they would meet the soldier chief at Fort Larned.[9]

The troopers had barely made camp when a sudden storm blew down from the Rockies and covered them with eight inches of snow. To complicate matters, the Indian chiefs

[6]Minnie Dubbs Millbrook, "The West Breaks in General Custer," in *The Custer Reader*, ed. by Hutton, p. 118.

[7]Custer, *My Life On The Plains*, p. 31.

[8]Letter, T.W.C. to Lydia Reed, 10 March 1867. Lawrence Frost Collection, Monroe County Historical Society, Monroe, Michigan.

[9]Millbrook, "The West Breaks in General Custer," pp. 35–37.

failed to appear on the date appointed. They sent word that they had discovered a herd of buffalo and were busy hunting. They further stated the snowstorm had greatly impeded their mobility. To the officers it sounded like some halfhearted excuses to avoid any confrontation with the soldiers.[10]

On Hancock's order, Custer moved his troopers to the Indian village, which was found with little trouble. But when the scouts approached the village they found it was empty. The Indians had escaped during the night.[11] Their memory of John Chivington's massacre of Black Kettle's peaceful Cheyenne village in Colorado in 1864 was all too fresh.

Meanwhile, back at Fort Riley, Tom and the other occupants also experienced memorable encounters with nature. Not long after the expedition left, a wild fire threatened to destroy the fort. Every able-bodied person emptied onto the plain to fight the conflagration. Mercifully the wind changed direction and the post was saved. Not long after the area experienced an earthquake, terrifying everyone.[12]

Armstrong and his command spent the next few weeks pursuing the Indians across western Kansas. The troopers experienced a new form of warfare in a new and strangely different country. The lush rich farms of the Shenandoah Valley were only a faint memory now. Western Kansas was barren in comparison. Trees were few and far between, usually near rivers and creeks. The tall prairie grass concealed ravines, trails, and the ever watchful Indians kept the column under constant surveillance. The vastness of the region, and the difficult terrain, complicated the ability to keep the command supplied with provisions. The command found itself on the verge of severe want. The problem of supply hampered the campaign for the rest of the summer.

---

[10]Ibid., pp. 118–119.

[11]Ibid., pp. 119–120.

[12]Custer, *Tenting On The Plains*, pp. 492–513.

While the Seventh could not locate the Indians at all, the Indians, on the other hand, had no trouble in finding victims. While Custer chased the Indians across western Kansas, the atrocities continued. Frustration grew among the high command. Custer received orders from Sheridan to cut loose from the rest of the command and range as far as he needed to find the marauding tribes.

Back at the fort, Tom gained strength with every passing day. He read Armstrong's letters excitedly, barely able to conceal his frustration at being left behind. Units of black infantrymen arrived at Fort Riley, and one man in particular had attached himself to the Custer household, hoping to impress Eliza, the Custer's black cook. The soldier quickly assumed Tom's chores, without any opposition from Tom.

But the presence of black troops was not without problems. Prejudice filled the command as officers berated and abused the soldiers. Many of the women professed apprehension because of the proximity of the black troops, and some began to carry pistols concealed on their persons. Tom worried about coming downstairs at night, afraid that a friend of Libbie's who was visiting might shoot him by accident.[13]

Other rumors ran through the fort. It was reported that many of the stage coach stops had been burned and the Indian depredations continued unabated. Tom even recounted to Libbie how he had heard that Fort Larned itself had fallen to the Indians. As it proved, these reports had no basis in fact.

The Hancock expedition, meanwhile, was still confounded by the elusive warriors of the plains. On the evening of 12 April a small band of warriors unexpectedly made their appearance. Hancock spoke to the Indians for some time, trying to impress upon them the futility of further hostilities. Hancock continued the conversation by telling the braves of his intention to continue on and meet with the chiefs of the

---

[13]Ibid., pp. 539–540.

tribes. A few days later the command drew near to a village and the warriors appeared, ready for war. A parlay was arranged and during the conversation Hancock made it known that he was determined to move closer to the Indian village. The Indians, however, abandoned the village, which Hancock promptly ordered to be burned.

The campaign proceeded on for the next few weeks with no positive results. The Seventh finally went into camp at Big Creek, Kansas, near Fort Hays. Tom, Libbie, and Colonel Smith arrived at the camp on 17 May. Armstrong was over-joyed to be reunited with his wife and brother. Tom was cer-tainly glad to be back with the command. Life at the post was too tame for him, especially with Armstrong out having all the fun. Their reunion, however, did not last long, as the com-mand received orders to continue their pursuit of the hostiles.

General Sherman was exceedingly displeased with the results of the campaign so far. Two months of campaigning had accomplished nothing. The Indian raids continued and the outrages committed against the civilian population grew daily. The army had ranged all over western Kansas, eastern Colorado, and western Nebraska with no success whatsoever. Sherman was determined to clear the area between the Smoky Hill River and the Platte of all hostile tribes. To this end he ordered Custer and the Seventh to resume their pur-suit of the Indians. The Seventh moved to Fort McPherson, then turned southward to Fort Sedgewick. From there the command moved to Fort Wallace and finally back to Fort Hays. The distance covered was approximately 1000 miles.[14]

Tom felt invigorated by the clean air of the plains. It felt good to be outside, and especially to be back with Armstrong. At night they dined together, discussing the day's march and recounting their past escapades. During their evening meal on 8 June they were discussing the personal habits of Major

---

[14]Frost, *Court-Martial of Custer*, pp. 36–37.

Wickliffe Cooper. They had barely finished their meal when they heard a gunshot. An officer rushed up with the news that Major Cooper had committed suicide. Tom and Armstrong hurried to Cooper's tent and found the unfortunate man lying on the floor in a pool of blood. Alcohol, the scourge of the western armies, had claimed another casualty.[15]

The command continued until reaching Fort Wallace where the command anticipated going into camp for several weeks. The troopers settled down to the welcome monotony of camp life while remaining ever vigilant for the possibility of attack. The horses and pack animals were tethered together, and the guards were doubled. At 8:00 P.M. bugler sounded Taps and the camp settled down to sleep. Armstrong was asleep in his tent when he was awakened by the sound of gunfire. Tom, the officer of the day, ran past his brother's tent shouting, "They are here!" The command quickly prepared for a fight, but the Indians had already run away.[16]

The command broke camp and moved out in pursuit. They had not gone far when they sighted a small group of Indians. Armstrong, Tom, and a few other men moved forward and through sign language made it known they wanted to talk. The two groups converged along a small creek, which separated them. Armstrong was surprised to find the Sioux chief, Pawnee Killer, seated on a pony across from him.

Tom kept his hand on his revolver as the conversation continued. He noticed the number of warriors facing them was increasing. It was clear to Tom that some treachery was afoot. Tom glanced at Armstrong who also had his hand on his pistol. Every few moments another warrior joined the war party. Armstrong made it known to Pawnee Killer that he would tolerate no more braves crossing the creek. He pointed to the bugler stationed between himself and the rest

---

[15]Ibid., p. 42.
[16]Custer, *My Life On The Plains*, p. 135.

of the command. Armstrong informed Pawnee Killer that if any more warriors approached he would signal the bugler and the rest of the soldiers would move forward. Custer told the chief he wished to come to the village and talk more. Pawnee Killer said he wanted gifts first, which Armstrong refused. Finally the warriors rode away.[17] The command moved out, intending to follow. The cavalry's horses, though, were no match for the Indian ponies, and the Indians quickly outdistanced the soldiers.

A few days later, the command very nearly fell victim to an old Indian trick. As the command moved across the plains, a small group of Indians appeared on the horizon. Captain Louis Hamilton, Lieutenant Custer, and the rest of A Troop were ordered to pursue them. The command moved out, and the Indians quickly disappeared below the distant horizon. When the troopers reached the top of the rise, they found the Indians were far ahead on the next ridge. The cavalrymen continued on, and when the Indians next appeared they had split into two groups. Captain Hamilton ordered Lieutenant Custer to take half of the command and pursue one group, while he chased the other. The troopers continued their pursuit, growing farther and farther apart. Suddenly Captain Hamilton found his command under attack. Hamilton ordered his men to form a skirmish line. They repulsed the Indian attack, and the men returned to the main force.[18]

From this point on conditions began to deteriorate. The sun blazed down upon the plains, scorching the grass and drying up the water holes. Day after day the sun beat down unmercifully. Dogs that had followed the command began to die of thirst. The horses and pack mules fared little better.

On 26 June the Seventh Cavalry finally ran into the Indians. A large war party of Cheyennes attacked the stage coach

---

[17]Frost, *Court-Martial of Custer*, pp. 55–57.
[18]Ibid., p. 57.

station at Ponds Creek, and attempted to run off the live-stock. Captain Albert Barnitz received orders to take his company and pursue the hostiles. The command rode for miles, and eventually caught sight of a band of approximately seventy-five warriors. The troopers gave chase across the plains, moving across the rolling hills and valleys. Just when they thought they were on another fruitless chase, they were attacked by nearly 300 warriors. Captain Barnitz ordered his men to dismount, and move forward as skirmishers. The attack continued for several hours, but eventually the Indians disengaged and rode away. The troopers sustained twelve casualties during the engagement.[19]

That same day another group of Indians attacked Lieutenant Cooke and a wagon train loaded with supplies. Lieutenant Cooke ordered the escort to dismount and form a protective cordon around the moving wagons. The Indians circled the wagons at a respectful distance, but could not compel the command to stop.[20]

Tom and the rest of the soldiers moved on to Riverside Station, where they learned that Lieutenant Lyman Kidder and ten men had been dispatched with supplemental orders for Custer. Armstrong reckoned that sufficient time had elapsed and the command should have encountered Lieutenant Kidder. They struck out again looking for any possible signs of the missing troopers. At length a trail was discovered and the bodies of Lieutenant Kidder and his men were found. A large war party had surrounded and overwhelmed Kidder and his men. They had all been mutilated beyond recognition.[21]

The command buried the fallen troopers in a common grave and continued on. They moved north, along the Platte River near the emigrant trails leading west to the gold fields

---

[19]Barnitz, *Life in Custer's Cavalry*, pp. 75–76.
[20]Ibid.   [21]Frost, *Court-Martial of Custer*, pp. 75–77.

in Colorado. The lure of untold riches proved to be too strong for some soldiers to resist. The desertion rate of the Seventh grew with each passing day. By the end of the Seventh's first year approximately 500 men had deserted.[22]

Men had been deserting in ones and twos all summer. On the evening of 6 July, Armstrong ordered Tom to reinforce the guard. Tom placed six men on stable guard and two officers to oversee the camp. During the night of 6-7 July, ten men deserted. Several stable guards had gone with them and one officer deserted the next day.[23]

As soon as a hasty breakfast was finished, the command moved south, away from the Platte and the western trails. The poor conditions, coupled with the proximity of the gold fields and the general feeling of ill will against General Custer, fueled the desire among many of the men to desert. The command rode 15 miles that morning, and stopped to give the horses time to rest. The men unsaddled their mounts and prepared a quick meal. Many men slept, hoping to catch up on some of the rest they had missed. The men had been in camp for about three hours when suddenly 13 men were seen racing across the prairie, heading to the north and the gold fields.[24] Six of the men were mounted while the others were on foot. The officer of the day woke his sleeping commanding officer. Armstrong and Tom raced to the edge of the camp. Armstrong ordered the bugler to sound "Recall." Shouts from Tom and Armstrong did no good, and the deserters continued to make good their escape.

Armstrong turned to Tom and excitedly said, "I want you to get on your horse and go after those deserters and shoot them down!"[25] Tom, Major Joel Elliott, and Lieutenant Cooke

---

[22]Burkey, *Custer Come At Once!*, p. 23.

[23]Frost, *Court-Martial of Custer*, p. 205.

[24]Ibid., p. 150.   [25]Ibid.

quickly saddled their horses and took off after the fleeing men. They pursued them for about twenty five minutes before they caught up with the men on foot. Major Elliott, in the lead, drew close to the men and ordered them to halt. Tom and Cooke rode up just as one of the deserters raised his carbine. The pistols of all three officers roared in unison, and the trooper fell dead while three of his companions were wounded. The deserters on horseback continued their escape.[26]

They placed the wounded men under arrest and brought them back to camp. In a loud voice, General Custer refused to allow the surgeon to attend to the men's wounds. Two hours later in private, Custer ordered the doctor to treat the men as best he could without drawing the attention of the command. With one exception, their wounds were not so serious that they required immediate medical attention. The man whose wound was serious did die, but the doctor later testified he would have died in any case. The men, however, did not know of Custer's direction to the doctor to treat the men. He wanted to show the rest of the command that desertion would be dealt with in a most severe manner.[27]

Tom and the command arrived at Fort Wallace on 13 July. The command had covered 81 miles in seven days. The men and horses of the command were exhausted from their grueling ordeal. Armstrong had hoped to meet General Hancock upon his arrival, but Hancock, had already departed the post. Tom and Armstrong also hoped Libbie would meet them at the fort, but she was not there.

General Custer decided to take a hand-picked detachment from the regiment and leave Fort Wallace. In his memoirs, Custer stated he left because he had received no orders and needed to be in touch with General Hancock. He went on to write that cholera had broken out in Kansas and he was

---

[26]Ibid., pp. 150–155.
[27]Millbrook, "The West Breaks in General Custer," pp. 134–135.

worried Libbie might be afflicted. Another more plausible reason could be that while at Fort Wallace, Custer received word his wife might be involved with another officer.[28]

Tom, Armstrong, and the rest of the detachment left Fort Wallace at sunset 15 July. They rode through the darkness, carefully picking their way across the Kansas prairie. Every ten or so miles they came upon a stage coach stop. Tom and Armstrong, riding in front of the column, warily approached the first stage coach stop when a shot rang out. A volley of bullets whistled over their heads and Armstrong immediately ordered the command about and moved themselves out of range. Very cautiously, a trooper inched forward to within shouting distance of the cabin. After a few well-chosen words passed between the soldier and the civilians, the command moved forward.

As Tom and the rest continued their journey, the command reached near exhaustion. The troopers became more and more strung out across the plains. Tom and Armstrong finally rode into Downer's Station the next day. Groups of stragglers followed, and the fatigued cavalrymen threw themselves down on the ground. A distant shout alerted Tom to several troopers racing across the prairie. When they arrived at the station, they informed the commanding officer they had been attacked by Indians and two men had been killed.[29]

The command rested a short period of time and struck out again. They straggled into Fort Harker at 2:00 A.M. on 19 July. They had traveled 210 miles in 67 hours. Custer learned that Colonel Smith was at Harker, and immediately went to the Colonel's quarters and woke him. He reported to Smith the condition of his command and his need for supplies. He also informed Smith of his intention to push on to Fort Riley. Custer left on the first available train going east.

---

[28]Leckie, *Elizabeth Bacon Custer and the Making of a Myth*, pp. 102–105.
[29]Custer, *My Life On The Plains*, pp. 207–211.

Armstrong arrived at Fort Riley and experienced a happy reunion with Libbie. The next morning the Custers were awakened by the officer of the day who informed Custer, by order of the Colonel of the regiment, he was to consider himself under house arrest pending charges of desertion and would await the pleasure of the Colonel.

Tom was informed that he and Lieutenant Cooke were to assemble a supply train and accompany it back to Fort Wallace. There they were to rejoin their respective commands.[30] The campaign which had begun with so much promise ended in dismal failure. The army had nothing to show for the months on the dusty plains except for saddle sores and worn out horses.

General Hancock had been under great pressure to bring the Indian depredations to a favorable conclusion. The conclusion, however, only served to send the participants scrambling to find someone to blame for the campaign's failures. Hancock pressed Colonel Smith to place charges of desertion against General Custer. To these charges were added additional charges of misconduct. The date of Custer's court-martial was set for 15 September and would be held at Fort Leavenworth. General Hancock, however, would not be present—General Sherman relieved him of command and replaced him with Major General Sheridan.

Tom was ordered to report to Fort Leavenworth as a witness for the prosecution. General Custer was found guilty on all charges and was suspended from rank and pay for one year. Armstrong and Libbie spent the first few months of their suspension at Fort Leavenworth, but when the Seventh moved out they went home to Monroe, Michigan. Tom returned to the Plains.

---

[30]Frost, *Court-Martial of Custer*, p. 86.

CHAPTER SIX

Kansas Aflame

Tom passed the winter of 1867-68 at Fort Leavenworth with Armstrong and Libbie, enjoying the best of the military society that the fort offered. In order to relieve the winter boredom, frequent parties were held, with each officer taking his turn. Tom enjoyed the gaiety as he moved from party to party. On 11 February, Tom found himself enjoying the merriment at an anniversary party for Captain and Mrs. Albert Barnitz. The festivities were proceeding nicely until Tom inadvertently stepped on Jennie Barnitz's party dress and ripped it so badly she had to excuse herself from her own party.[1] A few days later, perhaps to make amends for his carelessness, Tom invited the Barnitzs to another dance.

Meanwhile, in western Kansas the Cheyennes, Arapahos, Kiowas, and Comanches had gone into winter camps near the forts. The tribes traditionally roamed the Plains during the late spring into the early fall, but winter was their mortal enemy. The late summer and early fall were devoted to hunting, so that the tribes could lay up enough provisions to carry them through the winter months. But with the coming of the soldiers and the establishment of the forts, some tribes found it easier to winter near the whites. This was done so the tribes could obtain their badly needed provisions from the federal government as promised by Peace Commission which met with the tribes of the Southern Plains at Medicine Lodge

---

[1]Jennie Barnitz, *Life In Custer's Cavalry*, pp. 133–134.

Creek in October 1867. It became a habit of some tribes to raid and pillage during summer, seek peace in fall, and live off the federal government during winter.

Both sides made promises in order to obtain peace; promises that neither side intended to honor. During the early months of 1868, the tribes began to press the government to fulfill its pledge of guns and ammunition. The peace councils held during the fall guaranteed the Indians' food and other provisions if peace was maintained. While the government did supply the tribes with the promised foodstuffs, it tried to renege on the much desired weaponry. Now, with spring only a few months away, the Indians began to demand that the government keep all of its promises. General Sheridan was reluctant to distribute weapons to the tribes. He believed those same guns would be used against the white settlers, and the army would most certainly be sent against them.[2]

Tom and the other officers of the Seventh believed that spring would bring a resurgence of Indian depredations. But spring was a long way off, and the good times continued. Libbie's cousin, Rebecca Richmond, came to Kansas and spent several weeks with the Custers. With the threat of renewed hostilities in the spring, however, Miss Richmond decided to return home. Tom graciously helped her pack her belongings, and escorted Miss Richmond and her father to the railroad depot.[3]

On 2 March, Congress voted to reinstate Tom's brevet ranks. Tom had originally been breveted 1st lieutenant, major, and captain. In 1866, when he was mustered into the regular army, Tom was commissioned second lieutenant. His old brevet ranks corresponded to his old rank. His new rank was one grade higher, so his brevet ranks rose accordingly. Tom was breveted captain for his actions during the battle of

---

[2]Crawford, *Kansas In The Sixties*, pp. 287–288.
[3]Rebecca Richmond, *Life In Kansas With The Custers*, edited by Alice T. O'Neil (Privately printed, 1995) p. 21.

Waynesboro, Virginia, 2 March 1865. He was breveted major for his work in the battle of Namozine Church, 3 April 1865. Lastly, he was breveted lieutenant colonel for his gallantry at the battle of Sailor's Creek, Virginia, 6 April 1865.[4]

Meanwhile, the frivolity of life at Fort Leavenworth continued. A gala party was held on the evening of 23 March. Tom and his escort dined and danced to the music of the regimental band. A wonderful time was had by all.[5]

The weather, however, was changing and it would soon be spring. The days were becoming warmer, and the prairie grass was beginning to turn green and grow. As soon as possible, the Indians began leaving their winter camps near the forts and migrated onto the Plains. Soon after the winter camps broke up, news of Indian raids along the Smoky Hill route and along the Saline River raced across the Kansas prairie. The Indian raids, though, were not restricted to the white settlers. A war party of Cheyennes attacked a peaceful Kaw village near Council Grove, Kansas, but were repulsed with heavy losses.[6]

With the commencement of hostilities, the Seventh was ordered into the field, and desertion again became a problem for the regiment. Tom was assigned the task of pursuing deserters in early April. His pursuit took his command to the population centers of eastern Kansas, the closest point at which a runaway soldier could hide. He took time off from his tasks on 16 April to fall in with some friends and enjoy a few hours respite. He enjoyed a boisterous game of billiards, and afterward participated in a sing-a-long before departing to continue with his mission.[7]

Indian depredations intensified as the spring weather improved. Railroad gangs, stage coach lines, and farmers on the plains were easy targets for the roving bands of warriors. General Sheridan estimated there were approximately 6,000

---

[4]T.W.C. Service Records, N.A.
[5]Richmond, *Life With The Custers In Kansas*, p. 66.
[6]Crawford, *Kansas In The Sixties*, pp. 289–290.   [7]Ibid., p. 39.

hostiles in western Kansas and Nebraska. He countered this force with only 2600 cavalry and infantry stationed over the numerous forts of the region. It was clear that if peace was to be restored to the Plains more soldiers would be needed.[8]

General Sheridan gave Alfred Sully command, and ordered him to punish the guilty tribes. Sully's command chased the Indians all summer with little luck. Indian pressure became so intense that Sully's force had to withdraw to the comparative safety of Fort Dodge. General Sheridan felt the situation had deteriorated so much that he moved his departmental headquarters from Fort Leavenworth to Fort Hays, the western terminus of the railroad.[9]

Sheridan's request for more men was fulfilled by transferring seven troops of the US Fifth Cavalry to Kansas under the command of Major Eugene Carr. Carr, an able and determined commander, struck out with his command onto the plains to chase his foe.

At the end of May, Tom was ordered to leave Fort Leavenworth and move to Camp Alfred Gibbs on the Kansas plains. Tom's relocation came at a fortuitous time, as he had evidently reverted to his old habits of seeking solace from the bottle. Once again away from the influence of his family, Tom found he lacked the personal strength necessary to defeat his private demon. Fortunately, a young lady took him under her wing, and with her help and guidance he "reformed."[10]

In early July, Tom led a detail of ten men and scouted the area of Beaver Creek. Tom saw signs of Indians only a few hours old. He and his command followed the trail, but never came in sight of the hostiles. Tom did sight a small herd of buffalo, and he shot three in rapid succession with his pistol. His dog, Witch, surprised a wolf and, after a fierce fight, killed it. Tom returned to camp on 13 July and wrote Libbie a

---

[8]Sheridan, *Personal Memoirs*, pp. 297–299.
[9]Ibid., pp. 294–295.   [10]Barnitz, *Life In Custer's Cavalry*, p. 153.

long letter about his mission. He also stated that the regiment's acting commander, Major Joel Elliott, had ordered him to cut his hair. Tom was not sure he would comply with his commander's orders. Tom told Libbie he might have to have a "waltz" with Elliott over his hair.[11]

Not all of the tribes in Kansas were hostile. Many realized the futility of further resistance against the increasing numbers of whites. Some tribes remained close to the forts all the time for continuance of their government subsidies, and for protection from the hostile tribes. Camp Alfred Gibbs was no exception, and very soon after the post was established friendly Indians appeared in the area.

Tom held a common opinion of the "noble red man." He sympathized with their predicament. Even brother Armstrong stated that if he were an Indian, he would resist. But deep down, Tom held a very prejudicial opinion of the Native Americans. He saw them as savages surrounded by the modern world, an impediment to the growth of civilization. "I dislike having them around my tent," he wrote in one of his letters.[12] His brother officers knew of his aversion and did all they could to fill his tent with the unwelcome red visitors. Once inside Tom's tent they stayed for hours and invited themselves to all meals. Tom finally threw them out, or ordered his attendant do so.[13]

Visiting friends and relatives from the east were also frequent guests to the post. Easterners were curious about life in the Wild West. Many traveled west in order to experience that life, albeit on a modest scale, first hand. On occasion, Tom escorted visitors to the nearby Indian villages. The Easterners possessed a great curiosity about the Native Americans. Tom laughed to himself when the unwary sightseers found themselves confronted by the tribesmen, barely

---

[11]Letter, Thomas Ward Custer to Elizabeth Bacon Custer, 13 July 1868. E.B.C. Collection.
[12]Letter, Thomas Ward Custer to My Darling Sisters, 29 July 1868. E.B.C. Collection.
[13]Ibid.

modest in their summer dress. Women especially beat a hasty retreat at the sight of a warrior clad only with a breechcloth.[14]

Buffalo hunts were another obligatory ritual. Such hunts had become all the rage, with entire trains loaded with novice hunters who leaned out of the windows and fired indiscrimanently at the herds of buffalo they passed. Others preferred to hunt in the Indian fashion from horseback.

Tom and his dog, Witch, accompanied one such expedition. The Kansas summer was particularly intense, and the soldiers' dogs, which habitually accompanied the troopers on such forays, suffered from the oppressive heat. Tom's dog became acutely ill. Tom carried Witch on his horse, and tried to get the animal to drink a mixture of water and whiskey. All of this was for naught as Witch succumbed to the heat and died.[15]

On another hunt, Tom and several officers found a small herd of buffalo and gave chase. Brandy, one of Armstrong's dogs that he had left in Kansas with Tom, caught a calf but could not kill the animal. Tom shot the calf and killed two more buffalo. He then shot a third, which fell with a thud to the sunbaked Kansas prairie. Tom warily rode over to the buffalo, who suddenly jumped to its feet and charged Tom's horse. The buffalo struck with such force that the horse and its rider very nearly fell to the ground.[16]

While Tom seemed to be enjoying the late summer, other men were not as fortunate. General Sheridan, frustrated by the decided lack of military success in western Kansas, decided upon another tactic. He ordered his aide, Major George "Sandy" Forsyth, to assemble a hand picked force of 50 men for the purpose of pursuing the Indians. The unit moved out onto the Plains, and sought out their foe.

On 17 September, while scouting along the Republican River in northeastern Colorado, this elite unit found itself

---

[14]Letter, Thomas Ward Custer to Elizabeth Bacon Custer, Summer 1868. Merington Collection.
[15]Ibid.   [16]Ibid.

besieged by a force nearly six times their number. It was only through quick thinking by Major Forsyth that the command managed to repel the Indians' first attack. Forsyth ordered his men to seek the safety of a small island in the middle of the river. The fierce combat lasted for days, with the soldiers grimly battling overwhelming numbers. Almost all of the men were wounded, including Forsyth and the surgeon. Forsyth's pain was so intense that he operated upon himself to remove a bullet lodged in his thigh. A relief column finally arrived, and the battle of Beecher Island was over. But this battle did not bring about the desired end that Sheridan sought. The summer was fast slipping away without any resolution of the problem.

Late September found Tom in western Kansas, some seventy five miles from Fort Dodge. The weather was still temperate, but the wind off of the Rockies swept the prairie with an ominous sound. The early morning air became more brisk with each passing day. Tom wrote to Armstrong complaining the regiment had not been issued winter clothing. Tom went on to say General Sully was on his way to assume command of the regiment and possibly lead it in a winter campaign, or so he thought. Tom wasn't sure, but he was certain he wanted Armstrong to procure for him a couple of stag hounds.[17]

Unbeknownest to Tom, General Sheridan decided the events in Kansas needed another approach. General Sully and Major Carr both failed in their endeavors to deliver a decisive blow against the hostiles. The elusive warriors of the Plains proved to be more than a match for the staid tactics of the army. Sheridan decided the best way to deal with the Indians would be to launch a winter campaign.

During the summer months the Indians were too mobile to be caught by the military. The tribes were, however, vulnerable during the winter months. Sheridan proposed to move against them when they least expected with a strong force of

---

[17]Letter, Thomas Ward Custer to George Armstrong Custer, 23 September 1868. E.B.C. Collection.

cavalry and infantry. There was only one man whom Sheridan felt could lead the troops and bring about a suitable military solution: George Armstrong Custer. On 24 September, Sheridan wired Custer at Monroe," . . . can you come at once?"[18] Sheridan cleared the matter of Custer's suspension with General Sherman. Custer, chafing at the bit by his idleness in Michigan, lost no time in hurrying to the Plains. He breakfasted with Sheridan at his headquarters on 1 October.

The next morning, General Custer and an escort left the fort and headed across the Plains. That afternoon he surprised Tom and the rest of the regiment encamped at Bluff Creek, some thirty miles south of Fort Dodge. In the privacy of Tom's tent the two hugged and fell to wrestling with one another. Tom caught up with the family gossip while he and Armstrong ate dinner. They had barely finished when the camp was attacked by a band of hostile Indians. The warriors tried to lure the troopers into leaving the protection of their camp and give chase. By this time, though, the soldiers had learned that subterfuge all too well.[19]

The next day, the command broke camp and began to feel their way south toward the Indian Territory. President Andrew Jackson had, in the early 1830s, set aside the territory for the purpose of resettling the Indian tribes. The Five Civilized Tribes were sent here and had, by degrees, settled eastern Oklahoma, leaving western Oklahoma open to the militant tribes who moved in and out at will. The Indian tribes preyed upon the Kansas frontier, using the Indian Territory as a base from which they would raid, and then return with their spoils. This time their safe haven would not protect them.

The command continued moving south. Troopers on campaign were forced to forgo the niceties of civilization. Baths became very infrequent and not every trooper worried about his appearance. Tom, however, did take it upon himself to make an effort at cleanliness. In early October, the command made camp

---

[18]Sheridan, *Personal Memoirs*, p. 216.   [19]Custer, *My Life On The Plains*, pp. 218–219.

near a small creek, and Tom and a friend decided to take the
opportunity to take a bath. They had not seen any Indians for a
few days and they supposed they would be safe for the few minutes needed to scrub themselves. The two friends rode to the
creek, stripped off their uniforms, and began bathing. Suddenly,
their horses began to act jittery. Tom realized the horses were
skittish because they could smell Indians approaching. The two
troopers immediately waded out of the creek and ran to their
horses. There was no time to stop for their clothing or saddles as
every second counted. Tom seized his horse's mane and swung
himself up onto the horse. The two naked troopers galloped
away from the creek and headed back for the safety of the camp
as quickly as their horses would run. The Indians rapidly came
into view behind them, yelling and shrieking. The braves loosed
a volley of arrows at the fleeing soldiers with no effect. They
reached the picket line of the camp and everyone came running
to repulse the Indian attack. The warriors, however, had already
given up their pursuit. All that the surprised troopers encountered was the sight of the two naked men who were extremely
fortunate to have lost no more than their clothes. Since they
were on campaign, Tom did not carry any extra clothing. He
covered himself with a blanket, and duly made the rounds of his
brother officers borrowing the necessary items.[20]

A few days later, Tom experienced another hapless episode.
The dogs of the regiment accompanied the command across
the Plains. On 10 October, Armstrong's dog, Brandy, flushed
out a skunk from its den, and proceeded to maul the animal.
Tom dashed forward and tried to yank the dog off of the skunk
before any odorous damage could be done. Just as Tom pulled
Brandy away, the skunk turned and showered the two unfortu-
nates, and Tom lost his second set of clothes in a week. Being a
Custer, however, he decided to use his new aroma to play a
game on his brother officers. Arriving back at camp, he ran into

---

[20]Custer, *Following the Guidon*, pp. 18–19.

Captain Hamilton and apprised him of his malodorous intent. The two men entered a nearby officer's tent, now crowded with other men engaged in light conversation. Tom and Captain Hamilton entered and took up positions near the entrance of the tent. Before long comments began to issue from the assemblage concerning the fragrance of the night air. "Some dogs has been killing a skunk. I wonder where the brute is?" observed one occupant of the tent. Tom decided it was time to move on, and the two men quickly exited the tent. They walked down the line and found another tent full of comrades. Here, Tom again repeated his deviltry, exiting just as the company began to look for the odorous canine. Again Tom and Captain Hamilton ran out into the night, laughing at their puzzled friends. Finally, though, Tom had to confess to his new predicament and once again go begging for more clothes.[21]

Tom was able to redeem himself a few days later when the command encountered a landscape alive with hundreds of wild turkeys. He quickly shot five for the officer's mess.[22]

Never one to let anything hold him down for long, Tom quickly regained his old ways. He and Armstrong got into a row over stag hounds. Tom demanded that Armstrong give him a dog, Tom reminded Armstrong he had promised him one earlier. Tom assured Armstrong that Libbie would support him in his claim, and that his brother's memory was clearly declining. In a letter to Libbie, Armstrong, complained about his brother. "I might as well talk to a mule. You have some experience in determining how persistent a Custer is when seeking anything he really desires."[23]

The command continued their movement south. The weather was cooling and it rained intermittently. On 2 November, General Custer gave an order that many in the command profoundly

---

[21]Letter, George Armstrong Custer to Elizabeth Bacon Custer 10 October 1868. E.B.C. Collection.   [22]Custer, *Following The Guidon*, p. 12.
[23]Letter, George Armstrong Custer to Elizabeth Bacon Custer , 22 October 1868. E.B.C. Collection.

resented. Custer decided the Seventh would give a much better appearance if the regiment's horses were color coded. One company would be all bays, sorrels, and so on. The men, however, did not like the notion of giving up their horses with whom they had developed a special bond. But no amount of arguing could dissuade Custer from redistributing the mounts of the Seventh.

By 13 November the command was closer to the Indian Territory. The wagon train was placed in a column of fours, with two troops of cavalry in advance and rear, and three troops of cavalry on each flank.[24] The command now consisted of 450 wagons, eleven companies of the Seventh Cavalry, three companies of the Third Infantry, one company of the Fifth Infantry, and one company of the Thirty-eighth Infantry.[25]

On 18 November the command was well into the Indian Territory. The soldiers halted on a large plain, suitable for good grazing. The decision was made to make this location their base camp, which they christened Camp Supply. At this point, Armstrong became embroiled in a quarrel with General Sully over the command of the expedition. General Sheridan finally intervened and Custer was given command. Sheridan ordered Sully to return to Kansas and take command of Fort Harker. Sheridan had not called Custer out of suspension to have him play second fiddle to anyone. Sheridan wanted results and Custer had never disappointed him in the past.[26] Sheridan was frank in his orders to Custer:

> . . .proceed south, in the direction of the Antelope Hills, thence toward the Washita River, the supposed winter seat of the hostile tribes; to destroy their villages and ponies; to kill or hang all warriors, and bring back all women and children.[27]

The Seventh Cavalry prepared for a thirty-day campaign and moved out. Reveille sounded at 3:00 A.M. on 23 Novem-

[24]Benjamine Godfrey, "Some Reminiscences Including the Washita Battle, November 27, 1868," in *The Custer Reader*, ed. by Hutton, p. 162.
[25]Stan Hoig, *Battle of The Washita*, p. 77.
[26]Ibid., pp. 81–82.   [27]Ibid., p. 82.

ber. It began to snow that morning and continued all day. The snow became so dense that visibility was down to only a few feet. Tom, comfortable in his greatcoat, repeatedly wiped off the snow, hoping to prevent his coat from becoming any more wet. The snow caked on his hair, freezing, and breaking off. Armstrong rode in the lead, a compass in his hand to determine the proper direction. The snow finally stopped that night, but by then several inches blanketed the ground.[28]

Cheyenne Chief Black Kettle's village lay on the extreme western terminus of the Washita River valley. Further east in the valley, unbeknowest to Custer, lay scattered villages of other Cheyennes, Arapahos, Kiowas, Comanches, and Apaches. There were approximately 6,000 Indians in the 10-15 mile stretch of valley.[29]

Black Kettle had just returned from meeting with General William B. Hazen. Black Kettle had gone to talk with Hazen, hoping to persuade the army of his peaceful intentions. Hazen, though, informed Black Kettle that he could be of no help; troops were already in the field moving into the Indian Territory. Black Kettle returned to his village hoping to preclude a repetition of the infamous attack on his people in 1864 at Sand Creek, Colorado.

Upon his return, Black Kettle held a council for the local chiefs. He informed them of Hazen's warning about the troops moving toward them. Some of the chiefs scoffed at any notion of white soldiers moving through the drifting snow. Others agreed with Black Kettle. They had heard rumors of a large body of white soldiers to the north. Black Kettle finally proposed dispatching runners to find the soldiers, and inform them that the tribes were not on the warpath.[30]

On that same day, Custer sent a detachment of soldiers under Major Joel Elliott to locate the trail of the hostiles.

[28]Godfrey, "Reminiscences...", pp. 164–166.   [29]Hoig, *Battle of The Washita*, p. 93.
[30]Ibid., p. 94.

The trail was easy to find in the deep snow, and Elliott sent word back to Custer of his discovery of a fresh trail. The Indians were close.[31]

Armstrong ordered his bugler to sound "officer's call." Tom and the rest gathered around to hear their orders. Custer informed the officers that Major Elliott's command had accomplished their mission and found the tracks of a large war party heading toward the Washita. He informed the officers that the order for the advance would be given in twenty minutes.[32]

Tom immediately returned to his unit and informed the men they were moving out, and to open the supply wagons. Each man carried one hundred rounds of ammunition, a small amount of coffee, hard bread, jerky, and a small amount of forage for their horses. Tom, likewise, made haste in procuring those supplies he would need. All items deemed unnecessary would be left behind under the care of Tom's company commander, Captain Louis Hamilton.

Captain Hamilton drew the assignment of guarding the supply train during the battle. He was, of course, quite unhappy with the prospect of his unit marching into battle and his being left behind. He went to General Custer and pleaded to be reassigned so he could accompany his command. Custer informed him if he could find someone else who was willing to take his place he would be allowed to lead his men into battle. Finally, he located an officer suffering from a mild case of snow blindness who agreed to switch places with him. Hamilton informed General Custer and rejoined his command.[33]

The command moved out at 4 A.M. The bright moon sank below the horizon, and left the men in darkness. Sunrise found them still moving south. The landscape was a dazzling white in every direction. The snow was nearly a foot deep and the horses

---

[31]Godfrey, "Reminiscences...", p.167.
[32]Custer, *My Life On The Plains*, p. 303.   [33]Ibid., p. 309.

experienced some difficulty in forcing their way. Armstrong
sent the scouts out to find Major Elliott's trail. Finally, they discovered Elliott's tracks in the snow. The command increased
their gait, confident they were now on the right path. Custer
sent the scouts forward to overtake Elliott and order him to find
a suitable place to camp and await the rest of the command.

Late in the afternoon the command caught up with Major
Elliott's detachment. The troopers had been in the saddle
since before sunrise and the men and horses were hungry and
in need of rest. The command hastily made camp. The
troopers unsaddled their fatigued horses and placed their
grain sacks over the animals' heads. Small fires were permitted only under the cover of the riverbank. Tom quickly
brewed a hot cup of coffee and feasted upon hard bread and
jerky. Many men settled down for a quick nap.

By 10:00 P.M. the command saddled up and moved out.
The moonlight illuminated their way across the snow-cov-
ered landscape. The command was given for silence on the
march. The men could not even light their pipes for fear the
Indians would sight them and be warned. The only noise the
column made was the sound of the horses' hooves cracking
the surface of the frozen snow.[34]

Just after midnight the command stopped. Scouts in the
advance made signs for General Custer to come forward. One
of the scouts whispered he could smell smoke ahead. Custer
put his face to the wind, but could not discern any aroma of
smoke. The scout was adamant he could smell smoke, so they
were sent forward. They had not gone far when they discovered the remnants of a smoldering campfire. Suddenly they
heard the barking of a dog. Tom strained to pierce the silence,
and he thought he could hear the cry of an infant. The scouts
gestured for Custer to follow them. Armstrong, Tom, and the
other officers removed their sabers and quietly crawled up the

---

[34]Ibid., pp. 308–319.

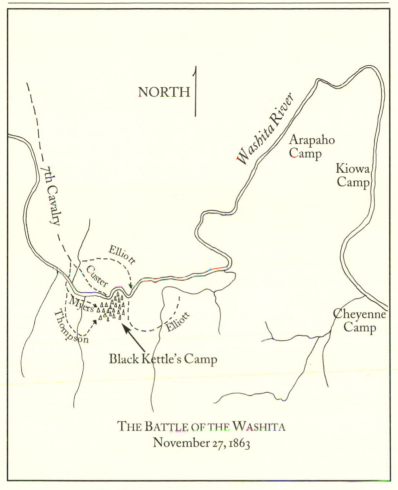

NORTH

Washita River

Arapaho
Camp

Kiowa
Camp

7th Cavalry

Elliott

Custer

Myers

Thompson

Elliott

Cheyenne
Camp

Black Kettle's Camp

THE BATTLE OF THE WASHITA
November 27, 1863

hill behind the scouts. Once on top they peered across the river
and saw the sleeping Indian village.

Tom and the officers scrutinized the encampment. After a
few minutes they moved back down the hill. After walking a
suitable distance they halted and surrounded General Custer
who quickly outlined his plan of attack. Major Elliott, commanding companies G, H, and M, was to circle the village,

giving a wide berth to avoid any noise, and take up positions on the east side of the village, just across the Washita River. Custer directed Colonel William Thompson, commanding companies B and F, to cross the Washita on the right and attack from the southwest. Colonel Edward Myers and companies E and I received orders to ford the Washita on the right with Thompson's command and attack from the west. The balance of the command under General Custer would attack across the Washita from the north. The command to enforce silence was repeated. Any dogs with the command were to be either muzzled, or killed to prevent any barking. The signal for the attack would be the regimental band, accompanying General Custer, playing the Seventh's battle song, "Garryowen."[35]

The respective commanders returned to their units, and moved out to assume their positions. Tom and Armstrong walked back to their headquarters area. Armstrong laid down and promptly went to sleep. The moon went down below the hills to the west, and the command was enveloped in darkness. Tom was cold, it always seemed to be coldest before the dawn, especially now, waiting for the attack to begin.

Armstrong woke after an hour nap. He looked to the east, but could see no sign of the dawn. Tom pointed to an unusually bright object hovering over the Indian village. Armstrong first thought that perhaps it was a flare, but he could not hear any repercussion. They finally realized it was a star, quite unlike any they had ever seen.

Slowly the darkness began to recede and the eastern sky began to lighten. Custer signaled for the command to mount. Seated in their saddles, the command scoured the darkness in front of them, trying to make out the outline of the village. Not a sound could be heard emanating from the tepees scattered along the Washita. A sudden tinge of apprehension swept through the command. What if the village was

---

[35]Ibid., pp. 320–323.

deserted? What if the Indians had discovered the troops earlier, and fled leaving everything behind them? A barking dog and the scouts reporting the discovery of the pony herd dispelled all such thoughts.[36]

Suddenly, a shot rang out from the opposite side of the village. Custer turned in his saddle and ordered the band to strike up "Garryowen." The first few notes erupted out of the instruments. The company buglers blasted out the notes of "Charge!" The regimental band played only a few more notes before their instruments froze. The song, however, had the desired effect. The emotionally charged troopers roared their approval, and the Seventh Cavalry swooped down from the four corners of the compass and into the village.

Tom struck his horse's flanks with his boots and shouted into the air. He held his reins with his left hand and carried his pistol in his right. His horse leaped into the icy Washita. Up ahead he saw dark figures in the half light running through the camp. His horse splashed out of the water and up the snowy embankment. The shouts and screams of the combatants filled the morning air. Tom fired his revolver at the moving figures. The lethal sound of gunfire exploded from all sides. There was no time to distinguish friend from foe, let alone men from women and children. Tom urged his horse forward and raced through the village.

Captain Hamilton, only a few feet in front of Tom, led his men into the village. He fired a few shots, when suddenly he was shot in the chest and died instantly. His body remained in the saddle for a few more feet, and then slowly fell to the ground.[37]

In such attacks all members of an Indian village became combatants. Young boys, women, and the elderly all joined in the fight to defend the village. In such a case they all became legitimate targets, and were dispatched without hesitation. Captain Frederick Benteen found himself con-

---

[36]Ibid., 330–335.   [37]Hoig, *Battle of The Washita*, p. 132.

fronted by a young boy who, in an attempt to get away, charged Benteen and shot at him several times. The boy fired twice more, wounding Benteen's horse who fell to the ground emptying Benteen from the saddle. The small warrior made it clear he intended to fire again. Benteen had no choice but to shoot the boy dead. Benteen later discovered the young warrior was Black Kettle's son.[38] In the space of only ten minutes the command had captured the village. The surprised occupants fled in all directions. The panic stricken warriors took cover behind trees, logs, and the river bank, and began to fire back into the village. The battle dissolved into a dozen small engagements between troopers and warriors fighting individually, or in small groups. Soldiers dismounted and moved forward as skirmishers to dislodge the embattled warriors. One by one the Indians were silenced.[39]

The troopers saw a squaw dash from a tepee with a young white captive. She darted in and out of the lodges, with the soldiers in hot pursuit. She saw more troopers coming to block her escape. Quickly, she reached into her blanket and pulled out a knife which she plunged into the terrified child. A split second later she fell dead from a soldier's bullet.[40]

Not all of the village's inhabitants tried to escape from the village. Scouts went from tepee to tepee telling the frightened occupants that they would not be harmed, and to come out. Those women and children who did try to run were being quickly rounded up and herded back into the village.

As Major Elliott entered the camp, he too saw the Indians attempting to flee in every direction. He saw a group of dismounted warriors racing off to the southeast. He turned in his saddle and asked for volunteers to join him in the pursuit. He quickly assembled some nineteen men for his detail. He

---

[38]Ibid., p. 133.   [39]Custer, *My Life On The Plains*, pp. 339–340
[40]Ibid.

turned to Lieutenant Owen Hale and shouted, "Here goes for a brevet or a coffin!"[41] Elliott ordered his detachment to give chase to the fleeing warriors.

Lieutenant Edward Godfrey and a few troopers gave chase to another group of warriors. Godfrey pursued the braves for almost two miles. As Godfrey's horse raced on, he became aware of some troopers yelling at him to stop. He turned to look at the men who were frantically making gestures, pointing ahead of him. Godfrey, very cautiously now, urged his horse forward and ascended the ridge in his front. Reaching the top, he saw before him in the valley below, dozens of tepees, with warriors running back and forth. He quickly retraced his path back to the command where he reported to General Custer his discovery of another Indian village, not more than three miles away. As Godfrey was making his report, other men reported they also had seen more Indians on the hills to the north.[42]

General Custer realized the situation had drastically changed, and the command was in peril from an unknown number of hostiles. He gave orders for the men to round up the captives, and to gather enough of the Indians' provisions to sustain them for the march back to Camp Supply. Custer turned to Godfrey and ordered him to destroy the pony herd.

Custer looked around, "Where is Elliott?" Tom and the others looked around, but no one could see him. Someone mentioned he might be chasing the escaping hostiles. Godfrey reported he had heard heavy firing from the opposite side of the valley.[43]

Custer ordered everything to be destroyed. One by one the Indian's lodgings were knocked down and set afire. All of their belongings quickly went up in smoke, which blackened the sky over the village. On the other side of the camp, Lieutenant Godfrey's men began the slaughter of the Indians' pony herd. At first,

---

[41]Godfrey, "Reminiscences . . .", pp. 122–123.
[42]Ibid.   [43]Ibid.

they tried to lasso the horses and cut their throats. The horses, however, were afraid of the soldiers, and so the men began to fire into the herd. Tom and Armstrong joined in the destruction, and before long some 800 horses were dead or dying.[44]

With the village destroyed and the ponies dead, Custer ordered the command to assemble. More and more warriors gathered on the hills surrounding the battlefield. Custer ordered two squadrons to mount and disperse the braves before they could attack. This done, he ordered the regimental band to play, and the command moved out. There was, however, still no sign of Major Elliott. But Custer felt he could not afford to spend any more time in the area. It would not be long before the assembling warriors would attack.

Tom tore a piece of cloth and bandaged his right hand. He had received a minor flesh wound from a stray bullet. It bled a lot, and was painful, but it was more of a nuisance than anything.[45]

A quick compiling of casualties revealed four men had been killed or mortally wounded during the attack. Another 15 men had been wounded, with a further 19 missing and presumed dead. The soldiers counted some 103 dead Cheyenne, with 53 women and children taken prisoners.[46]

With the command assembled, Custer gave the order and the band began to play "Ain't I Glad To Get Out Of The Wilderness." The command moved in the direction of the other villages. This act of bravado was a ruse, intending to frighten the neighboring tribes into thinking the soldiers intended to continue attacking the camps. The command marched until twilight, when Custer turned the command around, and the tired troopers retraced their steps. The soldiers and Indian prisoners began the march back to Camp Supply.

---

[44]Ibid., pp. 173–174. [45]Hoig, *Battle of The Washita*, p. 208.
[46]Ibid., pp. 139–140.

CHAPTER SEVEN

Big Creek

Tom and the battle fatigued troopers rode through the evening, not stopping until nearly 2:00 A.M. They rested a few hours, and were back in the saddle by daylight. The command reached its temporary base camp and recovered their belongings at around 10:00 A.M. Tom joined the other men and prepared his first hot meal in days. After finishing his meal, the march resumed, and Tom arrived at Camp Supply at ten o'clock that night.[1]

During the march, the Indian women observed their captors warily. They noticed the soldiers treated Armstrong with respect, befitting a great chief. The squaws introduced Armstrong to one of their number and, during the introductions, initiated a ceremony intending to marry him to the young woman. After a few moments of confusion, he realized what was happening. He thanked them profusely for the intended honor, but explained he was forced to decline their kindness.[2]

The day after the troopers arrived at Camp Supply, the command attended to the burial of Captain Hamilton. Tom, Armstrong, and General Sheridan were among the pallbearers who placed the flag draped coffin into an ambulance. Captain Hamilton's riderless horse led the mourners to a knoll overlooking the camp where, with military pomp and ceremony, they laid him to rest.[3]

---

[1]Custer, *My Life On The Plains*, pp. 375–376.
[2]Ibid., pp. 361–363.   [3]Ibid., pp. 394–396.

Tom found the next few days exceedingly busy. General Sheridan ordered the Seventh to resume its assignment of locating the remainder of the militant tribes. On 7 December, Tom and the command left Camp Supply. General Sheridan, desiring to see the battlefield of the Washita, accompanied the expedition. The command also wanted to try to locate the missing Major Elliot and his men.

The officers and men felt troubled about Custer's failure to ascertain the fate of Elliot, and a wide schism developed among the command. The men were already divided in their loyalty to their commanding officer. More and more, the officer corps of the Seventh found themselves choosing sides over the episode. Some sided with Custer, while those finding themselves at odds with their commanding officer, rallied behind Captain Frederick Benteen. The Elliot incident rapidly became a cancer which ate away at the fabric of the regiment.

The tenth of December dawned cold and bitter. Custer ordered the bulk of the command to remain in camp, while he and a small detachment accompanied General Sheridan to the battlefield. After a ride of an hour and a half the charred remains of the battlefield came into view. The village unfolded in front of them, a macabre sight with the morning sun shimmering on the frost-covered earth.

Tom saw hundreds of crows and ravens covering the ground. Wolves glanced up from their ghastly repast at the troopers who disturbed them. Tom and the troopers slowly rode forward. The birds reluctantly took flight, darkening the sky. The wolves, snarling and growling, grudgingly retreated before the approaching soldiers. Tom, Armstrong, and General Sheridan rode to the top of a small hill from which they surveyed the grisly scene.[4]

The remains of dozens of Indians lay strewn on the

---

[4]Keim, *Sheridan's Troopers*, pp. 143–145.

ground in front of them. Apparently, members of the neighboring tribes had been to the village and attempted to bury their fallen friends. The soldiers found some bodies wrapped in robes, and others placed in trees. The body of Black Kettle, however, could not be found, and so it was assumed his body had been taken away and buried.

The soldiers inspecting the village heard the sound of the scouts' horses galloping across the plain. The scouts excitedly rode up to the top of the hillock and reported to Custer their discovery of a trail of shod horses, leading away from the camp toward the southeast. The command assembled and followed the trail, which led across a small tributary of the Washita. As Tom ascended the far bank of the creek, he saw a body. The command continued following the trail and, within a few minutes, discovered Major Elliot and his men. Their mutilated bodies lay in a circle, not more than twenty yards across. Tom gazed in mute horror at the remains of his friends.

Each man had been disfigured, almost beyond recognition. Their bodies, all lying face down, exhibited numerous gunshot and arrow wounds. A few of the men were beheaded, or nearly so. All of their major body muscles were lacerated. Wolves continued the butchery that the Indians had started.[5] The gruesome scene reminded Tom of the Kidder massacre, and the wintry breeze suddenly seemed much colder. The grim faced soldiers attended to the somber task of burying their fallen comrades.

With the expedition to the battlefield complete, General Sheridan and his escort returned to Camp Supply. The Seventh Cavalry resumed their search for hostile villages. For the next twelve days, Tom endured a march over the most grueling terrain. It rained incessantly, turning the paths he traveled into quagmires of mud. The geography of the terrain made the march even more arduous, with many steep

---

[5]Ibid., pp. 143–144.

ravines, hills, and impassible rain swollen rivers and creeks. Some days the command barely covered eight miles. They realized the object of their mission, as many chiefs sought out the column and made overtures for peace.[6]

Tom and Armstrong celebrated the New Year of 1869 on the march. Armstrong wrote Libbie on 2 January that, "The Indian war is over."[7] There were, of course, some hold outs and to reach these Custer decided to form a forty-man detachment, and make a more concerted effort to reach the recalcitrant tribes.

Tom and the command moved out, following the northern range of the Wichita Mountains. They turned south toward the Red River, but the area proved to be barren of both Indians and game. Tom depleted his provisions, and found himself existing on the corn he carried for his horse. He remembered Indians sometimes fed their horses tree bark, so he tore some off of a tree and gave it to his mount.[8]

Tom, Armstrong, and the others endured the privations of the march as best they could, but they could not abide the misery of not receiving mail. At one point the mail carrier was in sight, but the river's current was so rapid he could not get across. They tried different methods of getting the mail across, but nothing worked. Tom volunteered to try to ford the river, and he urged his horse into the torrent. The animal tried in vain to swim against the current, but could not make it. Tom turned his horse around, and found it a difficult struggle to regain the river bank he had just left.[9] The men finally rigged a harness, and the mail was retrieved.

Armstrong decided that more progress might be made if he split the command. On 22 January he sent Tom and a

---

[6]Elizabeth B. Custer, *Following the Guidon*, p. 46.
[7]Letter, George Armstrong Custer to Elizabeth Bacon Custer, 2 January 1869. E.B.C. Collection.
[8]Hoig, *Battle of the Washita*, pp. 169–170.
[9]Custer, *Following the Guidon*, pp. 47–48.

small detachment to scout the Red River area for any signs of
the hostile tribes that had so far eluded their search. Tom
scoured the region for two weeks and returned on 8 February
with nothing to report. The column continued their march.

The mission was a hardship to both men and horses. The
men found ways of venting their frustrations, and the command structure began to fall apart. Armstrong decided that
discipline had become too lax, and took steps to improve it. He
ordered the arrest of those men who stepped out of bounds.
Tom and Captain George Yates, a Custer friend from Monroe,
Michigan, both found themselves under arrest for minor
infractions.[10] Yates took exception to Armstrong's treatment.
Other men also considered Custer a martinet; a petty man
bent on trivial details. Tom, however, took it all in stride.

Tom continued his normal banter with his brother, teasing
him about the time he spent writing to Libbie. Armstrong
spent hours writing letters, and was up long after everyone
else had gone to sleep. Tom often entered Armstrong's tent
early in the morning to find his brother still writing at his
desk. Letter writing was important to the Custers, and the
family thrived on being able to remain in some contact with
each other. They might endure the hardships of being separated from one another, but never tolerated the lack of mail.

Tom informed his brother of his irritation at Libbie's most
recent letter. It was too brief for Tom's liking. He told Armstrong to inform Libbie that "he was done with her from this
out."[11] This little irritation amused Armstrong, and he wrote
of it to Libbie. He also informed Libbie that Tom had
become a bit vulgar, but he felt she could reprimand him
when they returned.

On 15 March the column discovered a fresh Indian trail

---

[10]Letter, George Armstrong Custer to Elizabeth Bacon Custer, 8 February 1869. Mering-
    ton Collection.
[11]Ibid.

and followed it to an abandoned village. Tom saw numerous objects scattered about, discarded by the Indians in their haste to escape the approaching soldiers. The command remounted and moved out at a fast gait. They had not gone many miles when eight mounted warriors appeared. General Custer, using sign language, made it known to the braves he wished to speak with them. The Indians declared they belonged to Chief Medicine Arrow's tribe. Custer asked permission to speak to their chief. One of the warriors galloped back to camp, and in a while a large band of warriors approached. Among them rode Medicine Arrow, resplendent in his warrior finery.

After introductions, Custer inquired if Medicine Arrow held any white captives in his camp. Medicine Arrow replied in the affirmative. Custer asked to visit Medicine Arrow's camp, and continue their talk there, out of the wind. Custer and Lieutenant Cooke followed the warriors back to their village. Tom and the rest of the command moved to quickly encircle the encampment. The warriors, observing the movements of the white soldiers, became agitated and began riding their war ponies back and forth through the village. In the chief's tent, Custer watched as the tribe's holy man went through his ritual. The warriors passed the peace pipe from person to person, and after all had smoked, the medicine man emptied the contents of the pipe onto Custer's boots. He told Custer if he ever again attacked the Cheyenne he and his men would be killed.[12] Custer, sensing bad medicine was in the air, said he would leave, and their talk would continue tomorrow.[13]

The next day the chiefs came into the soldier's camp. Custer told Tom and other officers to stand nearby and, at his signal, take the chiefs prisoner. Custer turned to the chiefs and demanded the return of the captives, but the chiefs

[12]Utley, *Cavalier In Buckskin*, p. 73.
[13]Hoig, *Battle of the Washita*, pp. 173–177.

demurred. They became sullen and tense at the request, observing the proximity of Custer's officers. Custer could see their apprehension and so he stood up, unbuckled his gun belt, and let it fall to the ground. At once the Indians attempted to leave, but Tom and the other officers sprang upon them, disarmed them, and took them prisoner.[14]

Custer informed his prisoners that he wanted the white captives, and if they were not released he would order his men to hang the chiefs. Tense negotiations followed, and the soldiers placed the chiefs on horses with the nooses ready, when the white women were released. With this final success, the command ended their lengthy campaign, and rode back to Fort Hays.

As they approached Fort Hays, the Seventh heard the garrison's band playing the battle song of the regiment, "Garry Owen." The post commander, Nelson Miles, greeted the command and relieved the Seventh of their prisoners. Miles furnished the command with tents and provisions. The Seventh moved about two miles east of the post, and made their camp in a bend of Big Creek.

Hays City, Kansas, was the new home for Tom and the command. Hays was the end of the line for the railroad, and the big cattle herds coming up from Texas made Hays an important city. The town, only a few months old, already possessed a reputation on the frontier as a boisterous and hazardous place. Gunfights and funerals occurred with great frequency. The good citizens of Hays entrusted their safety, and the administration of law and order, to one James Butler Hickok, more commonly known on the frontier as Wild Bill.[15]

The camp at Big Creek was a welcome relief after almost an entire winter pursuing Indians across the southern plains.

---

[14]Ibid.
[15]Burkey, *Custer Come At Once!*, p. 60.

Now, with time on their hands, the soldiers found themselves fascinated by their Indian captives. Tom, also curious, often visited the Cheyennes, observing their peculiar lifestyle and customs. The captives gave Tom and Armstrong Indian names. The Indians named Armstrong *Montocke*, meaning "strong arm." They christened Tom *Mouksa*, meaning "buffalo calf."

During one of his visits to the captives Tom noticed a sick dog. A confirmed animal lover, he decided to return and find the dog and nurse it back to health. Tom diligently searched the compound looking for the animal. When he found him he was in the process of being boiled for the evening's supper. Tom gratefully refused the portion offered to him, and he left the prison area for the safety of his new home.[16]

Tom's new residence was a tent, fourteen by sixteen feet. Carpenters constructed floors in many of the tents to increase their comfort. Once finished, Tom adorned his tent with his captured trophies; Indian headdresses, shields, spears, bows and arrows, scalp locks, and various hides. He was especially proud of the assortment of live rattlesnakes he kept, each in its own special box.[17]

Tom became an expert in capturing the venomous creatures. When he encountered one of suitable length, he quickly took a coat and knotted one sleeve. He approached the reptile and pinned its head to the ground with the butt of his rifle, reached down and grabbed the snake's head with one hand and the body with the other. He stuffed the twisting serpent into the coat and tied up the other sleeve.[18]

Tom always took great delight in showing Libbie his latest acquisition. She entered his tent reluctantly, only after much protesting, and perched herself upon his bunk. Her eyes

---

[16]Custer, *Following the Guidon*, p. 94.
[17]Ibid., pp. 112–116.
[18]Ibid.

filled with terror as he opened the boxes and carefully extracted the snakes so she could admire them. Libbie advised Tom to place all of the snakes in one crate, so they could enjoy each other's company. Tom knew, however, if that were done he soon would have no snakes at all. "If you think, old lady, that after all the trouble I have been to, to catch these snakes to show you, I am going to make it easy for them to eat each other up, you are mightily mistaken."[19]

When not admiring, or adding, to his collection, Tom spent considerable time at Armstrong and Libbie's more spacious tent. The carpenters had constructed a deck which extended out the back of their tent, making a kind of elevated platform with a rail. The trio spent much of their time there; Armstrong reading, Libbie sewing, and Tom smoking. Tom jokingly referred to it as the "beer garden," much to Libbie's displeasure.[20]

Many new officers found assignment in the ranks of the Seventh while they were encamped at Big Creek. Captain Algernon Smith joined the regiment at this time. Smith gratefully accepted Tom's offer to share his tent until his own quarters were ready. It was, however, with great apprehension that Captain Smith approached his new home. At the opening of his tent, Tom chained his pet wolf. Smith eased himself around the growling, snapping beast as best he could. He entered the tent to find himself greeted by a chorus of rattlesnakes, unhappy at being awakened by the snarling wolf. Tom's dog, Brandy, habitually slept under Tom's bunk, and he did not take kindly to being disturbed either. Smith found himself surrounded, with no retreat possible. He was rescued by the propitious arrival of Tom, who roared with laughter at his guest's hesitation to make himself at home. That night Smith slept fitfully, acutely aware of every sound and of the

---

[19]Ibid.
[20]Ibid., p. 72.

possible enemy that lurked in the darkness. Smith moved closer to Tom, and piled his belongings on the opposite side of the bed, praying the two barricades would be enough to impede anything that might feel inclined to come up and visit.[21]

Happily, Smith soon found lodgings elsewhere, and was not unhappy at the prospect of losing his growling, hissing, and rattling tent mates. By this time, however, the two men had become fast friends. He even managed to have a little of the Custer penchant for mischief rub off on him. As he moved out of Tom's tent, Smith instructed his aide to liberate a few personal items from Tom. The pilfering reached such proportions that Tom had to put a stop to it, or he would find himself with no possessions left, except the snakes.[22]

In June the commander of the Seventh, Colonel Andrew J. Smith, was relieved of command and replaced by Colonel Samuel Sturgis. Armstrong and Tom left Fort Hays and traveled to Fort Leavenworth to confer with their new commander. Armstrong had applied for the position himself, but his request was refused. He did not carry the political influence necessary to affect such a request.

Tom and Armstrong returned, somewhat chagrined, to their post. The summer proved to be more quiet, thanks to the winter campaign. But the Custers found themselves inundated with tourists. During the course of the summer of 1869, they received nearly two hundred requests from friends wanting the Custers to assist them in the new national pastime, buffalo hunting. The summer of '69 passed with one expedition following on the heels of another, with an occasional horse race thrown in for good measure.

Tom joined Armstrong and Libbie on one such excursion in June. Armstrong arranged for one of his horses to run in a

---

[21]Ibid., pp. 125–126.
[22]Ibid., pp. 147–148.

race to be held at Fort Leavenworth. On 15 June they left camp and went into Hays City to catch the train east. As their carriage approached Hays, Tom dropped the leather curtain over the window. Libbie protested, but without success. Tom reprimanded her by saying, "Now mind, Old Lady, don't you try to look out of there if a crevice is left open. The town is nothing but a medley of disreputable people, and we don't wish you to see, or be seen."[23]

The trio sought a room for the night, but rooms were scarce. They wound up in the loft of one of the buildings which had been set up as a hotel room. There was no bed for Tom, so they made a pallet on the floor for him. Armstrong and Libbie went into the room first, changed their clothes and got into bed. They called Tom, who had been waiting patiently in the hall, and he took up his place on the floor. Tom pronounced Libbie, "the noblest Roman of them all."[24] Tom quickly fell asleep, but Armstrong had only feigned sleep. He picked up a shoe and launched it across the room against the wall. Tom shot up like a bullet ready for whatever, or whoever, it was he heard attempting to gain entry into their room. Armstrong roared with laughter.[25]

The rest of the night passed uneventfully. They overslept the next morning, and dressed hastily. They barely made it to the train before it left the station. As the train moved, Tom and Armstrong noticed that Libbie's toilet was not quite complete. The two brothers began to assist her with completing her dressing, to make her more "socially presentable." But being Custers, it was too good an opportunity to pass up and they became quite careless with dressing Libbie. In the end they collapsed with laughter which made their work impossible.[26] Eventually they arrived at Leavenworth and enjoyed their horse race.

---

[23]Ibid., p. 168.   [24]Ibid., pp. 173–174.
[25]Ibid.   [26]Ibid., p. 175.

In September the Custers found themselves playing host to two English lords who had come to the Plains to participate in a buffalo hunt. Tom showed them his rattlesnake collection, which made such an impression that several of his snakes were sent to England to be placed in zoos. On one day's hunt, Tom and Armstrong stole away from the Englishmen and hid themselves. They waited until the unsuspecting visitors were completely engrossed in their hunting, and then began shooting at them. The Englishmen, believing themselves under attack, beat a hasty retreat back to camp. In spite of this good natured interruption, the two Englishmen managed to kill twenty-six buffalo in three days of hunting.[27]

It was during this time that one of the many fictitious stories about Tom was supposed to have occurred. According to the tale, Tom became involved in a fracas with Wild Bill Hickok. The story relates that Tom, in a drunken stupor, tried to get his horse to jump up onto a table in one the local bars and dance. The horse failed to perform his feat, and Tom shot and killed the unfortunate animal. Hickok appeared and arrested Tom for discharging his firearm within the city limits. Tom was released to the care of his brother, and they returned to camp. Two men of Tom's company, however, decided not to let the episode pass. They went into town and confronted Wild Bill, who was more than a match for the troopers, and he shot them both, killing one and wounding the other. The historical evidence is clear that Hickok did shoot two members of the Seventh Cavalry, but no records exist naming Tom Custer as either having shot his horse, government property, or sending the two troopers into town to kill Hickok. The whole story, interesting as it may be, is a total fabrication. Another reason to discount the story is that Libbie made no mention of it in her writings. If such an incident had occurred, she might not have

---

[27]Ibid., pp. 83–85.

mentioned it out of embarrassment, but she definitely would have given a much different viewpoint of Wild Bill Hickok. The Custers were a tight family and if one member disliked someone they all tended to feel the same.[28]

In October, the Seventh received orders to report to their winter quarters. Tom and his troop remained at Fort Hays, while Armstrong and Libbie moved to Fort Leavenworth. Tom procured a vacant house on the post, which he furnished with new curtains and carpets.[29]

The winter months were usually quiet on the Plains, so Tom asked for, and received, a twenty-day leave of absence. Tom used his time off to join Armstrong and Lieutenant William Cooke on a trip east. Armstrong's trip was both official and personal. He traveled to Chicago to meet with General Sheridan and then on to Monroe, Michigan, to attend to matters concerning the estate of Libbie's late father. Apparently, Armstrong did not have the funds necessary to bring Libbie with him, and she stayed behind at Leavenworth. Armstrong's traveling companion, William Cooke, was a good friend to both Armstrong and Tom, and had served in the Seventh since its inception. He was born in Mt. Pleasant, Brent County, Ontario, Canada on 29 May 1846. He was one of thousands of Canadians who crossed the border and joined the Union Army. He served in the Eastern Theater in the 29th New York Volunteer Cavalry. He was mustered out of the service at the end of the war and joined the Seventh on 28 July 1866.[30] He sported a fine set of sideburns which he allowed to grow down to his chest, and was the fastest runner in the whole regiment.

---

[28]The earliest telling of the story that the author has found is in Richard O'Connor, *Wild Bill Hickok,* pp. 144-145, without any source cited. Rosa, *Wild Bill Hickock: The Man and His Myth,* makes no mention of the incident, and Burkey, *"Custer Come At Once!"* debunks the tale as apocryphal. Armstrong writes of Hickok in *My Life on the Plains* in an overall favorable manner.

[29]E.B.C. Collection.

[30]Ronald Nichols, *Men With Custer,* p. 66.

The trio arrived in Monroe, Michigan, on 13 December and remained to spend Christmas with their loved ones. The Custers introduced Cooke to a local maiden named Diana Darrah. A romance ensued between the bewiskered lieutenant and the Monroe maiden. Apparently, she had also enjoyed the attention of another Seventh Cavalry officer, Captain Myles Moylan. Tom told Armstrong to write Libbie and inform her of their matchmaking. Tom felt Diana would soon be able to "have Cooke on a string."[31]

Shortly before Christmas, Tom applied to have his leave extended. His request was granted and his leave was extended for three months. He returned to Fort Hays in March 1870. Indian depredations did not reach the fever pitch they had in earlier years. There were minor raids and encounters, but no major confrontations. In early May, Tom's troop M left the fort for summer duty at Camp Sturgis. On 11 June he led a detachment of 33 men, under the overall command of Captain Myles Keogh, thirty-five miles east of camp to protect a group of railroad workers. In August he participated in a scout along the Saline, Solomon, and the Republican rivers. Tom wintered again that year at Fort Hays. The spring of 1871 arrived, and Tom once again busied himself scouting the Kansas plains. On 16 March, Tom led his troop in a scout along the Solomon River. In April his troop scanned the area between the Solomon and the Republican rivers.[32]

The Seventh Cavalry experienced relative peace on the plains of Kansas in the spring of 1871. Storm clouds were, however, on the horizon.

---

[31]Frost, *General Custer's Libbie*, p. 186.
[32]Chandler, *Of Garyowen In Glory*, p. 37.

CHAPTER EIGHT

Reconstruction and the Northern Plains

While Tom and the Seventh Cavalry busied themselves with policing the Great Plains, other units of the army found themselves on Reconstruction duty in the South. The process of Reconstruction included four parts. The first part, and what would ultimately prove the easiest, involved the physical reconstruction of the ruined South. Devastation reached into virtually every state, with entire regions lying desolate. The other aspects of Reconstruction, the political, social, and economic restructuring of the South, proved to be virtually impossible to fulfill. Southern society galvanized itself into resisting the changes that the Radical Republicans in Congress attempted to impose upon them. The South might be defeated militarily, but would never submit spiritually to the North.

Out of the ashes of the vanquished Confederacy arose numerous militant organizations, determined to oppose what they considered to be the continuance of Northern aggression. Groups such as the Ku Klux Klan, Knights of the White Camilia, and the White Brotherhood became deeply entrenched in nearly every Southern state.[1] These groups used intimidation and brutality to secure their goals of continued white, Democratic rule in the South. These diverse

[1]Foner, *Reconstruction*, p. 425.

groups resolved to undermine the effects of the Reconstruction Acts and the Thirteenth, Fourteenth, and Fifteenth amendments. The Southern states did what they could through the implementation of the Black Codes and various Jim Crow Laws, but their final, and in many instances, most effective tools were the terrorist groups who roamed the countryside by night.

The election of 1868 demonstrated the power of the Klan. The Klan became the barbarous extension of the Democratic Party in the South. One Louisiana newspaper expressed the Southern perspective with these words:

> It is, indeed, unfortunate that (our people) should be compelled to have recourse to measures of violence and blood to do away with lawless tyrants and wrong doers . . . But who is to blame? . . . Assuredly not we people of the South, who have suffered wrongs beyond endurance. Radicalism and negroism . . . are alone to blame . . . Those northern emissaries of advanced political ideas, and of progressive social reforms . . . have met the fate they deserved.[2]

Violence erupted throughout the South, targeted at the freed blacks who were exercising their first act of suffrage. Ten percent of the black members of the 1867-68 constitutional conventions fell victim to Klan violence, with seven members assassinated. In Arkansas, terrorist groups murdered two hundred blacks during the campaign. Georgia listed 9300 blacks registered to vote, but election returns revealed that only eighty-seven men took their lives in their hands and actually voted. Violence reached a high in Louisiana where more than a thousand blacks were killed between April and election day in November.[3]

Blacks, however, were not the only targets of the Klan. Any whites who supported Reconstruction were also attacked. Carpetbaggers, Northerners who had come south

---

[2]McPherson, *Ordeal By Fire*, p. 544.
[3]Ibid., p. 426.

after the war to take advantage of the conditions, were special targets. Any member of the Republican party, carpetbagger or Southerner, was at risk of receiving late night visits from their robed neighbors.

Congress reacted by issuing the Force Acts of May 1870 and February 1871. This legislation decreed that anyone using coercion or violence to impede blacks from voting could be punished by fine or imprisonment. The Acts also gave the President the power to utilize the military if necessary, and place congressional elections under federal control.[4]

Violence continued unabated, especially in South Carolina. Between November 1870 and September 1871, the Ku Klux Klan ravaged the countryside night after night. It is believed that during this time period the Klansmen murdered eleven blacks, and savagely assaulted more than six hundred people. They also burned black schools and churches. One church was burned, rebuilt, and burned four times.[5] The black militia had been especially irritating to Klan members. Following an incident wherein a white man was killed by the militia, the Klan retaliated by removing arrested militia members from jail and executing them. More of the militia were arrested, and incarcerated. The governor of South Carolina ordered their removal to Columbia, but before the order could be implemented, the jail was stormed by several hundred Klansmen, and more militia were taken to a prearranged location and executed.[6]

The Federal Government finally had enough. President Ulysses S. Grant issued orders to the War Department to make the preparations to transfer several units of the Seventh Cavalry to Reconstruction duty in the South. Department commander General John Pope issued General Order Num-

Stampp, *The Era of Reconstruction*, p. 200.
[5]Trelease, *White Terror*, p. 365.
[6]Charles, *Narrative History of Union County, South Carolina*, pp. 223–227.

ber Four on 8 March 1871. The Seventh Cavalry was to be split up and assigned to various duty stations throughout the South.

Congress, meanwhile, debated and finally enacted legislation aimed specifically at the Klan. The Ku Klux Klan Act passed Congress on 20 April 1871. The act strengthened existing legislation and empowered the President with the authority to suspend the Writ of Habeas Corpus in those areas that, by presidential decree, were declared to be in a state of insurrection. Nine counties of South Carolina, including Union County, were named to the list of areas in anarchy.[7]

Tom, second lieutenant of Company M, received orders to report with his troop for assignment in South Carolina. Armstrong and Libbie were ordered to Elizabethtown, Kentucky. The units departed by train from Fort Hays on 23 May. They arrived at Louisville, Kentucky, on 28 May.[8]

The lengthy journey gave Tom and Armstrong time to think about their imminent separation, and they formulated a scheme. They approached Captain Benteen and attempted to talk him into allowing them to alter the orders by switching Benteen's assignment in Nashville, Tennessee, with Tom's in South Carolina. The two brothers tried to persuade Benteen that his assignment in Nashville would only be temporary, and he would then receive another assignment transferring him elsewhere. Benteen, always distrustful of the Custers, went to the Seventh's commander, Colonel Samuel Sturgis, and informed him of what the Custers had said. According to Benteen, Sturgis became angry and stated to him, in no uncertain terms, his opinion. "The lying whelp! There isn't a word of truth in it. Custer is trying to keep French's troop, in which his

---

[7]McPherson, *Ordeal By Fire*, p. 567.
[8]Melbourne C. Chandler, *Of Garryowen In Glory: The History of the 7th U.S. Cavalry* (Annadale, Virginia, 1960) p. 37.

brother Tom is first lieutenant, from going to South Carolina."[9] Captain Benteen's assignment was not changed.

Tom sadly said his goodbyes, boarded another train with his troop, and left Louisville on 31 May. On 14 June, they arrived in Darlington, South Carolina, located in the north-eastern part of the state. Tom's orders were to assist the local law enforcement officers by helping to suppress the Klan, locate and arrest those individuals engaged in the manufacture of moonshine whiskey, and assist with the collection of taxes.

The landscape of South Carolina was drastically different from the plains of Kansas. They found the dry heat of the windswept plains replaced by an almost oppressive humidity. The agriculture of the region differed accordingly. There were large fields of cotton, peanuts, and rice. Persimmon trees were in abundance, and after a few attempts they learned to eat the fruit only after the first frost. Many of the local black farmers raised watermelons, which the soldiers loved. Several days a week, wagon loads of watermelons found their way to camp. The men did not receive their pay on a regular basis, so Tom and other officers found them-selves having to either advance the men money, or at least promise the farmers that their bills would be paid. Unfortu-nately, few of the farmers ever received any compensation.[10]

Soon after Tom arrived, the Klan raided the home of a local union supporter. During the raid, the man's daughter sought to prevent her father's execution, and one of the Klans-man shot her in the leg which later had to be amputated. The enraged father managed to kill one of his assailants before he was murdered.[11] Warrants, however, were never issued even though everyone knew who the guilty parties were.

Tom and the troopers found themselves isolated in an

[9]Carroll, *The Benteen-Goldin Letters*, pp. 265–266.
[10]John Ryan Papers, pp. 125–129. Sandy Barnard Collection, Terre Haute, Indiana.
[11]Ibid., p. 127.

inhospitable environment, and sought their amusement in whatever ways possible. One diversion that Tom and the men engaged in was washing their horses in the small creek behind the camp. The men stripped off their clothing and rode their horses out into the stream. Once in the stream, the horses laid down on command and allowed the troopers to wash them. The fun began when new recruits arrived, and were ordered by Tom and the other officers to water their horses in the creek. Once in the water the mounts assumed their wash positions, much to the delight of the assembled officers and men who took great relish in the "baptism" of their new comrades.[12]

On 18 October, troop M received orders to move by rail to Spartanburg, located in the northwestern part of the state near the North Carolina state line. At Spartanburg, Company M was joined by troops B, E, and G all under the command of Major Marcus Reno. They were in camp for two weeks when they received orders to be ready to move out at midnight 7 November. Tom readied his troop and at the appointed hour moved out, heading southeast. They rode all night and arrived at Unionville just before dawn. The troopers quietly and quickly surrounded the town and sealed it off. Pickets were placed on every road and no one was allowed to leave. At the command the soldiers entered the town, served their warrants, and arrested several people.[13]

Tom and troop M continued their duty at Unionville for several more months. The men set up camp at the edge of town and settled in. With some amount of time on their hands, the men resorted to numerous diversions. Gambling was widespread in the camp. The first week of every month found Tom absorbed in this pastime. Their paydays were still not very regular, and the men resorted to using tobacco as a source of money. They also used it to barter with the

---

[12]Ibid., p. 130.
[13]Ibid., p. 131.

local shopkeepers for those necessities that the army did not provide.[14]

Tom asked for and received 27 days leave on 6 February, 1872. His leave was extended sixty days in March. Tom finally returned from leave on 1 May[15] Tom used his leave of absence to journey to Jersey City, New Jersey, and visit Lulie G. Burgess. Tom actively pursued many young ladies, but apparently Miss Lulie won his heart.

Lucia Gregory Burgess was born in June 1848 to John and Maria Burgess in Cooperstown, New York. The family later moved to Jersey City where Lulie's father opened a grocery store.[16] The circumstance of their meeting is lost to history. Tom always carried with him a small book entitled *The Words of Jesus*, that Lulie gave him as a present in June 1868. The book is inscribed, "For T.W. Custer. 7th Cavalry, U.S.A."[17] Evidently Lulie was in very poor health, as many of the letters that still exist mention her frailty. During this visit, Tom wrote to his niece, Emma Reed, and informed her that Lulie had not met him at the train station as she had not yet received his telegram notifying her of his imminent arrival. He went on to relate that Lulie had come downstairs for the first time in several days, joining him for duets on the piano.[18]

Upon his return to South Carolina, Tom reacquainted himself with another vice from his past, alcohol. Tom informed Armstrong by letter that several officers found themselves under arrest for drunkenness on duty[19] Tom did not mention to his brother that he too had succumbed to his old weakness.

---

[14]Ibid., p. 137.   [15]T.W.C. Service Records, N.A.

[16]Death Notices, *Freeman's Journal*. Cooperstown, New York. February 25, 1875. Vol. three, p. 81.

[17]Frost, *General Custer's Libbie*, p. 182.

[18]Letter, Thomas Ward Custer to Emma Reed, April 23, (year unknown), M.C.H.S.

[19]Letter, George Armstrong Custer to Margaret Custer Calhoun, November 29, 1871. Merington Collection.

One afternoon a fire broke out in town and Captain French ordered his men to assist in extinguishing the fire. One of the shopkeepers offered a barrel of whiskey if the troopers would save his safe. Several men imperiled their lives, and saved the store owner's safe. The barrel of whiskey was delivered to camp, but was commandeered by Captain French and Tom who drank it all.[20]

Action was the only remedy for such behavior. Tom received orders to have the troop ready to move out. Thirty men from companies M and E left camp at midnight, headed for Lawrenceville. They arrived before daylight and encircled the town. At sunrise they entered the village, accompanied by a United States Marshal who carried warrants for several people in the town.[21]

Some days later Tom participated in another raid at Jonesville. Tom received orders to capture two local men, known to be members of the Klan hierarchy. Tom directed his men to surround the house of the father of one of the men. As they lay in wait, two men approached the house. An informant whispered to Tom that they were the men they were after. The two men warily approached the darkened house. When the two men were close enough, the soldiers sprang out at them. One of the men escaped, but Tom tackled the other man and took him prisoner.[22]

Back in camp, Tom wrote to Armstrong informing him of their activities, and also asked his brother to procure a new mount for him. He did not receive a prompt reply to this letter and so he wrote to Libbie.

> Now Libbie if Armstrong is too confounded mean to write, I wish you would find out all you can in regard to what I have asked him, then write and let me know. I have not heard from Lulie for a week

---

[20]John Ryans Papers, p. 134.

[21]Ibid., p. 138.

[22]Charles, *Narrative of Union County*, p. 230.

or 10 days . . . but she don't seem to get much better . . . write oftener to you devoted brother.[23]

In a letter to his niece, Emma Reed, Tom facetiously announced his marriage. He stated that he heard from "your Aunt Lulu" every few days. He revealed she had gone to Cooperstown, New York, to try and regain her health. Tom hoped she would be well enough to come to South Carolina in January for a visit.[24] Lulie's continued poor health, however, prevented her visit.

That fall, rumors began to circulate that the Seventh would be withdrawn from duty in the South. Much of the power of the Klan had been broken, and the region was again peaceful and under the control of the local law officers. The continued need for troops was not necessary.

The enlistments of several men came due while in the South. Some reenlisted, while others took their discharges and found employment in the area. A few men even found wives for themselves among the usually unfriendly inhabitants. In November, Sergeant John Ryan of Tom's troop received his discharge from the service, and he distributed his belongings among the men. Tom took possession of Ryan's horse, but had to return it when Ryan came back to Unionville and reenlisted after being home only a few weeks. Tom tried to talk him out of his horse, but Ryan was adamant about getting it back.[25]

Ryan made it back in time as the troop received orders to break camp and make preparations to move back to the plains. On 24 December, troop M embarked by rail for Oxford, Mississippi. Tom, an inveterate animal lover, took with him two of his favorite hounds. They were in camp at Oxford for a

---

[23]Letter, Thomas Ward Custer to Elizabeth Bacon Custer, date unknown, Merington Collection.

[24]Letter, Thomas Ward Custer to Emma Reed, November 12 (no year), M.C.H.S.

[25]John Ryan Papers, p. 146.

short while when they received orders to relocate to a new camp just outside of Memphis, Tennessee.[26] Here, Tom was reunited with Libbie and Armstrong once again.

In the Seventh's two year absence from the Plains, much work had been accomplished on the railroads. The great expanse of the Plains, however, was not vast enough. With every mile that the railroads moved forward, they encroached upon the domains of the Native American tribes. Since the Treaty of 1868, the tribes had lived in an uneasy peace with the whites that encompassed them. The Treaty of 1868, arguably the best treaty any of the tribes received, was born out of Red Cloud's War 1866–1868. A gold strike in the Montana Territory caused a rush of white settlers who used the Bozeman Trail, which led through what is now northeastern Wyoming, to get to the gold fields. The government, without Indian approval, built several forts in the region to protect the white settlers as they passed through the Indian lands. This angered the various tribes of the Northern Cheyenne and Lakota Sioux who, through the leadership of the Lakota chief Red Cloud, fought to preserve their lands. Eventually, the Federal Government acquiesced to the demands of the Cheyenne and Lakota and closed the forts, and the Bozeman Trail which they protected. The tribes were also given all of western South Dakota as their reservation and portions of Wyoming and Montana as hunting lands. Red Cloud agreed to the treaty and led those tribes who followed him onto the reservation. Those tribes who did not follow Red Cloud remained outside the reservation, and outside the treaty. The increasing demand for land, however, was making the peace more and more fragile. President Grant believed that the railroads "will go far to a permanent settlement of all Indian difficulties."[27]

---

[26]Ibid., p. 153.   [27]Wert, Custer, p. 296.

The Custer clan in North Dakota. Left to Right, Brother-in-law James Calhoun (seated), Boston Custer (seated on the ground), Myles Keogh (standing, resting on one knee), Maggie Custer Calhoun (seated on the ground), Libbie Custer (seated above Maggie), George Armstrong Custer (standing with arms crossed), William Cooke (seated on ground with hat and long sideburns), Tom Custer (seated with upturned hat facing the camera). *Courtesy of Little Bighorn National Monument.*

The flood of civilization, and all that came with it, pushed the tribes into smaller and smaller areas. The wholesale slaughter of the great buffalo herds began in earnest with the building of the transcontinental railroads. The destruction of the buffalo escalated when the public became smitten with the craze for buffalo robes. Whole trains of novice hunters were taken west so they could lean out of the windows and kill the great beasts. Such widespread carnage continued until by the close of the century the great herds' numbers dwindled from the millions to only a few hundred. The government, realizing the role the buffalo played in the life of the Plains Indians, said nothing–knowing the end of the buffalo would be followed by the end of the Plains Indian's way of life.

The terminus of the Northern Pacific Railroad was Bis-

Amateur theatri-
cals at Fort Lin-
coln. Maggie,
Tom, and Lib-
bie. *Courtesy of
Little Bighorn
National Monu-
ment.*

marck, North Dakota, on the eastern side of the Missouri
River. The Northern Pacific began preparations to continue its westward expansion, but that would bring the railroad into contact with the tribes of the Lakota and
Northern Cheyenne who had refused the Treaty of 1868.
This unwanted invasion of their lands would most certainly
cause the tribes to violently resist the coming of the iron
horse, which they all knew would bring more whites into
their regions. The company appealed to the Grant Administration for protection for its employees. The Administration replied that it would do everything in its power to
assist the railroad.

The Dakota Territory was part of the military Division of
the Missouri. The Division extended from Chicago in the
east, north to the Canadian border, south to the Rio Grande
and the Gulf of Mexico, and west to the western foothills of

the Rocky Mountains. In command of the Division of the Missouri was Lieutenant General Philip Henry Sheridan. Sheridan received his third star in 1869 from his good friend President Grant. Grant allowed Sheridan to choose his own command, and Sheridan chose the Division of the Missouri.[28]

The northern plains were home to the Lakotas, Northern and Southern Cheyenne. Sheridan, according to his best estimates, believed these tribes to number approximately 175,000 members who were scattered over a million square miles of territory. The pacification, or subjugation, of these groups would be the job of those men that Sheridan placed in field command. Sheridan gave command of the Department of the Dakota to Brigadier General Alfred H. Terry. Sheridan was content with Terry as Department commander; however, he wanted an aggressive officer to serve as his field commander and he wasted no time in sending for his favorite. The Seventh Cavalry's new assignment was the terminus of the Northern Pacific at Bismarck. Fort Abraham Lincoln was to be located on the western side of the Missouri River, just across from Bismarck.

Sheridan anticipated trouble from the Lakota and Northern Cheyenne. The Lakotas had become increasingly belligerent, not only against white encroachment, but also against neighboring tribes. As the Lakota were being pushed from their lands by the never ending stream of white civilization, they in turn dislodged their neighbors, dislocating numerous tribes from their own ancestral homes. Intertribal warfare was quite common, but Sheridan believed it would not be long before the Lakota turned their hostility on the tide of white expansion.

To compound the situation, the Treaty of 1868, which gave the Lakota their reservation, had split the tribes. The

---

[28]Hutton, *Phil Sheridan and His Army*, p. 117.

question of Indian authority had always plagued the relations between the whites and Native Americans. The whites, used to the rule of one man or one legislative body, had problems with understanding the leadership roles of the chiefs. Whites took for granted that a chief spoke for his entire tribal group, not just the immediate group who followed him. Treaties were made with that understanding, and when problems arose the whites held the specific chief responsible for the actions of all of his tribal group. Red Cloud had signed the Treaty of 1868 and moved his people onto the reservation. The rest of the Lakota nation, under the nominal leadership of Sitting Bull, refused to acknowledge the treaty and the authority of Red Cloud to sign any such agreement, and would not live on the reservation. They chose instead to continue their nomadic lifestyle.

Tom and the regiment embarked on three steamers in Memphis for the trip up the Mississippi River to Cairo, Illinois, arriving there on 2 April. At Cairo, they loaded their baggage and horses into railroad cars and began the long journey north. The train stopped several times each day to allow the troopers to take their mounts out of the railroad cars to exercise and water them. The long ride ended at the terminus of the rail line just a mile short of the small town of Yankton, South Dakota.

The troopers unloaded their baggage and horses, while Custer surveyed the area and chose a place for their camp. The soldiers labored diligently, and after a few days their camp was constructed, just in time as events would prove. The command, used to being in the temperate weather of the south, now found that spring in the Dakota Territory was of a different nature. The morning dawned warm, but with threatening clouds in the west and a switching wind from the northwest gave portent that a turbulent change in the weather was upon them. Soon it began to snow and before long the cavalrymen found themselves in the midst of a blizzard. Custer ordered the men to break camp and seek sanctuary in town. Tom saddled his horse and dutifully followed his brother's orders. Armstrong and Libbie had found shelter in a shack belonging to a local man who agreed to rent it to them. Armstrong had fallen ill just as the storm broke and the surgeon ordered him to bed. Libbie nursed him through the howling night.[29]

Morning brought an end to the storm, but the snowfall was so deep that Armstrong and Libbie were stranded in their new home. Armstrong ate breakfast and felt better. Suddenly, they heard a knock on the cabin door. Libbie opened the door and found Tom standing in the snow with a basket of food and supplies in his arms. The shivering trio enjoyed a hearty breakfast.[30] The regiment slowly dug themselves out and found, to their amazement, they had suffered only minor casualties due to the inclement weather. Tom also learned such weather could disappear as quickly as it arrived. As a warm wind, called the chinook by the Indians, rapidly melted the snow. After a few days, the ground was sufficiently free of mud so the command could move out for their new home.

The column proceeded at a leisurely pace up the Missouri River. Each day brought a new revelation to Tom about his new environment. The country abounded with wild birds, which Tom took to shooting with great skill. The birds proved a delicacy, and the mess each night was filled with good food and talk between the family.

The family consisted of Libbie, Armstrong, Tom, and sister Margaret, now married to one of Tom's good friends and fellow officers, Lieutenant James Calhoun. Calhoun was born 24 August 1845 in Cincinnati, Ohio. He enlisted in the

---

[29]Custer, *Boots and Saddles*, pp. 11–13.
[30]Ibid., p. 17.

Civil War and fought with the Ohio infantry. After the war, he served with the regular army in Oregon and then in Arizona. He requested transfer to the Seventh Cavalry which was accomplished on 1 January 1871. He met Margaret while the Seventh was on Reconstruction duty in Kentucky, and he and Maggie were married in 1872.[31] The family ate their dinners together and enjoyed each other's company late into the night. Libbie soon fell into the habit of embellishing the tales of her experiences. Tom and Armstrong admonished her by saying, "Oh, I say, Old Lady, won't you come down a hundred or two?"[32]

After a few days of marching, the command entered the reservation land of the Lakota. The Lakota Indians were a confederation of several tribes, bound together by a common language, religion, and history. The Lakota confederation consisted of the Hunkpapas, Oglala, Brule, Miniconju, Two Kettle, Sans Arc, and Sihasapa. The tribes referred to each other as Lakota, the allies. The whites called referred to them as the "Sioux," a word derived from the Chippewa word for enemy.[33] The Lakota had received all of South Dakota west of the Missouri River as their reservation according to the Treaty of 1868. Several tribes approached the column and invited them to their camps. Tom saw firsthand the mighty warriors of the northern plains, warriors he would soon be fighting.

One day, a solitary Indian approached the camp on horseback. He was an elderly man who announced himself as The-Man-With-The-Broken-Ear, and he demanded to see the soldier-chief. Armstrong arrived and invited the old warrior to be his guest in his tent. The Indian nodded his assent, dismounted his pony, and entered Custer's tent, much to Libbie's terror. He seated himself and surveyed those white

---

[31]John M. Carroll, ed., *They Rode With Custer* p. 47.
[32]Custer, *Boots and Saddles*, p. 32.
[33]Utley, *The Lance And The Shield*, p. 4.

savages who surrounded him. Tom entered the tent, bowed, and extended his hand to the warrior. A broad smile creased Tom's face as he spoke to the Indian. "You conniving old galoot, why are you here begging and thieving when your wretched hands are hardly dry from some murder, and your miserable mouth is still red from eating the heart of your enemy?"[34]

Libbie found herself speechless at Tom's remarks. She was afraid the old warrior only feigned ignorance of white man's language, only to exact revenge later. They gave the warrior a small cup of alcohol, which he drank with great relish. One of the soldiers inquired if he would care for some more. "You bet!" the old man replied, much to Libbie's astonishment. The officers gave their visitor some more whiskey and continued to talk to him. They finally satisfied themselves that "you bet" was the only English that he knew. At length, he was placed back upon his steed, and he rode away.[35]

A few days later the column discovered a pole in the roadway in front of them. Suspended from the pole was a piece of red fabric and several locks of human hair. It was a warning not to proceed any further into the land of the Lakota. The command passed it by and continued on their way, and on 10 June the troopers arrived at Fort Rice.

---

[34]Custer, *Boots and Saddles*, pp. 65–66.
[35]Ibid.

Tom Custer Circa. 1870.
Courtesy Little Bighorn National Monument.

CHAPTER NINE

The Yellowstone Expedition

Tom and the column arrived at Fort Rice on 10 June. The fort, situated on the west bank of the Missouri River, was a collection of decidedly unimpressive log cabins of varying sizes enclosed by a wooden palisade. Photographs of the post reveal a certain bleakness, and the establishment appears devoid of the slightest detail of civilization. It was, as most western posts were, surrounded by miles and miles of barren countryside. After so many months in the South, Tom and the men of the Seventh must have experienced a pang of longing for the refinements of culture. Here, in this last outpost of civilization, the Seventh rendezvoused with the other units who would accompany them on the expedition up the Yellowstone.

There had been two other expeditions into the Yellowstone country. The first expedition occurred in the fall of 1871, under the command of Colonel J.N.G. Whistler. A second expedition followed the next year. This third expedition, the largest yet mounted, received orders to penetrate deeply into hostile Indian territory, so every precaution was to be taken.

General Sheridan gave the command of the expedition to Colonel David S. Stanley, who had led the second foray into the region. Stanley's orders from the acting Secretary of War, George M. Robeson, were as follows:

... Make a thorough examination of the region traversed, collecting and reporting all obtainable information in relation to the natural resources and capabilities of the country . . .[1]

To accomplish this task, General Sheridan issued Special Order No. 73 to department commander General Alfred Terry. Sheridan ordered the expedition to assemble at Fort Rice and be prepared to leave on 15 June. The command consisted of ten companies of the Seventh Cavalry, under the command of Lieutenant Colonel George Armstrong Custer. Also accompanying the expedition were four companies of the Sixth US Infantry, five companies of the Twenty-Second US Infantry, four companies of the Seventeenth US Infantry, two pieces of artillery, seventy-five Indian scouts, three hundred and fifty-three civilians, three hundred wagons, and four hundred and fifty heads of beef.[2] The expedition totaled over fifteen hundred men.

The five hundred mile march from Yankton was the first time the Seventh Cavalry had been together as one command in almost two years. During that interlude the command had become accustomed to a rather loose spirit of discipline. Custer, realizing the potential hardships that lay ahead in the weeks to come, sought to improve the conduct of the men. He issued a series of orders which, unfortunately, had an adverse effect. One of Custer's enlisted men later wrote: "Custer is not making himself agreeable at all to the officers of his command. He keeps himself aloof and spends his time in excogitating, annoying, vexatious, and useless orders, which visit us like a swarm of evils from Pandora's Box, small, numberless, and disagreeable."[3] The petty jealousies and feelings of resentment within the Seventh very quickly began to surface again.

It was the same old problem which had dogged Custer since he had arrived on the Plains. The men who found themselves in the frontier army were drastically different from those who had served during the Civil War. They were

---

[1]Frost, *Custer's Seventh Cavalry and the Campaign of '73*, p. 22.
[2]Wert, *Custer*, p. 303.   [3]Hutton, *Custer Reader*, p. 184.

not highly motivated by duty to their country; in fact, many of them were not even citizens. A large portion of the army in the West was made up of immigrants who signed up with the army in order to get themselves sent to the Plains. The rest was made up of those members of society who, for one reason or another, could not find their particular niche in life. Thieves on the run, husbands on the run, and all of those men in between, found themselves enlisting in the army. Such men do not readily give their allegiance to those they consider petty tyrants, and certainly do not find themselves highly motivated by thoughts of home and country.

Such men also inhabitated Fort Rice and the other forlorn outposts of the West. Libbie and Maggie Calhoun hoped to spend the time that the regiment was gone at Fort Rice. Upon arriving at the post, however, Libbie found she would not be able to stay at the post during Armstrong's absence. Apparently, the men of Fort Rice had already experienced the problems of having women on the post, and every entreaty of Libbie's was met with a resounding "No!" She said her goodbyes to her husband and Tom, and sadly made arrangements to go home to Monroe.[4]

Tom took advantage of the days of preparation before the command left by writing his will. On 19 June, he sat down and penned his last testament, leaving half of his estate to his mother, Maria, and the rest to his betrothed, Lulie Burgess. In the event that Lulie preceded him in death, all of his estate would go to Maria. The will was witnessed by Armstrong and Jimmi Calhoun. Tom never changed his will.[5]

The Yellowstone Expedition left Fort Rice on 20 June. The line of march was designed to take the command across what later became North Dakota, heading due west for the Yellow-

---

[4]Custer, *Boots and Saddles*, p. 70.
[5]Will of Thomas Ward Custer, Probate Court, Monroe County Courthouse, Monroe, Michigan.

Tom Custer
Circa. 1872.
*Courtesy Little
Bighorn National
Monument.*

stone River. This year's expedition would continue searching for the easiest route for the miles of iron track to come. The landscape of the Dakota territory was a drastic change for Tom. Gone were the lush growing fields of South Carolina, the magnolias and cypress trees, the large stands of evergreens and mighty oaks. Totally absent were the fields of cotton, rice, and watermelons. This region was even more barren than Kansas, and with each passing day, the landscape became more wild in appearance, even taking the name of "bad lands."

The first morning of the march began with breakfast at 3:30 A.M. Tom encountered a new vexation in the Dakotas in the form of grasshoppers. They found their way into everything, especially food. Tom found it necessary to hold his hand over his coffee to prevent invasions from the swarms of grasshoppers who seemed to cover everything. The first day's march was difficult at best. The tired troopers slept well that night, ignoring a thunderstorm and the driving rain.

The second day of the march was exceptionally hot. Tom saw numerous herds of antelope on the horizon. The temptation to shoot the animals became too great, and the troopers began firing. After a while, the firing became so general that it reminded Tom of a full scale Civil War battle. The only casualty this day was, unfortunately, one of Tom's beloved dogs, shot by accident.[6]

The first few days passed slowly as the command acclimated themselves to their new environment, and the long hours in the saddle. The routine of daily march began to finally take shape. The men arose at 3:30 A.M. for breakfast. The march commenced before sunrise, with General Custer and several companies of the Seventh Cavalry leading the way. The rest of the command followed at a slower pace, catching up with the lead units by late afternoon. Custer, in the advance, decided the course of the trail and determined a suitable campsite for the command. Every few days, the command rendezvoused with the steamer *Key West*, which brought supplies and the mail. This regimen continued for the duration of the expedition.

Since game was plentiful, and the need to conserve the beef herd great in the face of an uncertain future, Custer organized hunting parties to supplement the command's diet. Tom, and several other officers and enlisted men, were given the freedom to leave the column to pursue whatever game presented itself.[7] Antelope were so plentiful that one of the wagons actually ran over one of the animals. While observing the dead antelope, Tom remembered one of Libbie's tales of hunting in Kansas

---

[6]Frost, *Custer's Seventh Cavalry*, p. 49.   [7]Ibid., p. 73.

and laughed, telling Armstrong, "Well, by George, we can both beat Libbie's story now."[8]

The daily routine also came to include nightly games of chance. Tom joined his brother officers in an ongoing game of poker, and during the first few days of the march, Tom won five hundred dollars. Tom's brother-in-law, Jimmi Calhoun, however, was not as fortunate. Calhoun had absolutely no luck whatsoever with cards, and night after night he lost. Tom attempted to get him to listen to reason and stop playing. After all, Tom pointed out, Maggie would be so disappointed to find that her Jimmi had lost almost all of his money in games of chance. All of Tom's entreaties failed to make an impression upon Calhoun, however, and he continued to play and lose. In desperation to try and recoup his losses, Calhoun tried to borrow money from Tom. "Bunkey or no bunkey, you must keep your hand out of my haversack!" Tom replied to his luckless brother-in-law.[9]

Another Custer tradition also began anew. Armstrong engaged in long hours of letter writing, often writing on one letter for days at a time until they were a dozen pages or more in length. Tom pointed out to his brother that it was unnecessary for him to write a letter to anyone; in fact, it was impossible. Tom accused his brother of writing so much that he would have nothing to say to anyone that they had not already read in Armstrong's letter. Tom did, however, include two hundred and twenty-five dollars of his poker winnings for Libbie to deposit into his account, with twenty-five dollars to be sent home to Mother Custer.[10]

James Calhoun was not the only member of the command to find his evenings filled with negative diversions. Colonel Stanley suffered from the same malady as did many members of the frontier army, alcoholism. While the command assembled

[8]Letter, George A. Custer to Elizabeth B. Custer, 26 June 1873. Merington Collection.
[9]Ibid.   [10]Ibid.

at Fort Rice prior to the arrival of the Seventh, Tom Rosser, Custer's old classmate and former Confederate general, attempted to warn Stanley of Custer's aversion to drinking. Rosser, now the chief engineer for the Northern Pacific, proffered Stanley a little friendly advice. He cautioned Stanley that Custer would not tolerate what he perceived to be any delay, or interference, with the orders of General Sheridan which might arise from Stanley's dereliction of duty due to his drinking. Stanley, offended at Rosser's counsel, warned him he would not tolerate Custer's penchant for disregarding the orders of his commanding officer.[11] In a letter to his wife, Stanley stated that, "I have seen enough of him[Custer] to convince me that he is a cold-blooded, untruthful and unprincipled man. . . He is universally despised by all the officers of his regiment excepting his relatives and one or two sycophants. He brought a trader in the field without permission, carries an old Negro woman, and cast-iron cooking stove, and delays the march often by his extensive packing up in the morning. As I said, I will try, but am not sure I can avoid trouble with him. . ."[12]

The situation erupted on 8 July. Stanley observed General Custer's cookstove was, through necessity, the last item packed. The slow cooling stove caused an unnecessary delay in the movement of the wagons. Stanley, already irritated with what he perceived as insubordination in Custer's disobeying of orders, demanded the stove be abandoned. He also chastised Custer for allowing a civilian to use a government horse. In his defense, Custer pointed out that Stanley had already authorized the use of a government horse by another civilian, and he was only following Stanley's example. Stanley became incensed and ordered Custer placed under arrest. He ordered the cookstove be left behind and ordered Custer to ride in the rear of the column until further notice. Custer's sojourn in the rear of the command lasted only one day. Stanley sobered up

---

[11]Frost, *Custer's Seventh Cavalry*, p. 49.   [12]Monaghan, *Custer*, p. 342.

and rescinded the order of Custer's arrest. Custer reported to Libbie that Stanley came to him and apologized for the entire incident.[13] Tom sympathized with Armstrong's mistreatment at the hands of a man both men considered to be incompetent.

Tom saw the Yellowstone River on 15 July. He and Armstrong rode ahead of the advance party. They hoped to locate the steamer *Key West,* but the boat was nowhere in sight. Custer decided to take a small detachment and find the vessel. Tom and the troopers traveled thirty miles over extremely rough terrain. Tom viewed a landscape both wild and beautiful, unlike anything he had ever seen. The small group continued on and eventually found the steamer. Tom took advantage of the presence of the river boat, and he and Calhoun slept aboard. Custer sent several scouts back to guide the column to the rendezvous point. He also notified Stanley he had temporarily placed Tom in command of company B.[14] The rest of the command joined them the next day.

With their provisions replenished, the expedition continued moving west. Tom and Armstrong found time to hunt every day. On 22 July, Armstrong made a spectacular shot. He and Tom were in the advance of the column when a deer ran in front of them. Tom reached for his rifle and fired at the deer, but missed. Armstrong leaped off of his horse and raised his Remington sporting rifle, took aim, and fired. The deer kept running, unscathed by the brothers' gunfire. Armstrong again took careful aim at the fleeing deer and fired again. The deer fell headlong onto the ground. Tom let loose a yell and declared it "the best shot I've ever seen!"[15]

That evening Armstrong wrote to Libbie, and told her of the day's exploits. Tom entered the tent, rolled a cigarette, and reclined on Armstrong's bed to rest. Armstrong looked up from his work on his latest missive and again admonished Tom on his dereliction in

[13]Frost, *Custer's Seventh Cavalry,* p. 61.   [14]Ibid., p. 63.
[15]Letter, George A. Custer to Elizabeth B. Custer, 22 July 1873. Merington Collection.

his letter writing. Tom raised up and said, "I'd like to know what I could find to write after she reads that book from you!" Tom finished his smoke and left the tent, in search of a more interesting diversion. He returned later to find Armstrong still writing. He noticed several pages of the letter lay on his brother's desk. "What, are you still at work on this Old Lady's note? If you keep on you may make quite a letter of it," he said sarcastically.[16]

The next few days passed uneventfully as the command continued westward. Game continued to be plentiful and the men ate well, so well in fact that Tom's weight rose to 152 pounds.[17] The nightly games of poker continued, as did Tom's luck, and he sent Libbie another hundred dollars for deposit in his bank account.[18] But the quiet of the expedition was fast running out. They had advanced deep into the country of the non-reservation Lakota. Everyone felt it was only a matter of time before the command ran into the fierce warriors of the Plains.

The cavalrymen made camp on 2 August along the west bank of the Yellowstone River. They cooked their meals and played a few rounds of poker, when shots rang out. Tom reached for his weapon, but the Lakota disappeared. The next day, the command found the burial place of a Lakota warrior. Several of the troopers ransacked the grave in their desire for "trophies" they could send home to their families. Colonel Stanley became incensed at this barbaric behavior and gave orders forbidding the desecration of anymore Indian graves.[19]

The next morning found Tom, Armstrong, and Companies A and B in the saddle at 5 A.M., leading the advance. One of the Indian scouts, an Arikara named Bloody Knife who was fast becoming a favorite of Armstrong's, saw fresh signs of a small party of Lakota, probably the same ones who fired on the command the day before. Armstrong ordered Bloody Knife to follow

---

[16]Ibid.
[17]Ibid.
[18]Letter, George A. Custer to Elizabeth B. Custer, 27 July 1873. Merington Collection.
[19]Frost, *Custer's Seventh Cavalry*, p. 64.

the trail and the troopers moved out. For eighteen miles, Tom and the troopers rode across the windswept prairie with no sign, except hoofprints, of their elusive foe. At about 9 A.M., Bloody Knife rode up to Tom and Armstrong and stated they were now about twenty-five miles from the Rosebud River. Bloody Knife went on to say it was his knowledge that the Lakota routinely camped along the Rosebud, and with the pursuit of the war party headed that direction, it was probable they were still there. In any event, he warned, it would not be long before the soldiers found themselves under attack. In Bloody Knife's opinion, the cavalrymen had advanced as far as the Lakota would allow.[20]

Armstrong listened to Bloody Knife's words and decided that it would be more prudent to make camp, and wait for the rest of the command to arrive before continuing the advance. He gave orders for the men to dismount and make camp. The troopers allowed their horses to cool off, then took them to the river's edge to quench their thirst. The men moved closer to the banks of the Yellowstone, using it as a defensive line to protect their flank. A few men laid down to take a nap, while others kept a watchful eye on the horizon. Tom took off his coat, hat, and boots and laid down near Armstrong to take advantage of the uneasy respite. He quickly fell asleep.[21] The hot sun blazed down upon them, and a few more men succumbed to the temptation of sleep. Suddenly, a sentry broke the silence with the cry of "Indians!" Instantly Tom was on his feet, rifle in hand, and ready for action. Scanning the horizon, he saw six mounted warriors racing for the soldiers' horses. Armstrong ordered the bugler to sound "Boots and Saddles!" "Run to your horses, men! Run to your horses!" Armstrong shouted.[22] The men responded as one as they leaped into their saddles.[23]

Tom, Armstrong, and about twenty troopers gave chase to the warriors. The warriors saw the troopers racing toward

---

[20]Ibid., p. 66   [21]Hutton, *Custer Reader*, p. 206.
[22]Ibid.   [23]Frost, *Custer's Seventh Cavalry*, p. 66

them, stopped, turned their horses around, and raced back to the stand of cottonwoods a few hundred yards up river. Armstrong looked at Tom and ordered him and the rest of the troopers to fall back. Custer was suspicious as this was a frequently used ruse by the Plains Indians, one that cost Fetterman his life. Tom did as he was ordered and directed his men to halt their advance. Armstrong and his aide slowly rode on in cautious pursuit of the fleeing Indians. The Lakota finally came to a halt when they were parallel with the timber. Armstrong ordered his aide to return to Lieutenant Custer, and instruct him to pay attention to the small grove of trees near the river. As soon as his orderly galloped back, the Indians in front of Armstrong turned around and proceeded to advance. At that instant, hundreds of warriors exploded from the woods. The air filled with screams and war cries as the Lakota rushed upon the solitary rider in their front. Wasting not a second, Armstrong's horse reared into the air, turned around, and raced toward Tom and the waiting troopers.[24]

Armstrong streaked across the ground in a deadly race for his life. He shouted for Tom to dismount his men, but Tom could not hear his brother above the din of the approaching warriors. Tom, though, needed no such direction. When he saw the warriors racing across the plain he instinctively turned to his men and shouted, "Prepare to fight on foot!"[25] The soldiers removed their Springfields from their saddles and quickly dismounted. Every fourth trooper took the reins of the other three and held them tightly. The dismounted troopers moved forward into a skirmish line. The soldiers took their positions and Tom walked down the line shouting, "Don't fire, men, till I give the word, and when you do fire, aim low!"[26] Armstrong was now only a few feet from gaining the safety of his men, and once inside the line Tom gave the command. "Now, men, let them have it!" The troopers'

---

[24]Hutton, *Custer Reader*, pp. 209–221.   [25]Ibid.
[26]Ibid.

Springfields exploded in unison. A second volley quickly followed, and several of the onrushing Lakotas toppled from their horses. Meanwhile, the rest of the command under Captain Myles Moylan raced forward to support their embattled comrades. Tom ordered a third volley, and the Lakotas turned and fled. With this lull in the fighting, Armstrong ordered the troopers to move back to take advantage of the river. They were hopelessly outnumbered, and their only salvation was to prepare a defensive position that they could hold until the rest of the command under Stanley arrived.[27]

The troopers took up positions in a depression in the river bank which provided a natural line of defense. The Lakotas regrouped and prepared to attack again. The warriors split up, with some firing on the troopers from a distance, while others attempted to set fire to the tall prairie grass which fortunately would not burn. Unbeknownest to the soldiers, some of the Lakotas began moving along the river bank, using it to hide their movements into the rear of the soldiers' positions. The soldiers, however, noticed the suspicious behavior on their flank and discovered the Lakota warriors attempting to steal into their rear, and forcefully expelled them from their new positions. The battle continued from a distance until about 3 P.M., when the Lakotas began to stream away from the battlefield. Tom saw a large cloud of dust on the horizon, and deduced that it must be the rest of the command. With reinforcements near, Armstrong gave the order to mount and Tom and the soldiers pursued the retreating Lakotas, chasing them for several miles before halting and returning to link up with Stanley.[28]

Tom and Armstrong were not the only troopers to encounter the Lakota that day. Several miles away, Stanley's command also had their share of Indians. The column moved slowly across the plains. The day was extremely hot and, combined with the dust

[27]Ibid.   [28]Ibid., p. 218.

raised by the marching men, parched the throats of everyone. Water was on everyone's mind, and several men left the column without permission and headed for the nearby river to obtain water. Trumpeter Louis Hills of Company E was one of those men who raced to the riverbank. Sutler Augustus Baliran and veterinarian Dr. John Honsinger also left the column and rode toward a grove of cottonwood trees along the river where they dismounted and began filling their canteens. Hills looked up and saw the two men, and turned his attention back to filling the canteens in his possession. Suddenly, he heard screams and he turned his eyes back to the grove of trees and the two civilians. Hills watched in horror as the Indians attacked and murdered the two men. He quickly mounted his horse and raced back to the command to warn them of the danger.[29]

The deaths of the two civilians and the attack on Custer's advance party could not go unpunished. Stanley ordered Custer to locate the trail of the hostiles and give pursuit. The warriors did not take any precautions to disguise their trail and it was easy for the soldiers to follow. During the course of the pursuit, several dead Lakota ponies were discovered, as well as Dr. Honsinger's horse. The next day they came across the remnants of an abandoned village. Tom noticed a large number of items had been discarded by the fleeing Lakotas, a practice which meant great haste, a sign that they were close. The cavalrymen made camp near the deserted village. The following day, the command discovered another hastily abandoned campsite. Stanley ordered Custer to take the Seventh and give chase to the Lakota.[30]

Tom and the command reached the banks of the Yellowstone by the evening of 9 August. The men had been in the saddle for thirty-six hours following the trail of the elusive Indians. The river was deep, but two Indian scouts volunteered to cross to the opposite bank. With some difficulty they made

---

[29]Frost, *Custer's Seventh Cavalry*, pp. 75–76.   [30]Ibid., p. 79.

it across the river, and discovered the trail of the retreating hostiles. Tom knew the men and horses were exhausted, and felt grateful that Armstrong gave the order to make camp. The next morning, Tom and several other troopers attempted to cross the Yellowstone, but the current was much too swift. Custer ordered the men to build makeshift rafts in order to ferry the regiment across the raging river. By the time the rafts were constructed, it was too late to cross the river, and Armstrong ordered the men to make camp.[31] Sentinels were posted and Tom laid down fully dressed with his rifle by his side.

With the sun finally down, a cool evening breeze gave relief from the heat of the day. Tom and the men slept lightly, aware of the proximity of danger. At 4 A.M., Tom was jolted from his sleep by the sound of rifle fire. The sentries awoke the camp with cries of "Indians! Indians! They are firing from the other side!" Tom could barely make out the figures of a large number of warriors on the opposite bank of the Yellowstone. Armstrong quickly gave orders to his commanders. He ordered Captain Thomas French and his company to keep watch on the right flank downriver. He directed Captain Owen Hale and his men to guard the left flank and their section of the river. Captain George Yates and his command were directed to move forward, firing at the Indians on the opposite bank. Yates moved his men into a ravine and set about doing his work, raking the Indians with deadly accuracy.[32]

The Lakotas planned their attack well and began crossing the Yellowstone near Captain French's positions on the right flank. The attacking warriors took advantage of a ravine and began moving forward to infiltrate the soldiers' positions. Tom and Armstrong noticed the warriors using the natural contour of the landscape to creep toward their positions. Armstrong shouted for Lieutenant Weston to move his men into the end of the ravine and expel the warriors. Captain Hale moved his men to

[31]Ibid., pp. 83–84.   [32]Ibid.

support Weston's movement. Custer ordered the band forward and to play "Garryowen." At that moment, Tom and company B charged the Indians' right flank. The soldiers surged forward with a shout and the Sioux began to retreat. Armstrong, in the advance near Tom, suddenly fell to the earth. His horse had been shot from underneath him; he was, however, unhurt.[33] The melee continued for some time until the rest of the command made its presence felt by unleashing the artillery. Shells whistled over the heads of the cavalrymen, crashing into the warriors on the opposite shore. A few more well placed shots followed, and the Lakotas beat a hasty retreat. Later, a correspondent for the *New York Tribune* described the scene for his readers.

> "Forward!" Shouted the commanders, and away they went "pell-mell," the horses seemingly to share the eagerness of the men. There was no scattering or flagging. Every man keeps in his place. Weston and Hale on the left, Tom Custer plunging down the ravine on the right. Ditches, gullies, hills cannot stop them. Now Yates and Moylan are ordered to advance and support them, and add two more to the black columns dashing over the hills. No Indian would venture to stand before that whirlwind. Leaping on their horses they run for their lives. Hale and Weston succeed in getting within thirty yards of them and give them a volley from their carbines; McDougall speaks with his revolver. One conspicuous Indian in a red blanket, supposed to be Gall, an important chief, had his pony shot dead under him. He leaped on a fresh horse and got away. Seeing that with their jaded horses, wearied by the long march, they could not run down the Indians, they dismounted and gave them a volley from their carbines, then remounted and chased them till they had completed a run of eight miles. Lieutenant Custer on the left led his men on furiously. "He is a terrible rider," said one of our "casuals" to me. "I saw him fly over a ditch about 15 feet wide. The man after him missed it, and horse and rider rolled into the gully." Two or three times the Indians ahead of him, having a better start than those fleeing before the retribution of Hale, turned in their saddles and fired a volley which tore up the dust at the feet of their pursuers, but did no further damage.[34]

---

[33]Ibid., p. 84.
[34]Ibid.

On 16 August, Stanley informed the command that the expedition had reached its terminus and would start back east. The next morning, the men took advantage of their time in camp by washing their clothes, and themselves, in the Yellowstone. Suddenly, gunfire erupted from the opposite bank. The naked troopers hurriedly ran from the water to grab their weapons lying on the river's bank. A few shots were exchanged, but no real harm was done and the Lakotas left as quickly as they had come.[35] The next morning the command continued on their way back to civilization.

The return trip proved uneventful. The Lakota seemed content with the fact that the cavalry was leaving their lands, and did not attack the command again. The daily hunting forays began again. Armstrong killed another antelope. Tom, however, had still not killed one of the majestic animals. Tom decided Armstrong had too great an edge with his new Remington sporting rifle so he decided to even the score. He decided to borrow the prized rifle, and so he did at every opportunity. His own Winchester did not have the range of the Remington. Armstrong, noticed his rifle somehow "strayed" off on its own, and he sent his orderly to Tom's tent, where the rifle was miraculously discovered.[36]

The absence of the Lakota gave Tom a chance to relax and turn his attentions to other matters. The poker games began anew, with the usual results for Tom and James Calhoun. Tom found his brother-in-law was a rather thin skinned fellow who could not take a joke. This trait was definitely not in Calhoun's favor, and Tom smelled blood. The next few days became filled with verbal sparring between the two men. The evening mess opened the curtain for the evening's activities. Tom slowly began to needle Calhoun, who began a slow boil. Having heard enough, Calhoun responded angrily to Tom's tirade, which only

---

[35]Ibid., p. 91.
[36]Letter, George A. Custer to K.C. Barker, 6 September 1873. Merington Collections.

served to fuel Tom further. Finally, Calhoun reached his boiling point and angrily left the mess. Later, one of the regiment's horses died, and Tom accused Calhoun of deliberately starving the animal so he could better feed his own horse. Shortly after that incident, Tom again took the opportunity to harass Calhoun. Tom and the other officers seated themselves around the campfire. Tom turned the conversation to the celebrated showman, Buffalo Bill, now making his mark on the stage. One of the assemblage stated Buffalo Bill would probably earn twenty thousand dollars. Tom asked, "Is that so? By George, when we get back from this expedition why wouldn't it be good speculation for us to start through the states with (Antelope Jim) and (Vinagre,) [a play upon the Seventh's band leader's name] as the stars?" Calhoun recognized the jab as making fun of his hunting abilities and his responsibility as commander of the band with Tom's reference to 'Vinagre.' Calhoun did not respond to Tom's statement, other than to get mad and scowl at Tom. The men around the fire saw the irritation in Calhoun's face and began to laugh, which only exacerbated Calhoun's anger.[37]

During this expedition, Armstrong discovered taxidermy. One of the representatives of the Smithsonian noticed his interest offered to teach Armstrong the intricacies of the procedure. He was a quick learner, and became quite proficient in a short period of time. He became so good Tom badgered him into preparing an antelope head that he could send to Lulie. Armstrong prepared several specimens during the course of the expedition which he sent to various destinations.[38]

On 7 September the command was ferried across the Yellowstone River. Stanley ordered Custer to escort the engineers to Fort Lincoln, the new home of the Seventh Cavalry. Stanley's order was gratefully executed and Tom received his first glimpse of his new home late in the afternoon of 21 Sep-

---

[37]Letter, George A. Custer to Elizabeth B. Custer, 10 September 1873. Merington Collection.
[38]Letter, George A. Custer to Elizabeth B. Custer, 6 September 1873. Merington Collection.

tember. The Yellowstone Expedition was over. Tom and the
troopers had been in the field for ninety-five days, traveling
some four hundred and thirty-five miles.[39]

Fort Abraham Lincoln was created by act of Congress on 3
March 1873. The post was located on the west side of the Missouri River, opposite the growing town of Bismarck, Dakota
Territory. The fort lay below the western bluffs, just south of
Fort McKeen, an infantry post built for the protection of the
workers of the Northern Pacific Rail Road. Fort McKeen
consisted of three blockhouses, quarters for officers, and two
companies of infantry. The new installation was constructed
at the request of Phil Sheridan, who felt the cavalry would
best be qualified to guarantee the safety of the workers.[40]

Colonel George Dandy supervised the construction of the
new cavalry post. Two hundred men worked on the fort, using
nearly seven hundred car loads of supplies to build the post.
The carpenters built seven officers' quarters, a granary, office
and dispensary, guard house, commissary, Quartermaster
storehouse, three barracks buildings with attached mess
rooms, the necessary stables, ordinance depot, and finally, the
laundresses' quarters[41] The post held a total of six hundred
and fifty-five enlisted men and officers of the Seventh Cavalry, and two companies of infantry, the Sixth and Seventeenth, stationed at Fort McKeen. The rest of the Seventh
was quartered at Fort Rice, twenty-five miles to the south.[42]

Tom, meanwhile, moved into a two story frame house facing the parade ground and the Missouri River to the east. For
the next three years Fort Lincoln was Tom's home.

[39]Frost, *Custer's Seventh Cavalry*, p. 105.
[40]Goplen, *The Historical Significance of Fort Lincoln*, pp. 47–50.
[41]Ibid., p. 51.
[42]Ibid., p. 52.

CHAPTER TEN

Fort Lincoln and the Black Hills

Tom's new home at Fort Lincoln was one of the houses erected for the officers situated on the west side of the parade ground. He occupied half of the dwelling, while sister Margaret and Jimmi Calhoun periodically lived in the other half (officers were constantly bumped from their quarters by more senior officers, Tom bounced back and forth between living in his own quarters and living with George Armstrong Custer and Libbie). Armstrong and Libbie lived just next door.

Brother Armstrong occupied himself with preparing his new home for Libbie. He remained at the post for several weeks, getting all of their belongings unpacked. At last he was satisfied it was habitable for his bride, and he applied for a leave of absence so he could travel to Monroe and collect his wife. Before he left, he intrusted Tom to finish the supervision of the decorating of their quarters.

Armstrong, Libbie, and a companion from Monroe, Miss Agnes Bates, returned together in November. Armstrong and Libbie traveled by train to Bismarck where they boarded a wagon for the short journey to the banks of the Missouri River. The Dakotas were feeling the fury of an early winter, and the river was partially frozen. They rode across on the ice until they reached the point nearest the break in the ice shelf. They endured a perilous boat ride across the river to the opposite ice shelf, where Tom met them with an ambulance from the post.[1]

Tom arranged for a grand reception for Armstrong and Libbie. As soon as the wagon entered the parade ground, the band began playing the battle song of the Seventh, "Garry Owen." The entire post assembled to greet the returning Custers. Libbie found her new home aglow with lights and a grand reception ensued.[2]

With the return of their commander, the post settled into their daily routine. Tom found the inclement weather of the Dakotas a new experience after two years in the South. A gale force wind roared across the barren countryside. Snow fell, not vertically, but horizontally, finding its way through any gaps in the walls and windows. Temperatures dropped down to 40-50 degrees below zero. All water on the post froze. Men froze too, and they quickly discovered the worth of buffalo robes and coats. Custer restricted any outdoor activity while officers kept a strict watch on sentries, making sure they were warm and not falling victim to the intense cold. Men were detailed to make sure the fires in the officers' quarters and in the barracks never went out. On the evening of 5 February, Armstrong was, as usual, the last to retire. He went from room to room, inspecting the fires, stoking them if necessary, or checking to make sure the fire was extinguished if the room was not in use. Satisfied that everything was normal, he went to bed.

They were not in bed long when a strange sound woke them up. Libbie stated it sounded like the roar of large fire; definitely not the case Armstrong informed her, he had made sure before retiring. Libbie insisted that he get up and see what was wrong. Armstrong got out of bed and followed the noise to its source upstairs. He entered the first room and checked the stove, which contained only a few

---

[1]Custer, *Boots and Saddles*, p. 78.
[2]Ibid.

waning embers. He looked around the room and observed smoke snaking up from a hole burned through the floor. As he moved toward the plume to investigate, he noticed the wall seemed to reverberate with a rushing sound. Armstrong struck the floor with his fist and the charred wood gave way. He looked into the hole and saw a fire burning within the framework. He shouted to Libbie to get out of bed and wake Agnes. He attempted to force water and wet rags into the hole, but he could not reach the flame which appeared to be burning at the base of the wall near the chimney. Suddenly, there was a thunderous explosion and the room filled with smoke and sparks. Libbie jumped from her bed, frightened that Armstrong might be injured. Agnes Bates, in the room across the hall, woke up to find her own room ablaze. She frantically grabbed a wrap and ran from the room. Custer rushed down the steps, ushered the two women out of the house, and shouted "Fire!" The sentry on duty fired his weapon to awaken the garrison who raced to the scene.[3]

Tom dressed quickly and dashed to the blazing house. He discovered Libbie and Agnes outside, wrapped in blankets. Libbie frantically told Tom that Armstrong was still inside. Tom raced up the steps and into the house where he found Armstrong attempting to salvage their possessions. Unfortunately, very few of their personal belongings were rescued. The fire raced through the structure and the house burned to the ground.

The garrison rallied behind the Custers and provided enough items to help them rebuild their lives. Libbie and Armstrong relocated to temporary quarters in the other half of Tom's house. One of the first alterations they made was to cut a doorway in the wall so that the two living spaces could

---

[3]Letter, George A. Custer to Lt. Colonel William P. Carlin, 6 February 1874. Merington Collection.

be connected. Plans were immediately drawn up to rebuild their house.[4]

Garrison life was mundane in good weather, but winter exacerbated the monotony. The inhabitants of the fort made every effort to fill their free time with a diversity of amusements. Social gatherings filled a great deal of their time. They also engaged in sing-alongs, amateur theatrics, and diverse games of chance to occupy the long winter evenings. Each company took turns sponsoring dances.

Tom filled his free time by hunting with Armstrong. Together the brothers owned more than forty hunting dogs. Their hunts began as they had in Texas, with the blowing of their hunting horns. The blasting of the horns sent the dogs into a frenzy, and they immediately began yelping, barking, and racing for the doors. Tom and Armstrong vaulted into their saddles and raced away, accompanied by their enthusiastic canines. They returned with an assortment of wild game such as turkeys, deer, and antelope.

Tom also kept a buffalo calf as a pet. He escaped from his pen one day and entered the Custer home. He invaded the kitchen and snatched a bunch of carrots from the table. Custer's cook angrily chased the animal from the house and across the parade ground. The calf happily munched away on his carrots, much to Mary's chagrin.[5]

The carpenters, meanwhile, completed Libbie and Armstrong's new house in record time. Their new dwelling was much bigger than their old one, even sporting a wing addition that the Custers utilized as a ballroom. Tom left his quarters and moved into one of the upstairs bedrooms. Ensconced once again with Armstrong and Libbie, Tom's old lifestyle resumed. Tom, Armstrong, and Libbie found time to engage in riotous games of tag. Custer's orderly, sta-

---

[4]Ibid.
[5]Fougera, *With Custer's Cavalry*, p. 89.

tioned in the front hall, watched incredulously as his commanding officer pursued his wife and brother through the
house and up the stairs, yelling and screaming the entire
time.[6]

The newest arrival at Fort Lincoln, twenty-five-year-old
Boston Custer, occupied the other upstairs bedroom. Boston
arrived at Fort Lincoln anxious to encounter the Wild West.
Photographs of Boston reveal a rather gaunt young man.
Perhaps it was felt the climate of the west would improve his
health. He fit right in with the other family members, and
became the victim of a multitude of pranks from his elder
brothers. Tom took Boston under his wing and introduced
him to the members of the garrison. Tom also liberated any
necessary items, such as postage stamps, from Boston.[7]

The Custer home became the focal point of the Custer
"clan," those members of the family and loyal officers of the
regiment who supported their commander. The Custer family consisted of Armstrong, Tom, Libbie, Boston, Jimmi and
Margaret Calhoun. Their military family extended to Lieutenant Willie Cooke, who was a good friend to both Tom
and Armstrong. Other members of the clan included Captain and Mrs. Algernon Smith, and Captain and Mrs.
George Yates, who also hailed from Monroe, Michigan.
Captain Myles Walter Keogh filled out the circle. The Irish-
born Keogh had served for a time with the Papal guard in
Rome before immigrating to the United States. He joined
the Union cavalry during the Civil War and joined the Seventh Cavalry 28 July 1866.

The close-knit group filled their evenings with amateur
theatricals, with the family members assuming all the roles.
They all took turns performing in such plays as "Flora
McFlimsey With Nothing To Wear." They commemorated

---

[6]Custer, *Boots and Saddles*, pp. 117–118.
[7]Letter, Boston Custer to Emma Reed, 1 July 1874. M.C.H.S.

their thespian antics by posing for a series of photographs, showing Tom, Armstrong, Libbie, and the rest of the clan attired in their makeshift costumes.[8]

When the weather broke, Tom, Armstrong, and Libbie began their daily rides into the surrounding countryside. With the coming of spring, however, the Indians again made their presence felt. One day while riding, Armstrong and Libbie discovered the body of a murdered civilian near the post. Later, a rancher was found murdered and mutilated.[9] A few weeks afterward, a small war party of Lakotas attacked the post. They did no damage, and the only casualties were among the Lakotas. The fort experienced two more attacks in the following weeks.[10] On 10 June, a party of engineers, working within sight of the garrison, found themselves under attack by Lakota warriors. Fortunately, a detachment of troopers from Fort Lincoln had accompanied the railroad workers. The troopers organized a determined resistance, giving the surveyors time to escape. With the civilians safely back at the post, the cavalrymen began a slow retreat, fighting all the way back to the fort. Again, there were no casualties except among the attacking warriors.[11]

After months of limited activity and a decided increase in Indian depredations, the temperate weather allowed for the resumption of military drill. The coming of spring also allowed for the movement of civilization, as a steady stream of visitors arrived at the fort. Kate Garrett was one such visitor. She came to visit her sister Molly, the wife of Lieutenant Donald McIntosh of Company G. She arrived at Fort Lincoln a typical easterner, come to view at first-hand life in the Wild West. Upon her arrival, she was introduced to the officers of the Seventh Cavalry.

---

[8]Frost, *The Custer Album*, pp. 63–64.
[9]Custer, *Boots and Saddles*, pp. 126–129.
[10]Goplen, *Fort Lincoln*, p. 58.   [11]Ibid.

Tom took an immediate liking to young Kate, and wasted no time in demonstrating the Custer proclivity for practical jokes. After viewing a dress parade of the regiment, Kate observed that Tom wore his dress helmet very low over his forehead, making him almost unrecognizable. She confronted Tom and asked him why he wore his hat in such a fashion. He listened to her query, and looked around to see who might be listening. He leaned over to her and whispered, "It's a disguise. You see, they're after me for killing a Chinaman." Kate listened, astounded at Tom's confession. She walked away from Tom and kept his dark secret.[12]

The appearance of Kate and other visitors heralded the departure of some of the regiment's officers. Tom petitioned for a leave of absence on 7 April and he did not return until 28 May.[13] Before he left, however, he assisted Armstrong and Libbie with the planting of a garden. The army did not supply the men with much more than the absolute necessities of life. Fresh vegetables and fruit became delicacies that were highly cherished. The canned food industry began during the Civil War; the process, though, was not without its defects, and much of the food spoiled. The post, however, had to suffer whatever provisions the government sent them. In order to supplement their diets, soldiers were allotted space on the post to try their hand at gardening.

Tom labored over the small plot of ground, dreaming of enjoying the fruits of his labors. Among those vegetables planted was what he and Armstrong considered to be the reigning delicacy of the Plains: onions. They ate them raw, creamed, and any other way possible. Their dreams of culinary bliss, however, did not come true. One morning they awoke to find a swarm of grasshoppers descending upon the gardens. Tom ran into the kitchen, yelling for Libbie and the

---

[12]Fougera, *With Custer's Cavalry*, p. 84.
[13]T.W.C. Service Record, N.A.

cook to follow his lead. He grabbed a pot and spoon, and raced to the garden. He began beating the spoon on the pot, having read that such noise repelled the insects. He, Libbie, and Mary flailed away, filling the air with a cacophony of noise, all to no avail. The grasshoppers continued to eat until all of the sprouts were devoured.[14] It reminded Tom of one of the plagues from the Bible.

Tom, now with more free time on his hands, took it upon himself to teach Kate Garrett how to ride and shoot. Since her arrival at the post, every new acquaintance asked her about her equestrian and martial abilities. She confessed she could not ride, or shoot a gun. Tom took her riding and supervised her shooting every day, rain or shine. She complained to Tom of his daily efforts and wondered why he seemed in such a hurry for her to learn. He smiled and explained that, "Because once we leave for the campaign you won't have anyone to teach you." Tom's determination paid off, and she became an accomplished rider. One day while target shooting, she made a particularly fine shot. Tom was so pleased with her that he forgot himself and slapped her hard across the back as he exclaimed, "Golly, what a shot!"[15]

The campaign Tom spoke of was the imminent departure of the regiment to explore the Black Hills region. General Sheridan, accompanied by General Terry, arrived at the post on 24 April to discuss the scope of the expedition. General Sheridan ordered that Fort Lincoln be the point of origin for the expedition and directed all of the military units to assemble there. Tom anticipated the arrival of the rest of the Seventh, stationed at Fort Rice, in late June.

The Black Hills belonged to the Lakota by agreement in the Treaty of 1868. The Indians considered the region to be sacred. According to Indian religion, the Black Hills was the

---

[14]Custer, *Boots and Saddles,* p. 140.
[15]Fougera, *With Custer's Cavalry,* pp. 94–95.

equivalent of the Christian Garden of Eden. They believed all life began in the Black Hills, and the Great Spirit resided in the valleys and hills of the region. Frequent severe storms, and the general difficulty of the landscape, made the region inhospitable to the Native Americans. Whatever the belief of the particular tribes, they were all in unanimity on one point: they did not want any whites in the region. They claimed the territory by right of the treaty, and they were resolved to keep it.

The steady encroachment of the white civilization that sought to encircle them, combined with the ever increasing invasion of their sacred land by white miners, outraged the Lakota and Cheyenne. The Yellowstone Expedition of 1873 exacerbated their resentment. It was apparent to the Indians that the whites meant to infest their land, and ultimately tear it from them. Many of the tribes resolved to resist.

The attack on Custer's men during the Yellowstone Expedition caused great concern in Washington. The Secretary of the Interior counseled General Sheridan that the chiefs responsible for the attacks ought be arrested. Sheridan acknowledged the attacks on both civilians and the military by the Lakota had spiraled during the last twelve months. He explained, however, it would be impossible to chastise the tribes. There was no way to ascertain which tribes were responsible. Even if identifying the guilty tribe was possible, any action against the Lakota would likely elicit an aggressive response by the entire Sioux nation. General William T. Sherman, the commanding general of the army, counseled Sheridan by remarking, "I suppose we had better let things take their natural course until the mass of Indians commit some act that will warrant a final war . . ."[16]

The situation, meanwhile, deteriorated daily. Five thousand people had settled on lands promised to the Lakota by the Treaty of 1868. The settlers claimed the land was theirs,

---

[16]Hutton, *Phil Sherican*, pp. 285–286.

citing the provisions of the Homestead Act of 1862. Both the Lakota and the homesteaders demanded the protection of their rights according to the agreements made with both sides by the Federal Government.[17] As many times happened in Indian-white relations, the government made commitments to both sides that were impossible to honor. When compelled by events to choose between sides, the government embraced its own. The politicians left the army to enforce their decisions. The situation in 1874 had reached the point that the army had to respond to events.

Bitterness reached a fever pitch among the agency Indians during the late winter and early spring of 1874. The reservations filled with an incursion of non-reservation Indians who demanded the government supply them with provisions. The increase in the population on the reservations placed a strain on the resources of the government and created a scarcity of provisions. The Indians asserted the government was willfully starving them and responded with violence. They murdered the chief clerk at the Red Cloud Agency, as well as two soldiers from Fort Laramie. The Indians at the Spotted Tail Agency usurped control of the commissary and threatened more violence if anyone dared to interfere with the distribution of supplies. The military eventually intervened at the request of Columbus Delano, Secretary of the Interior and in charge of the reservations, and restored order.[18] Delano, however, insisted the military use restraint in dealing with the unhappy Indians.

This duplicity by Secretary Delano did not go unnoticed by General Sherman who told Sheridan:

> That letter from the Secretary of the Interior was meant to throw on us the blame in case of an Indian war . . . Everybody, even Mr. Delano, would be made happy if the troops should kill a goodly

---

[17]Athearn, *Sherman and the Settlement of the West*, p. 305.
[18]Hutton, *Phil Sherman*, pp. 287–288.

number of those Sioux, but they want to keep the record to prove
they didn't do it. We can afford to be frank and honest for sooner or
later those Sioux have to be wiped out or made to stay just where
they are put.[19]

The two generals decided a ring of forts encircling the
Lakota reservation, was necessary. The army constructed
Camp Robinson at the Red Cloud Agency and Camp Sheridan near the Spotted Tail Agency. Forts Lincoln and Rice
guarded the lands to the north, and Forts Sully and Randall
to the east. The only gap in the military's ring remained on
the western perimeter. Sheridan recommended that posts be
erected along the Yellowstone River. Most important, Sheridan insisted, was the necessity for a large military presence in
the Black Hills.[20]

Perhaps the actual motivation for the government's
actions regarding the Black Hills was the persistent rumor of
the presence of gold in the region. The Panic of 1873 discon-
tinued all progress on the extension of the Northern Pacific
Rail Road across the Dakotas. An economic disaster spread
throughout the United States. If the rumors of gold were
correct, then it might solve the depression and bring back
prosperity. The presence of gold in the Black Hills would
also resolve the Indian quandary. The government realized
that gold fever would cause a torrential avalanche of prospectors and settlers to the region. This influx of people, bringing
civilization with them, would end the Indians' dominance of
the region. To ascertain the truth of the rumors, two geologists were to accompany the expedition. Custer received his
orders from Sheridan and began to make the necessary
preparations for the campaign.

Not many days later the companies from Fort Rice arrived
at Fort Lincoln. Among those traveling with the column were

---

[19]Ibid., p. 290.
[20]Ibid.

Jimmi Calhoun and his wife, Margaret Custer Calhoun, and a joyous celebration ensued. The band broke into "Garry-owen," and the garrison turned out in force to greet their comrades. The arriving companies made camp near the fort.[21]

Tom, Armstrong, and other officers of the garrison also took up residence in the camp. It was warm and the cooling breezes made the climate more comfortable. Tom and Armstrong noticed Miss Garrett was a little unsure of the security in the tent which was her new home. Tom pondered for a moment and said, "Suppose we put a padlock on the inside for you?" Armstrong congratulated Tom. "Good idea!' he exclaimed. Armstrong turned to Kate and said, "Will that suit you?" Kate assured the two men the padlock would certainly alleviate her fears. Armstrong ordered one of the troopers to attend to the fixing of the padlock. Everyone had a great laugh at Kate's expense, and it took her years to live it down.[22] Unfortunately, her trials were not over.

One evening, after she had gone to bed, she heard what she believed to be a dog at the entrance of her tent. She thought perhaps the dog was either one of Tom's or Armstrong's, since their animals had the run of the camp. She called the dog by a collection of names she knew for those animals belonging to the Custer men, but the dog did not respond to any of them. She reached under her pillow and pulled out a piece of hard tack to lure the dog into her tent. The dog entered the tent and snatched the cracker from Kate's hand. She reached out and grabbed the dog, and tried to make it lie down on her floor. The animal would not, however, oblige and left the tent. A moment later, a gunshot jolted Kate from her rest. She sprang out of bed and stuck her head out of the tent to see what was wrong. The sentry explained he had just shot a large wolf that had come out of the young lady's tent. Armstrong

---

[21]Fougera, *With Custer's Cavalry*, p. 105.
[22]Ibid., p. 113.

gracefully tendered Kate his spot in bed and Kate spent the rest of the night with Libbie.[23]

Shortly before the expedition left, Kate fell in love with Lieutenant Frank Gibson. Tom and Armstrong decided to stage a buffalo hunt in their honor. The participants filled their baskets with food and moved onto the Plains. Earlier, a detachment of scouts from the fort located a small herd of buffalo, and sent back word of its location. The ladies were to stay out of harm's way while the men moved to the attack. During the course of the afternoon, a bull approached the ladies. Kate noticed the bull intended to charge one of the ladies, and she urged her horse to the attack. She rode alongside of the buffalo and shot him several times with her pistol. The gunshots drew the attention of Tom and the other men who raced to the defense of their loved ones. They arrived to find Kate standing proudly over her fallen buffalo. Tom and Armstrong severely reproached her for her careless behavior. They were, though, filled with pride at her foolhardy deed.[24]

These happy days, though, could not last forever. All of the troops and supplies for the expedition had arrived. On 1 July, Armstrong gave orders for the regiment to be ready to depart at 8:00 A.M. the following morning. At the appointed hour the band began playing "Garryowen," and the troopers mounted their horses and wheeled by fours into line. The officers inspected their respective commands and reported to General Custer that all was ready. Custer gave the command, and the troopers moved by companies into the line of march. The families and friends waved and cheered through their tears, suffering the fear of never seeing their loved ones again. The command snaked its way from the parade ground, up through the hills in the rear of the post, and onto the flat

---

[23]Ibid., pp. 129–130.
[24]Ibid., pp. 144–156.

prairie headed west. Tom rode for fifteen miles on the first day of march.[25]

The command consisted of ten companies of the Seventh Cavalry, the Seventeenth and Twentieth US Infantry, one hundred Indian scouts, guides, teamsters, wagon masters, newspapermen, one hundred ten wagons and three hundred head of beef.[26] Two geologists, a zoologist, a photographer, and several miners also accompanied the expedition. Army engineer Captain William Ludlow scouted the terrain to find a suitable place for future military posts.

Each morning, Tom, now in command of company L, readied his men for the day's travels.[27] Armstrong and his staff rode at the head of the column. The artillery, wagon train, and infantry followed. The cavalry rode alongside the column, guarding the flanks. The order passed from company to company: no hunting or straggling would be permitted.[28] The memory of the two civilians from the previous summer who left the column to get water and wound up being murdered by the Lakota remained fresh in their minds.

Jimmi Calhoun, acting assistant adjutant general for brother-in-law Armstrong, decided to keep a diary of the expedition in addition to his other clerical duties. His official duties involved transcribing all of Armstrong's orders and disseminating them among the officers. His unofficial daily entries tell of the miles traveled, the sights encountered, and a record of events occurring to him and his friends.

Tom loved the open range. The weather was wonderful and invigorating. Game was plentiful, and on 9 July Tom killed five antelope and captured a young rabbit.[29] But Tom

---

[25]Carroll and Frost, *Private Theodore Ewert's Diary of The Black Hills Expedition of 1874*, pp. 8–9.

[26]Wemett, "Custer's Expedition To The Black Hills in 1874," pp. 294–295.

[27]Frost, *With Custer in '74*, p. 12.

[28]Ibid., p. xxi.

[29]Ibid., p. 28.

realized that danger lurked behind every hill. He remembered the battles he fought the previous summer against the Lakota. He knew of the reverence the Lakota held for the Black Hills, and felt, as did most of the men, that the Lakota would challenge the soldiers' entry into the region. He was careful, and wisely so. A few days later, Tom saw a small party of Lakotas in the distance.[30]

Indians or not, the expedition continued onward. One of the zoologists unearthed the fossil remains of a dinosaur. Tom marveled at the size of the bone. He and Armstrong decided the creature must have been bigger than an elephant. The command pressed on, and Tom agreed with others who asserted this was the best foray on which they had ever been. A new friendship sprang up as Tom and Armstrong became good friends with Captain Ludlow, now a member the inner circle.[31]

Tom did find himself yearning for the relaxation of a good game of cards. Armstrong made it known such activity would not be encouraged during this trip as it had during the Yellowstone Expedition. Prohibition was the order of the day. Some men and officers, however, managed to procure several bottles of liquor which became evident during the campaign.

Armstrong filled his evenings with letter writing. His voluminous letters are filled with descriptions of the days' events and sights. Tom occasionally wrote, but as always found himself competing with Armstrong's lengthy missives. He did write to Libbie and facetiously ask her to clean his room for him while he was gone. Armstrong informed Libbie that she was to do nothing of the kind.[32]

On 11 July, Tom and Armstrong found a cave near their

---

[30]Letter, George A. Custer to Elizabeth B. Custer, 15 July 1874. Merington Collection.
[31]Ibid.
[32]Letter, George A. Custer to Elizabeth B. Custer, 15 August 1874. Merington Collection.

camp. The scouts reported that a white man lived in it at one time, and the Indians tried many times to shoot him, but were unsuccessful. Tom and Armstrong entered the cave and found the skeletal remains of the mountain man. His belongings littered the cave. They found a tin cup with initials on it and assumed the letters to be the initials of the dead man. In his letter to Libbie, Armstrong declared the initials to be the same as those of one of Libbie's old beaus. He and Tom agreed this explained the mysterious disappearance of Libbie's old flame. "Rather than meet such a fate as awaited him marrying you, Old Lady, he has chosen to seek out solitude in a cavern and there die."[33]

Tom, Armstrong, and Boston had a good laugh over Libbie's "old beau." Boston found himself glad to laugh at someone else's plight. Since the expedition began, everyone, especially Tom, had been busy making his life the butt of every joke. Boston's letters and actions reveal a young man who appeared to be either extremely naive, or lacking in certain areas of intelligence. Tom constantly took advantage of his brother's wide-eyed wonder. One evening while in camp, Tom picked up several smooth stones and presented them to Boston. He told his gullible brother that they were "sponge stones." He instructed Boston to keep them in water and after a few days they would soften. Boston dutifully did as he was told. Every evening he placed his stones in his cup and filled it with water. It took him several nights before he realized that his brother had lied to him and he was playing the fool once again.[34]

Being a Custer, however, he attempted to give as good as he got. Boston, just twelve when Tom left home, enjoyed the companionship of his older brothers no matter how much they teased him. He ate his meals with Tom, who never let up

---

[33]Custer, *Boots and Saddles*, p. 185.
[34]Letter, George A. Custer to Elizabeth B. Custer, 15 July 1874. Merington Collection.

about the quantity of food he consumed. Boston learned to do as he had done when they were boys back in Ohio: he ignored Tom.[35]

The command continued on with their exploration of the region. From time to time, they saw Indians on the horizon, intently watching the soldiers, but they did not approach, nor did they attack. On the morning of 26 July, Tom and the command discovered an abandoned Indian village. Tom noticed the campfires were still burning, and deer meat lay nearby on the ground. Tom knew that the Indians were very close. Armstrong ordered Bloody Knife and his Arikaras to find the trail of the Lakotas and determine where they had gone. The Arikaras had not been gone long when they came racing back to Armstrong with the news they had discovered the Lakotas.[36]

The troopers moved forward, following the Arikara guides. Before long, they located the camp. Armstrong directed one company to charge the camp while another took up positions between the warriors and their horses. Bloody Knife approached Tom and Armstrong and demanded the right to kill and scalp the Lakota. He told Armstrong he and his fellow Arikaras would attack the camp by themselves. The Lakotas were the hereditary enemies of the Arikara, and Bloody Knife demanded his right as a warrior to exact revenge for the murder of his people at the hands of the Lakotas. Armstrong refused, stating the expedition's purpose was to gather information, not to start a war. Bloody Knife pointed out to Custer that if the Lakota had spotted them first, they would not have hesitated to attack them. Bloody Knife's argument, however, fell on deaf ears. Custer had no intention of antagonizing the Lakotas.[37] Armstrong approached the camp under a white

---

[35]Letter, Boston Custer to Emma Reed, 2 August 1874, M.C.H.S.

[36]Frost, *Calhoun's Diary*, p. 54.

[37]Carroll and Frost, *Ewert's Diary*, pp. 45–46.

flag. The chief and three warriors approached and were taken prisoner to guarantee the safety of the command. The rest of the village fled. The old chief, One Stab, was held for several days and ordered to guide the column. The Arikaras, filled with anger at Custer's refusal to allow them to kill their enemies, became even more incensed at having to abide the presence of the Lakota chief. They guarded him day and night.[38]

Less than a week later, the expedition fulfilled its true goal. Calhoun reported in his diary that two miners discovered gold during the morning of 2 August.[39] Armstrong later reported to General Sheridan, "I have on my table 40 or 50 small particles of pure gold . . . obtained today from one panful of earth . . . it will be understood that there is no opportunity to make a satisfactory examination in regards to deposits of valuable minerals."[40]

Custer sent scout Charlie Reynolds and an escort to hurry this news to Sheridan. In spite of some amount of secrecy, the news leaked out as everyone knew that it would. Within a few weeks of the ending of the expedition, the Black Hills became the focus of a myriad of gold seekers. Dozens of mining camps sprang up within just a few weeks of the announcement. The government made only a half-hearted attempt to stop the illegal incursions. The Lakotas, however, reacted more forcefully.

Tom and the command, meanwhile, continued on with the exploration. On 3 August, they entered a valley teaming with wild berries. Tom could choose from wild blackberries, raspberries, strawberries, and cherries.[41] A few days later, the command entered a meadow carpeted with wild flowers. Tom reached down from his saddle and picked enough multicolored flowers to wreath his horse's head. Others placed

---

[38]Ibid.   [39]Frost, *Calhoun's Diary*, p. 60.
[40]*The Black Hills Engineer*, November, 1929, p. 280.
[41]Frost, *Calhoun's Diary*, pp. 67–68.

the flowers on their caps, in their pockets, and in the barrels of their rifles.[42]

Tom finally sighted Fort Lincoln on 30 August. He had been gone for sixty days and traveled eight hundred and eighty-three miles.[43] As the column approached the fort, the band broke into "Garry Owen." Libbie heard the first notes and broke into tears of joy. She hid behind the front door, ashamed to go outside and let others see her emotional reaction. In a few moments, she heard her husband's voice. She opened the door, ran down the steps, and threw herself into his arms. Tom and the others burst out laughing at Libbie's display. Through tear-filled eyes, Libbie looked upon the faces of her loved ones. Tom, Boston, and Armstrong were all deeply tanned and bearded. Their clothing was a hodge-podge of faded blue and white patches. But they were home, and they were all glad.

Before leaving on the expedition, Armstrong gave strict orders to his orderly to watch over Libbie and the house. As soon as the man heard the first notes of "Garryowen," he knew his mission was accomplished, and quickly disappeared. Armstrong and Tom dismounted their horses and walked up the steps to their house. The orderly appeared from around the corner of the house with an armful of puppies that had been born in their absence. His eyes twinkled as he staggered toward Tom and Armstrong. He reached the steps and fell down, thoroughly intoxicated. Tom and Armstrong broke into laughter. Armstrong thanked the soldier for his diligence to duty, and released him to go and find some quiet place where he could sleep off his own special joy at his commander's return. Libbie later wrote that she had never known of anyone who had gotten so drunk so quickly.[44] The Black Hills expedition was over.

---

[42]Goplen, *The Black Hills Engineer*, p. 274.

[43]Frost, *General Custer's Libbie*, p. 213.

[44]Custer, *Boots and Saddles*, pp. 158–160.

CHAPTER ELEVEN

The Clouds of War

Tom unpacked his bedroll and stretched across his bed. Rest, however, was out of the question. Tom's equestrian and sharpshooting protégé, Kate Garrett, had promised herself in marriage to Lieutenant Frank Gibson. They planned the wedding for the day after the return of the column from the Black Hills. Tom took part in the ceremony. He even swiped a taste of the icing before they cut the cake. Later, he joined in quarreling with the other unmarried officers debating which officer Kate should have married.[1]

With Kate and Lieutenant Gibson married, the garrison settled down to a more mundane existence. Armstrong and Libbie secreted themselves, enjoying each other's company once again. Tom and Boston continued their bachelor lifestyle. They sought the companionship of other men who, like themselves, were alone on the frontier. Occasionally they took their meals with their sister Margaret and her husband Jimmi.[2] On certain occasions the two brothers partied with their military counterparts in the infantry post up the hill.[3]

If Tom found the post boring, there was always the lure of Bismarck across the river. Bismarck was a typical frontier town, with all of the attractions of its more famous counterparts such as Dodge City and Hays City, Kansas. Saloons

---

[1]Fougera, *With Custer's Cavalry*, p. 197.
[2]Letter, Boston Custer to Emma Reed, 13 September 1874. M.C.H.S.
[3]Letter, Boston Custer to Emma Reed, 22 September 1874. M.C.H.S.

lined the main street, and soldiers took their relaxation there. A game of billiards could be had at the local sutler's store. If a more coarse type of entertainment was sought, that could also be found. Just across the river from the post, and outside the established city limits of Bismarck, grew a small, disorderly community known to everyone as the "Point."[4]

Tom and his friends frequently sought their amusement in Bismarck. Boston often accompanied Tom, and the brothers involved themselves in whatever activities caught their fancy. Several times their amusements made them lose track of time, and they were late in returning to the post. This always meant missing the evening meal, much to Boston's displeasure. Tom took it all in stride, and lost weight.[5]

The officers also took turns in sponsoring dance parties in their quarters. Tom and Boston shared quarters together, next door to Maggie's. Tom gave his first dance of the season in early November.[6] It was a modest party, but a great success with all who participated. Tom made plans for a more elaborate party, given a few weeks later.

The party, however, would have to wait. During a visit to the Standing Rock Agency in late December, Charley Reynolds happened to be present at a ceremonial dance. Reynolds observed a warrior reenacting one of his brave deeds. Reynolds, who understood the sign language of the Lakota, watched in fascination as the warrior danced out his tale. As the warrior's story unfolded, however, Reynolds realized the warrior was responsible for the deaths of at least one of the two civilians during the Yellowstone Expedition. He discreetly obtained the warrior's name, Rain-In-The-Face,

---

[4]Goplen, *Ft. Lincoln*, p. 56.
[5]Letter, Boston Custer to Emma Reed, 4 October 1874. M.C.H.S.
[6]Letter, Boston Custer to Emma Reed, 8 November 1874. M.C.H.S.

and quietly left the campfire. He arrived at Fort Lincoln and made his report to Armstrong.[7]

Armstrong decided that Rain-In-The-Face must be brought to justice. He ordered Tom and Captain Yates to take a detail of fifty men and accompany Charley Reynolds to the Agency and arrest Rain-In-The-Face. Tom and the detail traveled to Fort Rice and augmented their force with another fifty men. They arrived at Standing Rock on the day the monthly supplies were issued. To put the suspicious Indians at ease, the troopers let it be known they were on their way to the Red River area to investigate reports of cattle theft. To reinforce the ruse, a detail of twenty-five men left the agency for the Red River region. Tom and four other troopers entered the agency store, and strategically arranged themselves, and waited.[8]

Tom stood in the store for hours, waiting and watching as the Indians came into the store for their supplies. The warriors covered themselves with their blankets to ward off the cold, making Tom's identification of Rain-In-The-Face more difficult.[9] The warriors eyed the soldiers warily, talking in low whispers among themselves. The braves cast furtive glances at the soldiers, cautiously lowering their blankets from their faces to talk to the agent. Immediately, Charley Reynolds tensed. He moved, keeping his eyes upon one of the warriors at the counter. Reynolds made eye contact with Tom, and nodded his head.[10]

Tom moved closer to the warrior. Rain-In-The-Face sensed the presence of the soldier, and began to open his blanket, uncovering the rifle in his hands. Tom lunged forward and threw his arms around the warrior. The soldiers

---

[7]Carroll, ed., *The Teepee Book*, p. 565.

[8]Ibid., pp. 566–567.

[9]Custer, *Boots and Saddles*, p. 171.

[10]Carroll, *The Teepee Book*, p. 567.

maneuvered to impede any interference from the Indians in the store. Tom grappled with Rain-In-The-Face for possession of the rifle. Another soldier came to Tom's assistance and assisted in subduing the warrior, securing his arms behind his back. The excited Indians ran from the building, shouting to the warriors outside what had just happened.[11]

As Tom exited the store with his prisoner, they encountered a large crowd of Indians, many armed with the new Winchester repeating rifle. The soldiers were surrounded.[12] Charley Reynolds shouted to the Indians the reason for the arrest of Rain-In-The-Face. It made no difference to the angry warriors and they pressed closer, shouting menacing threats to the soldiers. Tom dragged his prisoner to a horse and pushed him up onto the saddle. Captain Yates ordered the men to form two lines around the prisoner. Yates told Reynolds to tell the older warriors in the crowd to use their influence and control the younger braves. Yates warned the Sioux that if anyone attempted to interfere with the arrest of the prisoner, he would order the men to open fire. The Indians changed their tactics, and tried to bargain with Tom and Yates for Rain's release, offering themselves as prisoners. Yates refused and informed them that he must take Rain to Fort Lincoln for trial.[13]

The escort forced their way through the crowd. Daylight was fast fading, and Yates feared moving in the darkness. He commandeered a tepee and placed Rain there under guard. A crowd of Indian women appeared and surrounded the tepee, singing and chanting songs all night. Later on, a young woman stepped out of the darkness and warned Yates not to leave the reservation that night.[14]

The next morning, the troopers made ready to leave. The sullen Indians gathered about the soldiers. Someone shoved a note into Yates' hand, warning him not to return by way of

---

[11]Ibid., p. 567.   [12]Ibid., pp. 566–567.
[13]Ibid., pp. 606–607.   [14]Ibid.

the bluffs. Earlier, Tom observed a large group of mounted Indians galloping away from the agency, heading in the direction of the bluffs. Tom and the detail left the agency and avoided the bluffs, arriving safely at Fort Lincoln where Rain-In-The-Face was placed in the guardhouse.[15]

Armstrong interrogated Rain several times before he finally confessed to the murder of Dr. Holsinger. Rain spoke freely with Armstrong, but became sullen and antagonistic when Tom entered the room. He told Tom that he intended to kill him, and eat his heart. Tom listened to Rain's threats and smiled. During the three months of his captivity, several Indian delegations came to the fort to visit Rain, and to try and intercede on his behalf. One evening, Tom was enjoying an amateur theatrical production when the play was interrupted by a frantic bugle call. He and the other officers raced to the guardhouse to find that Rain and another prisoner had escaped.[16]

Friendly Indians, advised of the escape, furnished Rain with a horse and provisions. He left the area and the reservation, joining the free-roamers on the Plains. Before he left, he repeated his oath to take his revenge on Tom.

The winter snows slowed the arrival of mail from the east. Letters and newspapers from friends and loved ones were always eagerly anticipated by Tom. Sometime in March of 1875 came the one letter that deep in his heart he knew would one day arrive. His fiancé, Lulie, died of consumption on 16 February 1875 in Mont Clair, New Jersey. Her family had her remains taken by train to Cooperstown, New York, for burial in the family plot.[17] The exact status of their relationship at the time of Lulie's death is unknown. Tom's name is not mentioned in any of Lulie's death notices, nor is he men-

---

[15]Ibid., pp. 607–608.

[16]Ibid., p. 609.

[17]*The Freeman's Journal,* February 25, 1875. Cooperstown, New York.

tioned in her will. Tom, however, never changed his will leaving her half of his estate, in spite of the fact that she preceded him in death.

Tom surely realized their relationship was a dream at best. Lulie's failing health would have never tolerated life on the plains. The only way Tom could have married her would have been to resign his commission and move back east, something he would have never done without Armstrong and Libbie.

Spring came late to the Northern Plains. The fort was still snow bound on 1 May. To break the monotony, Tom hitched up his horses to his sleigh and took his companions for a ride. After the ride, he put away his sleigh and team. He went back to his room, and wrote a letter to his niece, Emma Reed, telling her of his outing the day before. It was Sunday, and the post was quiet. Tom confessed he always felt lonely on Sundays. He told Emma that he, Armstrong, and Libbie, hoped to come east next summer, to celebrate the centennial.[18]

The summer passed quickly and in late September Tom, Cooke, Armstrong, and Libbie traveled east. They stopped in Monroe, and visited with the family. After a few days, they continued on to New York where they attended the theater.[19] Tom's leave of absence, however, expired and he returned to Fort Lincoln without Armstrong and Libbie on 25 November. Upon his arrival, he sat down and wrote a letter to the War Department. He was fourteen days late in arriving at Fort Lincoln, and had to report his reasons for his delay. The War Department seemed satisfied with Tom's explanations.[20]

Less than a week later, on 2 December, Tom was promoted to captain and given command of company C. He was

---

[18]Letter, Thomas Ward Custer to Emma Reed, 2 May 1875. M.C.H.S.

[19]Custer, *Boots and Saddles,* p. 208.

[20]Letter, Thomas Ward Custer to Emma Reed, 17 December 1875. M.C.H.S.

very happy with his promotion, but he still found it difficult to resume the monotony of the post in winter after all the excitement of New York City. He decided to liven things up a bit, so he hitched up his horses to the sleigh and took his friends on a ride across the snow covered plains. But even the weather conspired against him, and a chinook wind quickly melted the snow, canceling anymore sleigh rides.[21]

Without Armstrong and Libbie, the post seemed lifeless. To occupy his time, Tom busied himself with harassing his sister, Maggie. Tom made several trips a day to Maggie's house, coming and going at will.[22] Maggie was not as playful as Libbie, and Jimmi had no sense of humor at all. Tom loved them dearly, but they were no substitute for Armstrong and Libbie.

During the evening of 17 December, Tom made his customary appearance at Maggie's. He was restless and, unfortunately, the Calhoun's did not alleviate his boredom. Tom suggested they all go over to Algernon Smith's quarters. Tom assured Maggie and Jimmi that Mrs. Smith had baked a mince pie that she would cheerfully share with them. The expectation of a mince pie enticed the Calhouns, and they agreed to go with Tom. They all trooped over to the Smith's, who greeted them enthusiastically. Tom entertained them all, but it became apparent to the Calhouns that there was no mince pie. After a while, they excused themselves and went home, irate with Tom for placing them in such an embarrassing situation.[23]

The evening, however, was not a total loss. Tom and Mrs. Smith used the time to plan a dance. The next evening the guests danced the night away in Tom's parlor. His bedroom served as the ladies' dressing room, and Boston's bedroom filled in as the men's smoking room. The Smith's parlor became the sitting room. The arrangements worked very

---

[21]Ibid.
[22]Ibid.
[23]Ibid.

well, and everyone enjoyed themselves immensely. The guests thanked Tom and Mrs. Smith for their hospitality, and hoped they would plan another such evening very soon.[24]

Christmas proved to be very lonely for Tom. A few days after the holidays he received a letter from Libbie. She counseled him to be prudent in his spending and to bypass the sutler's store, especially the bar. She admonished him to refrain from card playing, and to avoid the temptations of evil influences that surrounded him. Libbie ended her letter by saying, "Oh, Tom, if I find that the boy I loved, and prayed over, has gone downhill. . . Oh, if only you had a companionable wife."[25] Libbie remembered how Tom behaved when away from her steadying influence. Tom possessed a dependent personality, and needed a strong personality from whom to draw strength. When left on his own, or in the company of those with less moral character, he quickly assimilated the behavior patterns of his peers.

Libbie believed matrimony to be the savior of young officers.[26] Whenever a young officer transferred to the Seventh, Libbie always inquired about their marital status. When single officers arrived at the post, Libbie counseled them about the positive influences of marriage. Many times she lamented over particular officers, and how they could be so much better with the steadying influence of a wife. Tom especially worried her. She knew of his weaknesses and feared for him. She hoped he would have found the right young lady by this time and settled down. She knew Tom dallied with numerous young ladies, but Lulie Burgess seemed to be the one who captured his heart. Libbie knew Tom would never leave Armstrong, they were inseparable.

---

[24]Ibid.

[25]Merington, *The Custer Story*, p. 277.

[26]Custer, *Boots and Saddles*, p. 181.

Libbie also knew Armstrong contemplated leaving the army; he certainly wanted to. He dabbled in all sorts of schemes in order to find his niche in the business world. But was he doing that for his own good, or did he too realize that only by leaving the West would Tom be able to marry the girl of his heart? Were Armstrong's forays into the world of business strictly for himself, or was their another motive?

Armstrong also wrote Tom from New York. He expressed ignorance about any possible promotion that might, or might not, happen in the near future. He told Tom he expected a summer campaign against the recalcitrant tribes who refused to live on the reservation. Armstrong informed Tom, ". . .there will be lively work before us. I think the 7th Cavalry may have its greatest campaign ahead."[27]

The campaign Armstrong spoke of was the result of the Black Hills Expedition and the discovery of gold. Since that time, hundreds of miners had invaded the Black Hills in search of the shiny metal that the Lakota said drove white men mad. Initially, the government tried to keep the miners out of the region, but that proved both physically and politically impossible. In September of 1875, a government commission came to the Great Sioux Reservation to meet with the Indians. The government officials attempted to purchase the Black Hills, without success. The Lakoata became enraged, and the officials felt lucky to get away with their lives.[28]

By late summer, General George Crook estimated at least a thousand miners were roaming the Black Hills.[29] Earlier, Sheridan had notified General Terry, "Should companies now organizing at Sioux City and Yankton trespass on the Sioux Reservation, you are hereby directed to use the force at your command to turn the wagon trains, destroying

---

[27]Merington, *The Custer Story*, p. 277.
[28]John Gray, *Centennial Campaign* (Norman, Oklahoma, 1976) p. 21.
[29]Hutton, *Phil Sheridan*, p. 294.

the outfit and arrest the leaders, confining them at the nearest military post."[30]

This quandary proved most unfortunate to the Grant
Administration. The discovery of gold struck the government
on several levels. First of all, it made relations between the
Lakota and the federal government tenuous at best. The
Lakota viewed the government's encroachment into their
reservation as an illegal invasion, in clear violation of the
treaty as they understood it. Three times the Lakota endured
the military's incursions into their reservation. Secondly, the
government found itself stuck in the quagmire of a financial
depression. The Panic of 1873 halted the progression of the
Northern Pacific Railroad and numerous other projects across
the country. The discovery of gold could help alleviate the
financial distress of the economy. There was talk that the gold
strike might be as big as the strike in California in 1849. Without the proper scientific investigation, there was simply no
way to know for sure the extent of the wealth lying on the
ground waiting to be picked up. Lastly, because of the discovery of gold and the treaty with the Indians, the government
found itself fighting both sides, forced to enforce laws and
regulations that the government did not believe in and, in
fact, wanted to violate. Ulysses S. Grant pondered the various
aspects of his dilemma, and eventually found his solution.

In their attempt to forge an honorable peace, one with
which both sides could live, the government signed the
Treaty of 1868. The treaty promised to assist the Lakotas in
becoming civilized. The Federal Government promised to
provide the Lakotas with schools, teachers, clothing, and the
seeds and implements necessary for the Lakotas to learn
farming. The government further promised to provide food
for the tribes for four years.

---

[30]Ibid., p. 293.

That same government, though, informed the reservation Lakota it now considered those rations to be gratuities, subject to termination without violation of the treaty. The chiefs went to Washington, to discuss this new threat with the Great White Father. The Great White Father, however, informed his children his benevolence was discretionary. He further told the Lakota he was powerless to control those people who were invading the Lakota lands in search of the yellow rocks. Grant offered the Lakota twenty-five thousand dollars for the land along the Republican River, which they ultimately accepted.[31]

One of the codicils of the treaty stipulated that a three-fourths majority vote was needed to amend the document. This agreement, which the government felt was more than gracious, now turned against them. The commission made clear that there was no way the government would ever get three-fourths of the Lakotas to agree to give up the Black Hills. In fact, it would be difficult to get a simple majority. The government now regretted its legal goodwill. The treaty, however, did contain enough legal loop holes that Grant could maneuver to a possible solution.

On 3 November, Grant convened a high level meeting at the White House. In attendance at the conference was the new Secretary of the Interior Zachariah Chandler, Secretary of War William Belknap, General Phil Sheridan, and General George Crook. Before this elite group of men, Grant outlined his proposed solution, war. The only legal way the government could obtain the Black Hills was to push the Sioux into a corner from which their only escape would be armed resistance. Once the tribes went on the warpath, the government could declare the treaty null and void. The assembled dignitaries listened in approving silence.[32]

---

[31]Gray, *Centennial Campaign*, p. 18.   [32]Ibid., pp. 25–26.

Grant understood perfectly the political dilemma which faced him. For months he had been trying to devise a strategy that would resolve his predicament. He tried to sound out Secretary of the Interior Columbus Delano about his opinions on the subject, but found him to be less than agreeable about the possible solution that Grant contemplated. It was obvious to Grant that Delano had to go, and pressure was applied. Delano eventually resigned, and Grant named Zachariah Chandler as his replacement. Chandler, in his interview with Grant, made it clear he was very agreeable to Grant's objectives.[33]

Grant now got down to the details. He turned to Generals Sheridan and Crook and instructed them that the directives forbidding any trespassing into the Black Hills would no longer be enforced. They would, however, remain on the books. He further informed the two generals he expected them to begin the necessary military planning for immediate action against the non-reservation Lakota.[34] Grant turned to Secretaries Chandler and Belknap and told them that he expected them to begin compiling a list of outrages perpetrated by the winter roamers. If necessary, he added, fabricate the charges.[35]

The military solution to the dilemma was a long time in coming. General Sherman spoke of it many times and did not hesitate to voice his convictions to the Administration. "We could settle them in an hour, but Congress wants the patronage of the Indian Bureau and the Bureau wants the appropriation without any trouble of the Indians themselves." Sherman believed the nation was foolishly going into debt by both feeding and fighting the Indians.[36] It was a waste of money that Sherman well knew how to solve.

[33]Ibid.   [34]Ibid.
[35]Ibid.   [36]Althearn, *Sherman and the Settlement of the West*, p. 307.

The various members of the meeting went back to their respective posts and began their preparations. First of all, steps must be taken to make clear the government's innocent status in the matter. A few weeks later, on 3 December, Secretary Chandler wrote to Secretary Belknap:

> . . . steps to be taken to compel the hostile Sioux to go upon a reservation and cease their depredations, I have the honor to inform you that I have this day directed the Commissioners of Indian Affairs to notify said Indians that they must remove to a reservation before the 31st of January next; that if they neglect or refuse so to move, they will be reported to the War Department as hostile Indians and that a military force will be sent to compel them to obey. . .[37]

Secretary Chandler directed the Indian agents to stop selling weapons and ammunition to the Lakota. The agents notified the Lakota they would no longer be permitted to hunt in the unceded territory. It was clear the government was pushing the Lakota into a corner from which the only escape was war. The government closed the hunting lands, stopped the sale of guns and ammunition, and threatened to stop the issuance of rations. There was no other avenue left open to the Indians but become farmers very quickly, or fight.

The final legal formality was the letter Secretary Chandler wrote to the non-reservation Lakotas, informing them they were to surrender themselves to proper authorities, and take up residence on the Great Sioux Reservation by 31 January 1876. This letter was intended to mollify the public conscience and furnish the government with legal ground on which to stand. Of course no one mentioned just how the non-reservation Lakotas were going to receive the letter, let alone read it and understand it. It was also unknown how the tribes were going to move hundreds of miles in the dead of winter. There was no way the tribes could, or would submit.

---

[37]Gray, *Centennial Campaign*, p. 31.

On 1 February, Chandler formally handed the problem of the Lakota over to Secretary Belknap and the War Department. "The said Indians are hereby turned over to the War Department for such actions on the part of the army as you deem proper under the circumstances."[38] The government's position was legally in place.

Meanwhile, the Northern Plains was in the grip of a fierce winter storm that paralyzed all movement. At Fort Lincoln, Tom and the rest gathered near their fires to keep warm. As the commander of his own troop, Tom was required to make sure the men and horses received adequate food and shelter. He kept a close eye on the sentries. The wind was so strong that some men were blown off their feet while attempting to walk their duty. It was necessary to relieve the sentries every hour, to make sure no one froze to death.[39]

Armstrong and Libbie were also caught by the inclement weather. They were returning to Fort Lincoln by train and found themselves marooned by the huge drifts of snow several miles east of Bismarck. The train was snow bound for several days and food was running out. In desperation, the men climbed up a telegraph pole, cut the wire, rigged up a makeshift telegraphy office, and sent an urgent message for help. Before long, the keys tapped out a reply. It was Tom! "Shall I come out for you? You say nothing about the Old Lady, is she with you?" Armstrong and Libbie asked the telegrapher to tell Tom that Libbie was indeed present. Libbie asked the man to tell Tom not to come after them; it was too dangerous. The return message from Tom exhibited the Custer trait of bull-headedness; he was on the way! Armstrong and Libbie settled back into their seats and waited. The time crept slowly by while Libbie anxiously scanned the horizon for any sign of her beloved brother, all the while ter-

---

[38]Ibid., p. 36.
[39]Fougera, *With Custer's Cavalry*, p. 245.

rified he would freeze to death. Suddenly, she heard the unmistakable sound of Tom's war-whoop! She looked out of the window and saw Tom waving at them from his sleigh. He entered the train and they hugged and laughed. Libbie pretended to scold Tom, but her happiness was very visible.[40]

Tom and Boston cheerfully gave up their bachelor quarters and moved back in with Armstrong and Libbie.[41] Once again, Tom felt secure and his boredom vanished. The days of boisterous camaraderie returned to Fort Lincoln. Before leaving, the Custers had obtained a piano. The piano was very popular, and it was played incessantly. Tom also enjoyed the piano, although he could not play it. What he lacked in musical training, he made up for in zeal. It was debated by some whether or not Tom was playing the piano or abusing it. Tom's musical cacophony assaulted the ears of the household, who begged and pleaded with him to stop. Even Armstrong occasionally implored Tom to "stop feeling about for that tune!"[42]

When not playing the piano, Tom happily fell back into his winter routine. Every Friday night, the garrison held dances. Private theatricals were performed, either in the Custer's parlor, or in the post "theater." Tom feasted on cake, frozen custard, and ham sandwiches.[43] The routine was periodically interrupted by visitors to the post.

One day, Tom was riding the train, returning from one of his leaves. A missionary was also traveling aboard the train, and when the train stopped he got off and began preaching at one of the stations. Tom also got off to stretch his legs and walk around a bit. Tom was attracted by the missionary's religious fervor and began to listen to his message. Before long

---

[40]Custer, *Boots and Saddles*, pp. 213–215.

[41]Ibid., p. 193.

[42]Custer, *Boots and Saddles*, p. 179.

[43]Ibid., p. 182.

an indifferent crowd gathered, some paying attention, others not. The missionary attempted to lead the crowd in the singing of a hymn. The old man sang with the same ardor that he had exhibited with his preaching, the crowd, however, did not respond. Tom watched as the preacher continued singing, seemingly oblivious to the fact he was alone. The old man's zeal, and his predicament, struck a chord in Tom's soul. He enlisted the assistance of another traveler and they joined the minister on the platform, lending their voices to his in song. Tom encouraged the audience to join in, and before long the crowd was singing the praises of the Lord.[44]

The train blew its whistle and the passengers rushed to get aboard. Tom introduced himself to the minister, who gave his name as Mr. Matchett. Tom escorted the minister back to the train and engaged him in conversation all the way to Bismarck. Tom invited him to join them at the post for religious services and he happily accepted.

Mr. Matchett held religious services in the parlor of the Custer home. He thanked God for His generosity and many blessings, and for the health and protection of those who received him into their home. He told the assemblage of God's love and assured them of eternal life. He assured them they would all meet again in heaven.

---

[44]Ibid., pp. 205–207.

CHAPTER TWELVE

The March

While Tom busied himself with winter routine, the military campaign against the Lakota began to take shape. General Phil Sheridan, that diminutive bundle of Irish energy, hounded his officers to get the campaign underway as soon as possible, "Unless they are caught before early spring, they cannot be caught at all!"[1] Sheridan believed a winter campaign necessary, to bring the recalcitrant Lakota to terms. He realized once the weather broke, the elusive Lakota would be in their element and be very difficult, and expensive, to track down. Sheridan remembered very well the debacle of the campaign in Kansas in 1867-68. The army spent months in the field and millions of dollars, with no results. Sheridan solved that problem by unleashing Custer in the dead of winter in 1868.

Sheridan planned to employ the same strategy again. Converging columns of soldiers would enter the Indians' domain and defeat them. The warriors of the Northern Plains would be attacked by columns from western Montana, Wyoming, and the Dakotas. In reality, Sheridan understood that probably only one or two of the columns would encounter the Indians, with the other column performing in the task of herding the Indians into the attacking columns. It had worked brilliantly before, and Sheridan knew that it could work again.

On 10 February, Sheridan notified the commander of the department of the Dakotas, General Alfred Terry, to begin the

---

[1]Sarf, *The Little Bighorn Campaign*, p. 21.

necessary preparations for the impending campaign. Terry wrote to Sheridan of his plans, which were quite rudimentary,

> "I think my only plan will be to give Custer a secure base well up on the Yellowstone from which he can operate, at which he can find supplies, and to which he can retire anytime the Indians gather in too great numbers for the small force he will have."[2]

Terry ordered General John Gibbon to assemble all the available troops in western Montana, and position his force along the north bank of the Yellowstone, in order to obstruct the Indians' crossing the river and escaping, or enlarging the area of operations. Inclement weather, however, prohibited Gibbon from taking the field for weeks.

General George Crook and his command left Fort Fetterman in Central Wyoming in late February 1876. His command consisted of twelve companies of the Second and Third Cavalry and the Fourth Infantry, totaling over 900 men. On 17 March, Colonel Joseph Reynolds and a portion of Crook's command attacked what they believed to be a Lakota village along the Powder River, near present day Sheridan, Wyoming. The village was a Cheyenne camp, and the attack proved to be a debacle. The soldiers initially succeeded in capturing the village. The Cheyenne counterattacked and forced the soldiers to abandon the village, filled with much needed supplies, and their own dead and wounded. Before their retreat, however, the soldiers managed to destroy most of the village and its supplies, leaving the Cheyenne improvished. Crook, though, later preferred charges against Reynolds and several other officers, whom he declared were derelict in their duty.[3] Sheridan's great winter campaign ended in failure. Crook failed him, but did manage, by attacking the Cheyenne camp, to cause them to band together with their Lakota brothers, ensuring the spring campaign would find the Indians' numbers greatly increased.

---

[2]Ibid., p.23.   [3]Hedren, ed., *The Great Sioux War*, p. 9.

Gibbon's column never made it onto the Plains due to the severe weather. Terry's other column, under Custer, also failed to take the field. The Seventh was dispersed in several different posts, and the weather made it impossible to bring the regiment together. But Custer was far from idle.

Tom and Armstrong poured over the dispatches detailing the crumbling winter campaign. In March another dispatch arrived, ordering Armstrong to appear before the Senate of the United States. The Senate planned to hold hearings on possible criminal activities involving Secretary of the Interior, William Belknap. Armstrong had been very vocal in his criticisms of the Secretary and his various agents, and the Senate wanted to hear more. Belknap, hoping to avoid the proceedings, resigned on 2 March. The Senate, however, decided to continue with the hearings. Armstrong left Fort Lincoln on 21 March.

With Armstrong away, Libbie spent considerable time in the company of Margaret and Jimmi Calhoun, sleeping in their quarters most nights. Tom and Boston followed Libbie over to their sister's house, and made themselves right at home. Tom was bored, and he and Boston talked the dreary winter evenings away. Night after night, Libbie and Maggie dropped hints that they were tired and wished to retire. Tom and Boston, however, were oblivious to the subtleties of polite conversation. The two women decided on another course of action and, when bedtime arrived, they got up and began undressing. The brothers beat a hasty retreat when confronted by the appearances of women's undergarments.[4]

Maggie, unlike Libbie, was not a woman to trifle with. She grew up in a house full of brothers and she knew how to take care of them. She never hesitated to lash out and slap her tormenting brothers if she felt they needed it. If that failed, she closed her fist and beat them, husband Jimmi included.[5]

---

[4]Letter, Boston Custer to Emma Reed, 2 April 1876. M.C.H.S.
[5]Merington, *The Custer Story*, p. 301.

When she finished applying her discipline, she warned her brothers that worse would follow if they did not behave.

When not at Maggie's house, the clan assembled in Armstrong's home. Here Tom engaged in endless games of billiards. Tom and Boston played pairs with Libbie and Mrs. Smith. The two brothers argued every night over which one of them would have to take Libbie. Both decried her ability and bemoaned their hard luck of being forced to take her as a partner.[6]

Meanwhile, in Washington, Armstrong enjoyed the diversions of the city. He frequently found himself in the company of leading Democratic leaders of Congress. Armstrong's political acumen had never been very astute, and his courting of Grant's opposition party did not go unnoticed by the Republican president. Tom and Libbie poured over his letters which he filled with names and places of the high and mighty. He related the news he heard about Crook's winter debacle. Smugly he wrote, "I guess the authorities will conclude that it is not every Tom, Dick, and Harry who conduct a successful campaign against Indians."[7]

A few weeks later, Armstrong appeared before the Senate Committee. During his testimony, Armstrong spoke freely of what he knew about the business practices of the Indian Agents. Custer's testimony was a mixture of hearsay and innuendo. At one point, he implicated President Grant's brother, Orvil, as being an accomplice of Belknap.

The newspapers reported every word of the hearing, and even remarked how splendidly Armstrong was attired in his black coat and light pants, clothing he had borrowed from Tom. In his next letter, Armstrong jokingly told Libbie to inform Tom that he was going to charge him for all of the free publicity that his clothes had gotten him.[8] Armstrong's high times, though, came to an abrupt halt.

---

[6]Ibid.

[7]Letter, George A. Custer to Elizabeth B. Custer, 10 April 1876. Merington Collection.

[8]Merington, *The Custer Story*, p. 292.

Grant had heard enough. Armstrong's brazen temerity, and lack of political savvy caused the president to explode. In a fit of anger, Grant wrote an order removing Armstrong from field command in the upcoming expedition. Armstrong tried to see the president, but Grant refused to see him. With the permission of General Sherman, Armstrong left Washington to return to Fort Lincoln. Upon his arrival at St. Paul, he met with General Terry. Here Armstrong found a telegram waiting from General Sherman, lambasting him for failing to meet with the president. Armstrong explained his predicament to Terry, a lawyer in civilian life. Terry helped Armstrong draft a telegram to Grant, "I appeal to you as a soldier to spare me the humiliation of seeing my regiment march to meet the enemy and I not share its dangers."[9] Terry and Sheridan also sent telegrams to the president asking for clemency. Grant finally relented, and on 8 May sent a telegram to Terry rescinding his earlier order, much to Terry's relief.

Tom and Libbie greeted Armstrong when he returned to Fort Lincoln on 14 May, in the company of General Terry. The entire twelve companies of the Seventh had collected and were camped just south of the post. Row after row of white tents stretched across the rolling plain. Tom had moved his belongings into his tent several days earlier. Armstrong and Libbie now joined him in the tent city on the plain.[10]

The day held one last bit of official business for Tom. Fred Girard returned with several Arikara Indians as scouts for the expedition. Tom met with them, and the post surgeon examined each one. They passed their medical exams, and Girard led them into Armstrong's office. The Arikaras entered the room and looked around, many of them had never been in a house before. Tom raised his right hand and told Girard to translate for him. Girard turned to the braves and in their language told them to raise their right hands. Tom recited the

---

[9]Utley, *Cavalier In Buckskin*, pp. 161–163.
[10]Custer, *Boots and Saddles*, p. 217.

oath of allegiance, which Girard translated, and the ceremony was over.[11]

"Reveille" sounded at 4 A.M. Tom raised from his bed and wiped his eyes. He greeted Boston, his tentmate, and quickly dressed. Tom exited his tent to find the entire camp shrouded in fog. Custer's cook, Mary prepared a large breakfast for the family, which they quickly ate. At 5 A.M. another bugle call echoed across the plain and the tent city disappeared in a matter of a few minutes. Tom and Boston took down their tent and stowed it away on the company wagon.[12] Tom carried the rest of his equipment to the picket line and saddled his horse. Tom made the rounds of his troop, making sure everything was done and accounted for. At 7 A.M. the bugles blasted "Boots and Saddles" and the men mounted their horses.

General Terry decided to march the command through Fort Lincoln, perhaps to impress the families of the soldiers with the strength of the command. For the first time, all twelve companies of the Seventh were together, totaling thirty-two officers and seven hundred and eighteen enlisted men. Also accompanying the expedition was Company B, Sixth U.S. Infantry, Companies C and G of the Seventeenth U.S. Infantry, and one company from the Twentieth U.S. Infantry with three Gatling guns. Lieutenant Charles Varnum commanded the thirty-nine Indian scouts accompanying the expedition. There were one hundred and fifty wagons, a mule train, cattle herd, and the necessary teamsters and packers.[13] The command quickly fell into line, company by company. Armstrong, Libbie, and Maggie mounted their horses and placed themselves in front of the command. Tom took his place at the head of Company C, next to his second in command Lieutenant Henry Harrington. The guidons of the individual companies barely moved in the chill, damp air. Armstrong turned

[11]Graham, *The Custer Myth*, p. 28.
[12]William O. Taylor, *With Custer On The Little Bighorn*, p. 18.
[13]Sarf, *The Little Bighorn Campaign*, pp. 67–69.

in his saddle and gave the command, "Forward!" Each company commander in turn shouted the command to his men, and the Seventh began to move.

The command first moved past the camp of their Arikara scouts. The scouts' women and children stood outside their teepees, singing and chanting their goodbyes. Their warriors answered them by beating on their drums and taking up their songs. Libbie felt a chill at the lament, and wished they would quit, but the dirge continued for miles.[14]

The soldiers continued their line of march through Laundress' Row. Here the wives and children of the enlisted men gathered to say goodbye. Tears flowed down the cheeks of the women as they called out their loved ones' names. The small children, quite taken with the procession, gathered up sticks and fell into line, mimicking their fathers and friends. The column next moved into the fort proper, and the regimental band broke into "The Girl I Left Behind Me." As they entered the parade ground, Armstrong gave the command to halt. He dismissed the married men from the column to say their last goodbyes. Tom looked at his friends, and felt the heartache of such a parting. As if to boost his spirits and those around him, Tom shouted out, "A single company of that," he said pointing to the regiment, "can lick the whole Sioux nation!"[15] Those who heard the boast shouted their approval, while the wives forced a smile across their faces and nodded in agreement, silently praying to God that Tom was right.

Armstrong turned to his bugler and "Boots and Saddles" sang out again. The men kissed their loved ones once more, and returned to their horses.[16] The command reformed and continued its movement through the fort. The column turned to the left, and moved between the houses on officers' row and up the bluffs behind them. At this point an atmospheric phenomenon occurred best described by Libbie Custer.

---

[14]Custer, *Boots and Saddles*, pp. 217–218.   [15]Merington, *The Custer Story*, p. 296.
[16]Windolph, *I Fought With Custer*, p. 53.

From the hour of breaking camp, before the sun was up, a mist had enveloped everything. Soon the bright sun began to penetrate this veil and dispersed the haze, and a scene of wonder and beauty appeared . . . As the sun broke through the mist a mirage appeared which took up about half of the line of cavalry and thenceforth for a little distance it marched, equally plain to the sight on the earth and in the sky.[17]

Libbie later realized what a portent this ghostly image proved to be.

Near the infantry post, the column converged with the supply wagons. The single column continued moving west, away from Fort Lincoln. Tom and Armstrong joked with Libbie and Maggie while they rode, trying to lift their spirits. The column rode twelve miles that first day. They made camp along the Heart River, and Armstrong allowed the paymaster to pay the men their wages. The post sutler accompanied the column so he could collect the money owed to him. This angered many men, but Armstrong realized if they had been paid at the post many of them would have indulged in the many pleasures of Whiskey Point.

The next morning, Libbie and Maggie accompanied the paymaster back to Fort Lincoln. The two women tearfully kissed their loved ones goodbye and begged them to keep safe. Tom kissed and hugged Libbie and Maggie. Armstrong assisted Libbie in mounting her horse, and she thanked him through tear-filled eyes. She watched as Tom and Armstrong mounted their horses and swung into line. Libbie and Maggie turned their mounts, and moved along side the paymaster and the escort. The two groups rode away from each other in opposite directions. Libbie and Maggie stopped their horses on a small hill, and turned to watch their loved ones ride off into the distance.[18]

The troopers' mood lightened somewhat over the next few

---

[17]Custer, *Boots and Saddles*, p. 218.   [18]Ibid., p. 219.

days. Tom enjoyed the open air and the vast expanses over which they rode. Game was not as plentiful as it had been during the Black Hills Expedition, but Tom still found time to do some hunting. Tom and Armstrong, took their nephew, Arthur Reed, hunting with them. It was the first excursion for young Arthur, called Autie by the family, on the Great Plains. Armstrong took out his Remington Sporting rifle and killed a wild cat. Tom killed a black tailed deer, and sent part of it to the mess for the enlisted men.[19]

On 24 May, Tom was relieved of command of Company C and placed on Armstrong's staff as an aide. He took his tent and pitched on officers' row, near Armstrong's. He also kept a sharp eye out for odd looking stones and petrified wood. His niece, Emma, loved the pretty rocks and begged her uncle to find some for her. Tom doted on Emma, going so far as telling her that he would adopt her.[20]

General Crook's Wyoming column left Fort Fetterman on 29 May, two weeks behind schedule. His command, the largest of the three, consisted of ten companies of the Third Cavalry, five companies of the Second Cavalry, and 300 infantrymen, totaling fifty-one officers and over 1,000 soldiers. In support of Crook's column was a pack train of eighty-one men and 250 mules and 116 teamsters driving 106 wagons.[21] The Indians had kept a careful watch on Fort Fetterman ever since Crook's ill-fated winter campaign. They were watching the day his column left the fort, and every day thereafter.

The Dakota column continued their movement, unaware of Crook's delay. A few days later, Tom saw the Little Missouri River. On 30 May, Armstrong decided to take a small command of four companies and scout the river bank for any signs of hostile Indians. The command covered nearly fifty miles, but found nothing. Along the way, Autie Reed's horse stepped

---

[19]Letter, Thomas Ward Custer to Emma Reed, 26 May 1876. M.C.H.S.
[20]Ibid.   [21]Sarf, *The Little Bighorn Campaign*, pp. 74–75.

into a bed of quicksand. Terrified, Autie leaped off the horse and into the river. Tom roared with laughter and could not resist teasing his nephew. "Are you looking for specimens?" Tom shouted.[22]

The foray quickly assumed the air of a Sunday outing, and Tom enjoyed the day immensely. While they were scouting the valley, Tom, Armstrong, and Boston moved out ahead of the command. They rode through various gullies until they were several hundred yards away from the rest of the men. Tom and Armstrong urged their horses ahead of Boston's. Boston's horse began to limp, so he dismounted and began to tend to the horse's hoof, dislodging a rock. Tom and Armstrong used those few moments to move their horses out of sight and ride behind their brother. They dismounted and climbed a small grass covered hill. They moved quietly through the grass until they could see Boston, scanning the area for any sign of his missing brothers. Tom and Armstrong cocked their rifles and shot at Boston, just missing him. Boston jerked back on his horse's reins and galloped toward the distant column. To hurry him along, Armstrong fired one last shot over his head.[23] They quickly overtook their frightened brother, laughing all the way back to the column. During lunch, they recounted Boston's adventure to the other officers who enjoyed the tale immensely. They resumed their march and arrived back at camp at 6 P.M.[24]

The march continued the next morning across the windswept plains. They crossed the Little Missouri and one wagon turned over while attempting to move up the west bank. Tom observed the predicament the wagon was in, and waited for Boston to cross the river. As soon as his hapless brother's horse moved up the embankment, Tom reached out

---

[22]Letter, Thomas Ward Custer to Emma Reed, 30 May 1876. M.C.H.S.

[23]Custer, *Boots and Saddles*, pp. 269–270.

[24]Willert, *Little Bighorn Diary*, p. 69.

and pulled Boston off of his horse and sent him into the river.[25] Later, the Custer men ate lunch in Armstrong's tent. Boston took off his gloves and laid them down while he ate. Tom waited until Boston's attention was focused on his food, reached over, and stole his gloves.[26]

That afternoon, though, the good times disappeared as the weather began to change. The sky darkened, and by evening it began to rain. Everything was soaked the next morning, so the command remained in camp. The wind turned cold during the night, and the rain changed to snow. When Tom awoke on the morning of 1 June he found the camp snowbound! It snowed for the rest of the day, and the command spent another day in camp, trying to keep warm. The snow continued intermittently during the next day, and the temperature plummeted. Finally, on 3 June at 5 A.M., the column moved out. Tom bundled himself against the biting north wind, while the temperature dropped to thirty-five degrees.[27]

On 4 June the column sighted fresh signs of buffalo, and Indians.[28] That evening after the Seventh made camp, Tom took time to write to his niece, Emma, informing her of her brother's progress. Tom wrote Emma relating how Autie found five missing cattle, and praising his endurance of the hardships of the march. He went on to say that he had found some sage hen chicks and he gave them to Mary, the cook, to raise.[29] The next morning the command continued west, reaching the headwaters of Beaver Creek by afternoon.[30]

On 10 June, General Terry ordered six companies of the Seventh, under Major Marcus Reno, on a twelve day scout toward the Tongue River. Terry ordered Reno to scout the Tongue to its confluence, looking for any signs of the Indians,

---

[25]Letter, Boston Custer to Emma Reed, 31 May 1876. M.C.H.S.
[26]Ibid.   [27]Ibid., p. 85.   [28]Godfrey, *The Field Diary of . . .*, p. 4.
[29]Letter, Thomas Ward Custer to Emma Reed, 5 June 1876. M.C.H.S.
[30]Godfrey, *Diary,* p. 5.

and rendezvous with the rest of the command along the Yellowstone River. Armstrong, somewhat miffed that he was not given the command, did not try to conceal his displeasure, nor his confidence that Reno would find nothing. Reno assembled his command and left around 3:30 P.M.[31] The rest of the command moved out the next morning, headed for the mouth of the Powder River.

The command moved over difficult terrain the next few days. In spite of the physical difficulty of the land, the time passed uneventfully. The expedition still possessed the air of a delightful excursion. Tom and Armstrong caught several fish, which they fried for their breakfast on 17 June. That evening, Tom could not resist throwing dirt clods at Boston, who was trying to get some sleep. The next day, Tom saw a flock of wild geese overhead. He quickly pulled his rifle from its scabbard, aimed, and fired. Unknown to Tom, Armstrong had seen the same geese and fired, not only the same time, but at the same goose.[32]

The Wyoming column, however, did not spend the day in the same lazy fashion. Lakota and Cheyenne warriors attacked Crook's column early in the morning of 17 June along Rosebud Creek. The battle raged for hours, with the Indians and soldiers moving back and forth across the rolling hills and valleys. The Indians withdrew after six hours of vicious fighting. Crook's command suffered only nine soldiers killed and twenty-one wounded. The real loss to Crook was the ammunition expended to repel the Indians. The men were down to only fifty rounds per man, not enough to sustain them in another battle. Faced with the reality of the ammunition crisis, and the certainty of another fight if he continued northward, Crook decided to fall back upon his base of supply.[33] Sheridan's three columns were now down to two.

---

[31] Willert, *Little Bighorn Diary*, p. 118.
[32] Custer. *Boots and Saddles*, pp. 273–274.
[33] Robinson, *A Good Year To Die*, pp. 148–149.

Meanwhile, back at Fort Lincoln, the newest issue of *Galaxy Magazine* arrived containing Armstrong's article on the fight along the Yellowstone in 1873. Libbie eagerly read the article and wrote to her husband, sending her congratulations on his latest literary effort. The article contained several paragraphs of praise for Tom. On 20 June, Libbie wrote a letter to Armstrong relating her approval of his article, and his praise of Tom. "You appreciate his (Tom) valor as a soldier, you do not want to be puffing your own family. Mother will be so pleased for 'Tommie.'"[34]

On 18 June, the Seventh camped at the confluence of the Tongue and the Yellowstone. Here the men busied themselves with fishing, bathing, and taking their rest. A few days earlier, Tom and Armstrong pulled down an Indian burial scaffold. They opened the covering and gave Autie Reed the dead warrior's moccasins, and bow and arrows for souvenirs.[35]

Reno, meanwhile, stumbled upon the trail of the tribes. He discovered several campsites, and determined that the trail led west, toward the valley of the Little Big Horn. Technically, Reno had disobeyed Terry's orders in advancing so far. The astounding aspect of which, as Armstrong later pointed out, was that having gone so far out of his way to discover the hostiles, he went no further after discovering their trail. As Reno intimated to Terry in a message, "I can tell you where the Indians are not . . ."[36] On 20 June, Reno, Terry, and Gibbon rendezvoused at the confluence of the Yellowstone and the Tongue rivers on the steamer, *Far West*.

The conference got off to a bad start when Armstrong began berating Reno for his failure to ascertain the exact location of the hostiles. There was no love lost between the two men, and their tempers quickly reached the boiling point. Terry broke up the argument, and moved the meeting to the

---

[34]Merington, *The Custer Story*, p. 305.
[35]Ibid., p. 307.
[36]Sarf, *The Little Bighorn Campaign*, p. 51.

business at hand. In spite of Reno's failure to learn exactly where the Indians were, he was correct in his statement about knowing where the Indians were not. The trail Reno discovered led toward the Little Big Horn. The Indians might be there, or by now be farther west, in fact, almost anywhere within a hundred mile radius. The only thing to do was to send the cavalry in pursuit. Terry offered Armstrong all of the cavalry for this purpose, but he declined. He felt the Seventh strong enough for any hostile force it might encounter. Much has been written about what happened at this conference, especially in light of the events that followed. It is clear, from what is known, that Terry expected Custer to trail the Indians and attack them. Terry expected his command and Gibbon's to act as an anvil, while Custer became the hammer. It was hoped the two columns could act in some slight way together, but only in so far as they would both be in the same general area, chasing the same foe. There would be no way the two could remain in close contact with one another; the terrain and the hostiles precluded that. The orders Terry gave to Custer were broad and vague through necessity. In the face of such an uncertain situation, there was simply no way Terry could give concise orders. He understood that situations change and necessitate flexibility. He did not want to hamper his columns by issuing orders specifically detailing them to precise actions and locations. He could not anticipate the movement of the tribes, so he could not issue such orders. After the event, Terry tried to paint a picture of Custer in disobedience of his orders, but that was done to try and shift blame for the disaster from Terry to Custer. It must also be remembered that no one had any knowledge of Crook's defeat. Terry still believed Crook's column was in the field and heading toward them.

After the conference on the *Far West* ended, Armstrong met with his officers. He told the men to prepare for a fifteen day march, and to appropriate such supplies that would be necessary. "Well, gentlemen, you may carry what supplies you please; you will be held responsible for your companies. . . You had better carry along an extra supply of salt; we may have to live on horsemeat before we get through."[37]

Tom, meanwhile, busied himself writing what proved to be his last letter. He wrote again to his niece, Emma, and told her the regiment was collecting fifteen days rations for their chase of the Sioux. He hinted they might be gone longer, if necessary. He told his niece he expected to return to Fort Lincoln "if we make a success of this trip."[38] He closed his letter by telling Emma about his nephew, "Aut is getting along first rate, he is going with me of course."[39] Later that evening, Tom joined Armstrong and several others in a poker game that lasted until the early hours of the morning. Champagne flowed freely during the game, and no doubt several men had headaches the next morning.[40]

A heavy north wind greeted Tom on the morning of 22 June.[41] It had been a short night, and Tom was suffering from the effects of too much socializing. He got up, took down his tent, and packed his belongings. Armstrong ordered the men to pack away their sabers before leaving camp. Tom deposited his saber in a wooden crate along with the other officers and men who had brought them along. He took his letter to Grant Marsh, captain of the steamboat, *Far West*, for delivery.

Boston gave careful consideration to going along with Captain Marsh. During the last few weeks he had taken every opportunity to learn as much as he could about piloting the river boat. Armstrong ran into Marsh earlier and verified that Boston was indeed going with the boat. At the last minute, however, Boston decided to go along with his brothers.[42]

---

[37]Willert, *Little Big Horn Diary*, p. 204.
[38]Letter, Thomas Ward Custer to Emma Reed, 22 June 1876. M.C.H.S.
[39]Ibid.   [40]Ibid.
[41]Gibbon, *Adventures On The Western Frontier*, p. 131.
[42]Willert, *Little Bighorn Diary*, p. 213.

Terry ordered another review of the troops, and notified Armstrong to parade the Seventh before himself and General Gibbon. At noon, Tom moved his horse into the front of the column with the other members of the staff and prepared to move forward at his brother's command. General Gibbon later wrote,

> At noon the next day, General Terry, accompanied by myself and General Brisbin, rode to the upper end of the camp to witness the departure of Custer and his fine regiment. The bugles sounded the "Boots and Saddles," and Custer, after starting the advance, rode up and joined us. Together we sat on our horses and witnessed the approach of the command as it threaded its way through the rank sage-brush which covered the valley: First came a band of buglers sounding a march, and as they came opposite to General Terry they wheeled out of the column as at review, continuing to play as the command passed along. The regiment presented a fine appearance, and as the various companies passed us we had a good opportunity to note the number of fine horses in the ranks, many of them being part-blooded horses from Kentucky, and I was told there was not a single sore-backed horse amongst them. General Custer appeared to be in good spirits, chatted freely with us, and was evidently proud of the appearance of his command. The pack-mules, in a compact body, followed the regiment, and behind them came a rear-guard, and as that approached Custer shook hands with us and bade us good-by. As he turned to leave us I made some pleasant remark, warning him against being greedy, and with a gay wave of his hand he called back, "No. I will not," and rode off after his command.[43]

Tom rode throughout the afternoon. The pack train proved to have no end of trouble and slowed the column considerably. The troopers traveled twelve miles, and went into camp on the left bank of the Rosebud Creek. After dinner, Armstrong ordered his bugler to sound "Officers' Call." Tom and the other officers assembled in Armstrong's tent, sitting on the ground around his camp bed. Armstrong informed the officers that no more bugle calls would be sounded, unless in an emergency.

---

[43]Gibbon, *Adventures On The Western Frontier*, p. 131.

From this time forward, the men on stable guard would wake the company commanders at three A.M. and the command would move out by 5 A.M.[44] Armstrong continued by saying the company commanders were all experienced men, and until further notice, all the necessary commands would emanate from them. The only commands to come from headquarters would be to break camp and when to go into camp. Armstrong cautioned all the troop commanders about staying within supporting distance of each other, not to get ahead of the scouts, or lag too far in the rear of the column.[45]

Tom and the other officers noticed the excited state of the Indian scouts, making signs amongst themselves about too many Lakotas. Armstrong now addressed those concerns. He told the officers he estimated that the hostiles numbered somewhere between a thousand and fifteen hundred warriors, certainly no more than that. General Terry, Armstrong continued, offered him the Second Cavalry as reinforcements, but he refused. He told General Terry he was sure the Seventh could whip anything they came across, and if not, the additional troops would not make any difference. Besides, he did not want to spark any inter-regimental jealousies between the two commands. He also refused the Gatling guns, as he was afraid they would slow down his command.[46]

He then advised that the next few days would entail easy marches, probably about twenty-five to thirty miles a day. He cautioned the officers to impress upon their men the need to conserve as much of their supplies as they possibly could. It might be a long time before they saw the steamer again, and their fifteen day march might go on a lot longer and farther than planned.[47]

Armstrong quite suddenly asked the officers if they had any

[44]Taylor, *With Custer On The Little Bighorn*, p. 27.

[45]Graham, *The Custer Myth*, p. 134.

[46]Ibid., pp. 134–135.   [47]Ibid.

suggestions they wanted to make. Tom looked around the tent at the faces of his fellow officers. Many of them appeared shocked at Armstrong's remarks. The officers met Armstrong's query with silence, and the meeting broke up.[48]

Lieutenants Edward Godfrey and George Wallace quietly picked their way back to their campsite in the darkness. After a few moments, Wallace turned to Godfrey and said, "Godfrey, I believe General Custer is going to be killed!" "Why, Wallace," Godfrey replied, "What makes you think so?" "Because I have never heard Custer talk that way before."[49]

The command moved on time the next morning. The landscape was more difficult now, and Tom and the command moved back and forth across the Rosebud several times. Tom thought the valley of the Rosebud extremely beautiful. Several stands of timber and copious rosebushes lined the river's bank, giving the river its name.[50] Later in the day, Tom saw Reno's trail from a few days earlier and the command turned to follow it. He also saw signs of several Indian camps along the river. [51]

The next morning found Tom in the saddle by 5 A.M. He rode only a few miles when a large campsite came into view. Armstrong called his officers together and the rest of the command dismounted for a rest. Very obviously the Indians had recently held an important ceremony here. They discovered a fresh scalp, belonging to a white man. The scouts explained the Lakota had performed a Sun Dance ritual. The scouts also reported sighting pictographs in which the Lakota boasted of knowing about the soldiers, and not being afraid.

The Lakota occupied this campsite for several days in early June. Sitting Bull led the Sun Dance ritual, a yearly tradition among many Northern Plains Indians. During the course of the ritual, Sitting Bull fasted and prayed, while strips of his skin were ritually cut off. During the ceremony, he fell into a

[48]Ibid.   [49]Ibid.
[50]Godfrey, *Diary of The Little Bighorn*, p. 9.   [51]Ibid.

trance and experienced a vision. He saw bluecoats riding toward their encampment. The soldiers fell out of the sky and into the Sioux camp, and he heard the voice of the Great Spirit say that because the soldiers did not listen, he was giving them to the Lakota. A few days after this vision, the Indians attacked and defeated General Crook's column along the Rosebud. Sitting Bull's divine revelation, reinforced by the defeat of Crook, gave the Lakota and Cheyenne a heightened sense of spiritual power.

While Tom and Armstrong went over the camp with the scouts, another incident occurred. Armstrong's personal guidon, a red, white, and blue swallow tail with crossed sabers, fell to the ground. Lieutenant Edward Godfrey of troop K saw the flag fall and picked it up. He pushed the staff back into the ground and turned to walk away, when it fell again. This time, Godfrey embedded the staff in a sage brush and pushed it into the ground. Lieutenant George Wallace of company G also witnessed this incident, and later mentioned to Godfrey he considered this a bad omen.[52] Armstrong ordered his staff to collect the officers of the command at his tent around 9:30 P.M. A single candle illuminated the headquarters tent. Armstrong stood up and told Tom and the assembled officers the scouts had reported the trail of the hostiles led over the divide, toward the Little Big Horn. Armstrong expressed his desire to move the command in pursuit, and get as close as possible by morning. He intended to conceal the command by daylight, locate the Indian camp, and be in position to attack at dawn on the morning of the 26th.[53]

The meeting ended, but some of the officers stayed behind and began singing. Custer sat down in his camp chair and listened to Tom and other officers sing "Annie Laurie," and several other songs. Curiously, they ended with the *Doxology*,

---

[52]Godfrey, *Diary of The Little Bighorn*, pp. 8–9.
[53]Graham, *The Custer Myth*, p. 136.

"Praise God From Whom All Blessings Flow." It was a somber moment, and each man became lost in thought. At that moment, hoping to lighten the situation, someone began "For He's a Jolly Good Fellow." A few half hearted laughs were heard, and they wished each other good night.[54]

Before he retired to rest, Armstrong sent for Lieutenant Varnum and Fred Girard. He ordered the men to take the scouts and ride all night to the high place that the Crows had told him about, and see if they could spot the camp of the Sioux. The rest of the command would follow them in a few hours. Varnum sent Girard to inform the scouts, while he stayed to talk with Custer. Varnum asked for permission to take Charley Reynolds with him. He wanted a white man along so he could have someone to talk with. Custer gave his permission and the scouts left the camp.[55]

After a few more hours rest, the command moved out around midnight. The troopers found it more than a little difficult to move in the dark. The soldiers attempted to follow the trooper in front of them across the blackened landscape. Sometimes they were following the noise of those in front. There was certainly no lack of noise, as horses and men groped around in the dark. The clanking of accouterments, braying of mules, and the ever present profanity of the troopers guided many a soldier through the darkness. Armstrong halted the command at around 5:00 A.M. and the men cooked their breakfast.

Varnum and the scouts reached Crow's Nest at around three in the morning of 25 June. Varnum laid down to try and catch up on his sleep, while the scouts went to the top of the hill. After about an hour, Varnum got up and went to the summit. The excited scouts told Varnum about a big village in the distance. Varnum looked down into the valley before him. In

[54]Taylor, *With Custer On The Little Bighorn*, pp. 30–31.
[55]Carroll, ed., *Custer's Chief of Scouts*, pp. 86–87.

the dim morning light he could see two teepees, one of which was fallen down. The scouts told him to look farther, beyond the ridge line to the west. They told Varnum they could see an immense pony herd on the far bluffs. Varnum strained his eyes, but could not see anything. The scouts became exasperated with him and told him to look for what looked like worms in the grass, but Varnum could still not see what the Indians said they saw. He did believe, however, that they could see something.[56] The scouts also pointed out the smoke in their rear, indicating the presence of the command. Varnum sent several scouts back to inform General Custer, and to bring him to the Crow's Nest.

The scouts arrived at camp a little after 7:00 A.M. and notified Custer of what they had seen. Armstrong, Tom, Bloody Knife, and Red Star sat around the campfire in silence. Armstrong looked over at Tom, then motioned to Bloody Knife. "Your brother, there," Custer said, pointing at Tom, "is frightened, his heart flutters with fear, his eyes are rolling with fright at the news of the Sioux. When we have beaten the Sioux he will then be a man."[57] Perhaps they all laughed nervously; perhaps the comment passed in silence. In any event, Custer gave the necessary orders for the command to move out, and rendezvous with the scouts at Crow's Nest. He was also informed that a mule had strayed from the command. Custer ordered a detail to back track and find the missing animal.

---

[56] Ibid., p. 87.
[57] Libby, *Arikara Narrative* (Glorieta, New Mexico, 1976) p. 90.

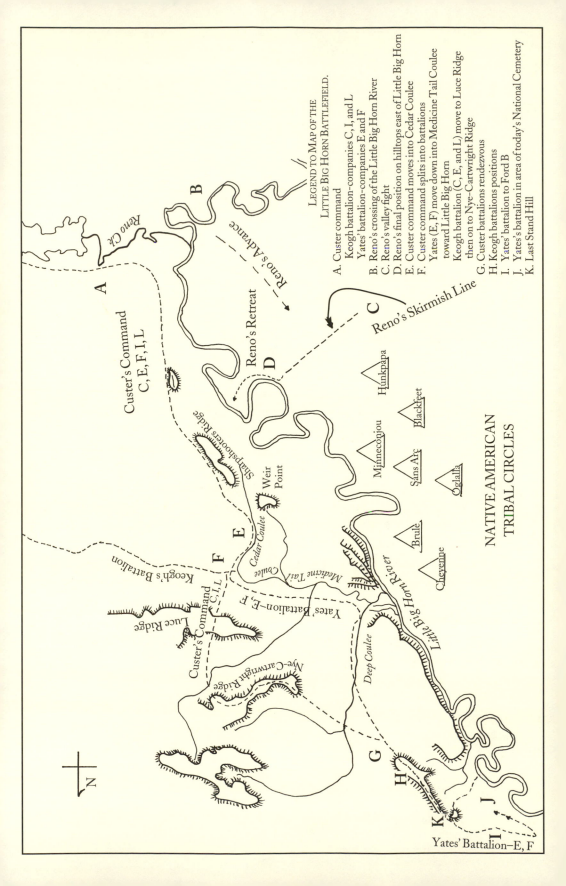

N

A

Reno Cr.

B

Reno's Advance

Reno's Retreat

Custer's Command
C, E, F, I, L

Sharpshooters Ridge

Weir Point

C

Reno's Skirmish Line

D

Hunkpapa

Blackfeet

Minneconjou

Sans Arc

Oglalla

Cedar Coulee

Brule

Medicine Tail Coulee

Cheyenne

NATIVE AMERICAN
TRIBAL CIRCLES

E

F

Keogh's Battalion

Luce Ridge

Custer's Command
C, I, L

Yates' Battalion—E, F

Nye-Cartwright Ridge

Little Big Horn River

Deep Coulee

G

H

K

J

I

Yates' Battalion—E, F

LEGEND TO MAP OF THE
LITTLE BIG HORN BATTLEFIELD.

A. Custer command
   Keogh battalion-companies C, I, and L
   Yates' battalion-companies E and F
B. Reno's crossing of the Little Big Horn River
C. Reno's valley fight
D. Reno's final position on hilltops east of Little Big Horn
E. Custer command moves into Cedar Coulee
F. Custer command splits into battalions
   Yates (E, F) move down into Medicine Tail Coulee
   toward Little Big Horn
   Keogh battalion (C, E, and L) move to Luce Ridge
   then on to Nye-Cartwright Ridge
G. Custer battalions rendezvous
H. Keogh battalions positions
I. Yates' battalion to Ford B
J. Yates's battalion in area of today's National Cemetery
K. Last Stand Hill

CHAPTER THIRTEEN

Soldier of the Lord

Armstrong halted the command in a depression near the base of the Crow's Nest. Red Star identified the lookout point to Tom and Armstrong and they rode ahead of the column toward the hill. From his vantage point on the hilltop, Varnum had seen the approach of the command, and descended the hill to meet his commander. He intercepted Tom and Armstrong a few hundred yards from the hill and made his report. Varnum told Armstrong the scouts reported a large village in the valley of the Little Big Horn, but confessed that he could see nothing. Armstrong listened intently while Varnum finished his report, and said he would have a look for himself. He turned to Tom and ordered him to return to the column to await further orders.[1]

As they ascended the hill, Varnum informed Armstrong that the region was alive with numerous small bands of hostiles. One band came near enough to the Crow's Nest to entice Varnum and the scouts to attempt an ambush, but without success. Varnum also stated he observed another band of hostiles on the far bluffs to the north watching the approach of Custer's column.[2] Armstrong said nothing, but continued up the hill.

Tom galloped back to Cooke and explained that Armstrong had ridden to the top with Varnum. A few other offi-

---

[1]Carroll, *Custer's Chief Of Scouts*, p. 88.
[2]Ibid., pp. 87–89.

cers rode up, and someone suggested they retire and have a smoke. Tom, Cooke, Jimmi Calhoun, Lieutenant Myles Moylan, Lieutenant Godfrey, and Lieutenant Winfield Edgerly found a ravine that suited their needs. The men made their cigarettes, and began to review the day's proceedings. At one point, Cooke turned to Lieutenant Edgerly who jokingly remarked that he would have the opportunity to "bathe my maiden saber that day."[3]

From his position on the west face of the Crow's Nest, Armstrong scanned the horizon. Varnum pointed west to the far ridge line and directed his commander's vision into the valley beyond. Armstrong focused his eyes on the valley some fifteen miles distant, but a haze hung over the horizon which obscured the valley of the Little Big Horn. The half-breed scout, Mitch Bouyer, assured Armstrong the village was there. "I have got mighty good eyes and I can see no Indians," Armstrong exclaimed.[4] Bouyer translated Armstrong's statement to the Indian scouts who expressed indignant disbelief. Bouyer turned back to Armstrong and stated, "If you can't find more Indians in that valley than you ever saw together before, you may hang me!"[5] Armstrong was taken aback at Bouyer's declaration. "It would do a damn sight of good to hang you, wouldn't it?" Now it was Varnum's turn to be startled; the general rarely used profanity.[6]

In spite of the morning's information before him, Armstrong declared that in his judgment the situation had not changed. He reaffirmed his belief that the hostiles had not discovered the troops, and his strategy of waiting out the day and attacking the next morning was still operational. The scouts and Bouyer began to argue with him, pointing out all the different bands of Indians in the immediate vicinity that had unquestionably seen the column. The argument contin-

[3]Clark, ed., *Scalp Dance*, p. 24.   [4]Ibid.
[5]Ibid.   [6]Ibid.

ued as Custer made his way from the lookout point, back to the top of the hill. Suddenly he stopped. Something in the distance caught his eye. Varnum turned to look and saw the column moving in the direction of the Crow's Nest. Varnum heard Custer exclaim to himself, "Who in the mischief . . ."[7]

Armstrong and Varnum mounted their horses and hurried down the side of the hill toward the approaching column. Tom galloped up to meet them. "Tom," Armstrong shouted, "who in the devil moved those troops forward?" Tom was silent. Armstrong did not pursue his question. His mind was racing; reevaluating the events of the morning. No matter how much he disliked what he had seen and heard, he could no longer dismiss the facts in front of him. The column had been detected by the hostiles who might even now be spreading the alarm in the Indian camp. He turned to Tom, lowered his voice, and said, "My orders and intentions were to remain in camp all day and make a night attack on the Indians, but they have discovered us and are on the run."[8] The next bit of information galvanized his intentions.

Tom reminded Armstrong of the missing pack mule, and how men had been sent back upon the trail to retrieve the animal. Tom informed Armstrong that the soldiers had found the missing mule surrounded by Indians. They exchanged a few shots with the Indians, and recovered the mule with its box of hard tack.[9] Tom's news corroborated the necessity for immediate action, and Armstrong shouted for the trumpeter to sound "Officers' Call." The officers, surprised by the sound of the bugle, assembled quickly. Lieutenant Godfrey recalled the meeting:

> He recounted . . . the scouts had seen several Indians moving along the ridge overlooking the valley through which we had marched, as

---

[7]Nichols, ed., *The Reno Court of Inquiry*, p. 134.
[8]Graham, *The Custer Myth*, p. 251.
[9]Godfrey, *Diary of the Little Big Horn*, p. 10.

if observing our movements; he thought the Indians must have seen the dust made by the command. At all events our presence had been discovered and further concealment was unnecessary; that he had not intended to make the attack until the next morning, the 26th, but our discovery made it imperative to act at once, as delay would allow the village to scatter and escape. Troop commanders were ordered to make a detail of one noncommissioned officer and six men to accompany the pack; to inspect their troops and report as soon as they were ready to march; that the troops would take their places in the column of march in the order in which reports of readiness were received, and the last one to report would escort the pack-train.[10]

The column assembled and moved westward, toward the divide between the Rosebud and the Little Big Horn valley. Shortly past noon, after crossing the divide, Armstrong halted and divided the command into battalions. Major Marcus Reno received command of companies A, G, M, all of the Arikara scouts, and several civilian scouts, totaling nearly 150 men. Captain Frederick Benteen's battalion consisted of companies D, H, and his own company K, totaling approximately 115 men. Captain Thomas McDougall and company B, reinforced by men from each of the other companies, commanded the pack train, approximately 145 men.[11] Custer retained companies C, E, F, I, and L, totaling approximately 210 men under his immediate command. Before they proceeded though, he further divided the five companies into two battalions. Captain Yates commanded the first battalion of companies E and F while Captain Keogh, the senior captain, commanded companies C, I, and L.

Custer ordered Captain Benteen and his command to move to the left, cross the bluffs into the next valley, and attack any hostiles he encountered. Benteen ordered his column left oblique and moved out, unsure exactly of Custer's

[10]Ibid., p. 10.
[11]Sarf, *The Little Bighorn Campaign*, p. 188.

orders. He later received two messages from Custer, instructing him to continue his scout across the next ridge, and the next, until he came to the valley of the Little Big Horn. Benteen considered this to be a foolhardy assignment and a great waste of time. The hills were very steep and it took an interminable amount of time to move from ridge to ridge. It became obvious to Benteen that he was on a wild goose chase; there were no Indians in front of him. At approximately 1330 hours he decided to abandon his fruitless venture and regain the trail of the main body of the command.[12]

While Benteen was busy crossing the ridges to the south, Custer and Reno continued west, toward the valley of the Little Big Horn. They followed Ash Creek, later renamed Reno Creek, which the scouts said emptied into the Little Big Horn. Reno's men crossed to the south bank, while Custer's command paralleled them on the north bank. They traveled for several miles when they came to the location of the lone teepee which had been sighted earlier in the morning by Varnum and the scouts from the Crow's Nest. It was now approximately 1400 hours.

Fred Girard, one of the civilian scouts, moved ahead of the column. He passed the lone teepee and ascended a small knoll. The ground was much torn up with the signs of the camp moving westward, toward the Little Big Horn. He saw another small hillock a few dozen yards away and decided to ride there. Once atop the knoll he scanned the area toward the Little Big Horn and saw a group of Indians racing toward the river. He turned in his saddle and shouted back at Custer, "Here are your Indians, running like devils!"[13]

Custer halted his command at the site of the lone teepee. His mind raced for a few moments when he turned to Cooke and snapped out his orders in his customary excited stammer.

---

[12]Graham, *The Custer Myth*, pp. 179–180.
[13]Nichols, *The Reno Court of Inquiry*, p. 84.

After a few sentences to Cooke, Custer turned in his saddle, removed his hat, and gestured to Reno to cross the creek. Reno gave the order, and his men crossed the creek. Lieutenant Cooke rode up to Reno and told him to move his command to the front. As Reno listened to his instructions, he noticed the Indian scouts stripping off their clothing in preparation for battle. Reno's command continued in the advance for a few hundred yards when Lieutenant Cooke again galloped up to Reno. "General Custer directs you to take as rapid a gait as you think prudent and charge the village afterwards, and you will be supported by the whole outfit," said Cooke.[14] Reno directed the scouts in front to continue the advance while the rest of the command followed. Reno and Custer's command continued their parallel course for several hundred more yards. The distance between the two commands increased, though, as Reno's men galloped toward the Little Big Horn. As an afterthought, Custer ordered Lieutenant Cooke and Captain Keogh to follow Reno's command to the river and observe the crossing.

Reno's men arrived at the Little Big Horn and began to ford the river at approximately 1500 hours. The horses were extremely thirsty and took this opportunity to drink which caused some delay in crossing the river. It was with some difficulty that the troopers urged their horses out of the stream and up the far embankment. Once on top of the riverbank, the soldiers moved onto the valley floor. Major Reno halted the battalion and gave orders for the soldiers to tighten their saddle girths and reform their companies.[15] This accomplished, the command moved down the valley and swung into line of battle with two companies in front and one in the rear.

---

[14]Ibid., pp. 560–561.
[15]Graham, *The Custer Myth*, p. 241.

Girard, Varnum, and several other scouts, had already crossed the river and were several hundred yards ahead of the command. Girard heard the Arikara scouts shouting that the Lakota were coming to meet them. Varnum later stated that he saw:

> . . . quite a large body of the Indians some little distance off and they were running away from us and then running back, running back and forth across the prairie and toward us and in every direction, apparently trying to kick up all the dust they could . . .[16]

Girard decided to return to the command and inform them of what he had seen. He rode back and reported first to Major Reno, and then, seeing Lieutenant Cooke and Captain Keogh on a small hillock on the east bank of the Little Big Horn, Girard crossed the river and reported his observations to them. Cooke listened to Girard's report of the Indian's reactions and said, "All right, I'll go back and report." Girard turned his horse around, recrossed the river, and returned to the fight.[17]

Armstrong, meanwhile, ordered his command to halt along Reno Creek and allow the animals to drink. While the horses quenched their thirst, Daniel Kanipe of C troop saw 60-70 warriors on the bluffs above the column to the north, and reported his sighting to Lieutenant Harrington. Lieutenant Harrington relayed the information to Tom and Armstrong. Custer directed the command to move out and up the bluffs.[18]

The troopers rode up the bluffs, using a ridge back for their trail. They came out on top of the bluffs several hundred yards between what would later become Reno's defensive position on the hill top and an Indian position called Sharpshooter Ridge. Armstrong halted the command again

---

[16]Nichols, *The Reno Court of Inquiry*, p. 141.
[17]Ibid., p. 87.
[18]Hammer, ed., *Custer in '76*, pp. 92–93.

for approximately ten minutes. From his vantage point Tom saw Reno's command moving down the valley toward the Indian camp. Armstrong gazed intently at the hundreds of teepees dotting the valley floor. Someone offered that the warriors might be out on a buffalo hunt; since they had seen tracks back on the trail that might have been made by hunting parties. Armstrong looked at his officers and men and said, "We will go down and make a crossing and capture the village." Several nearby troopers heard his remark and enthusiastically broke into a cheer. Custer barked out the commands, "Attention! Fours right! Column left!" The troopers accomplished the commands and the battalion continued its movement northward.[19]

Reno's battalion continued moving down the valley to a point about a hundred yards from the village. Reno halted the command and ordered the men to dismount and advance in skirmish formation, with every fourth man holding the horses of his companions. The horse holders led the animals into some woods along the Little Big Horn on the right for shelter. The skirmish line moved forward approximately a hundred yards when both sides began firing. The Indians had been moving back toward their village as Reno's men approached, but when the soldiers stopped and dismounted, the Indians advanced. The left flank of the soldiers' line was in the air, and the warriors began to move around the line. After a few minutes of skirmishing, the Arikara scouts on the left flank gave way under the pressure of the Lakota warriors and abandoned the fight, further jeopardizing the soldier's position.[20]

Custer's command, meanwhile, continued northward, toward a large hill that dominated the landscape from which the entire valley could be seen. From their vantage point, several troopers saw Reno's command in the valley. The entire

---

[19]Ibid., p. 100.
[20]Godfrey, *Custer's Last Battle*, pp. 23–24.

command heard the growing crescendo of gunfire, indicating that Reno was in contact with the enemy. Several men began to cheer and wave their arms in support of Reno's men, and in anticipation of their own imminent participation in the battle. This noise excited the horses, and several troopers lost control of their mounts and galloped out of their ranks ahead of Tom and Armstrong in front of the command. Custer shouted to the men, "Hold your horses boys, there are Indians enough down there for all of us!"[21]

Tom and Armstrong had not yet seen the entire village, but had observed enough to know that it was larger than anything they had anticipated. Armstrong turned to Tom and instructed him to send a messenger back to McDougall and the pack train. Tom galloped over to Daniel Kanipe and ordered him to go back on their trail and find Lieutenant McDougall and tell him, "Hurry up—cut loose any loose packs, unless ammunition packs." As Kanipe turned his horse around, Tom shouted after him, "And if you see Benteen tell him to come on quick—a big Indian camp!"[22]

Reno's men continued to move forward. The Indians, meanwhile, rode back and forth kicking up a tremendous dust cloud which all but obscured the village. Other warriors rained down bullets and arrows upon the skirmish line from every direction. The soldiers and scouts returned the fire, loosing a fusillade of bullets upon the southern part of the village, the Hunkpapa camp, killing several women and children.[23] At that moment, the ground seemed to open up before the soldiers' eyes as scores of Indians scrambled out of a ravine just in front of the skirmish line.[24] Several hundred warriors now descended upon Reno's command. The left

---

[21]Hammer, *Custer in '76,* p. 94.
[22]Ibid., p. 93.
[23]Hardorff, *Hokahey! A Good Day to Die!,* pp. 32–35.
[24]Nichols, *The Reno Court of Inquiry,* pp. 561–562.

flank, in peril since the scouts ran away, began to collapse under the intense firepower of the Indians. The warriors moved around the end of the skirmish line and fired into the soldiers from the rear. The right of Reno's line had anchored itself on the woods, near the river and was initially secure. The Indians, however, moved from their camp into the woods, using the trees as cover. Reno realized his command was in imminent danger of being surrounded and destroyed in their present position.

Reno ordered company G to withdraw from the skirmish line and move into the woods and expel the infiltrating Indians. This, however, left a gap in the skirmish line, and Lieutenant Moylan quickly extended his command to cover the empty space.[25] Moylan sent word to Reno that the entire line was in dire peril. Reno came to Moylan's position, evaluated the situation, and gave orders for companies A and M to withdraw from the skirmish line into the safety of the woods.[26] The line quickly fell back into the timber, and the battle continued.

Tom heard the escalating gunfire from the valley floor indicating that Reno was heavily engaged with the hostiles. Two messengers from Reno had overtaken the command and reported that Reno was meeting stiff resistance. It was clear to Tom that something must be done to relieve the pressure upon Reno's command, but nothing could be accomplished from the command's present position upon the bluffs. The column continued moving northward, toward the coulee the scouts said led directly to the Little Big Horn.

The command reached the bottom of a prominent high point along the bluffs directly in front of Cedar Coulee. Custer and his orderly, trumpeter John Martin, ascended the

[25]Ibid., p. 216.
[26]Ibid., pp. 216–217.

hill, later named Weir Point. From his vantage atop the hill, Custer could finally see the valley in its entirety. The Indian village stretched for several miles along the Little Big Horn, ending near the ford the scouts had told him about at the head of Medicine Tail Coulee. Looking to his left, down the valley, Custer observed a huge dust cloud just south of the village. Gunfire from Reno's attack had become one continuous roar. Custer, however, could not discern Reno's command through the swirling clouds on the valley floor. He took out his field glasses and moved his gaze back and forth, vainly trying to determine Reno's position. He continued looking at the village for a few moments when he lowered the glasses and said, "We have got them this time!"[27]

Custer and Martin rode back down the hill to the waiting command. He rode up to Tom, apprised him of the situation, and ordered the command to move into Cedar Coulee. The command rode a few dozen yards into the coulee when Custer stopped the column. Custer turned to Martin and said, "Orderly, I want you to take a message to Colonel Benteen. Ride as fast as you can and tell him to hurry. Tell him it's a big village, and I want him to be quick and to bring the ammunition packs." Martin snapped to attention and said, "Yes Sir!" Martin turned his horse to leave, when Cooke stopped him. "Wait, orderly, I'll give you a message." John Martin, an immigrant whose real name was Giovanni Martini, had been in the United States for only three years and Cooke did not trust his mastery of the language. Cooke took out his notebook and hurriedly wrote Custer's order. He tore the page from the book, handed it to Martin, and reiterated Custer's order, "Now, orderly, ride as fast as you can to Colonel Benteen. Take the same trail we came down. If you have time, and there is no danger, come back, but otherwise stay with your company."[28]

---

[27]Brininstool, *Troopers with Custer*, p. 189.
[28]Ibid.

Martin acknowledged the order and galloped up the coulee, back onto the ridge.

Martin rode hard across the ridge top, listening to the gunfire from the valley. He came to a spot on the ridge where he could look down into the valley and saw Reno's men falling back into the timber.[29] At that moment, the sound of gunfire erupted from the rear. Martin turned in the saddle and saw Indians firing at him from the bluffs behind him. He kicked his horse and took off at a dead run over the trail, staying low on the saddle to avoid being hit. He had ridden several hundred yards when a solitary rider appeared on the trail ahead. Martin pulled back on the reins; afraid it might be an Indian approaching. At that moment the figure waved to him; it was Boston Custer. Boston rode up to Martin and asked the location of the General and if the command had encountered any hostiles. Martin motioned to the rear and said the command was back down the trail, heading toward the river, and it had not yet gone into battle. Boston expressed his desire to catch up with his brothers. Martin told him to be careful. The countryside was full of Indians. Boston replied, "Well, I am going to join the command anyhow." As he spoke, Boston noticed Martin's horse had been shot, and he brought that fact to the courier's attention and galloped off.[30]

Meanwhile, the battle in the timber continued to escalate in noise and confusion. The Indians, using the river bank for cover, began to infiltrate the woods. The warriors in the open grew in ever increasing numbers, and began to encircle the woods. The troopers' position grew more precarious as the moments passed. They had already expended a good deal of their ammunition, and to stay here under fire was to court

---

[29]Ibid., p. 190.   [30]Hammer, *Custer in '76*, p. 104.

disaster. Reno, overcome by the ferocity of the Indians' resistance, remembered that Custer told him he would be supported by the entire command. But the entire command was nowhere to be seen! Reno turned to ask Bloody Knife a question, but at that moment a bullet slammed into the rear of Bloody Knife's skull and exploded out his forehead, sending a shower of blood and brains into Major Reno's face. Stunned by the specter of death so close to him, Reno shouted, "Mount!" The men who were nearby and heard him above the din of the battle, mounted. Reno sat upon his horse a few moments and shouted, "Dismount!" The men complied with the order, but as soon as their feet hit the ground, Reno again shouted, "Mount!" At that moment, Reno struck his horse with his spurs and raced out of the woods, followed by those men close enough to hear him, or those lucky enough to see him.[31] All cohesion within the battalion now dissolved.

Reno led the men in a hell-bent race to the river and to the bluffs on the other side. The Indians could not believe their eyes! They quickly attacked the retreating troopers and shot man after man. To the warriors, the soldier retreat bore all of the characteristics of a buffalo hunt. They rode alongside the panic-stricken soldiers and shot them at point blank range. Many soldiers continued to blaze away in the timber; unaware that they had been abandoned. Once they realized the precariousness of their situation they also took advantage of the confusion to find hiding places, and prayed to catch up with the command later.

Reno and the remnant of his command splashed across the Little Big Horn and lunged up the river bank. There was no place to go but up, and the soldiers raced for the comparative safety of the bluffs overlooking the river. Upon gaining the heights, Reno ordered his men to prepare a defensive

---

[31]Willert, *Little Big Horn Diary*, pp. 302.

perimeter along the ridgetops to repel the Indians. Strangely, though, when the Indians were most assured of victory, their presence dissipated. Word quickly spread among them, "More soldiers to the north!" Many warriors had seen Custer's battalion as they rode above the battle in the valley. The Lakota warrior, Runs The Enemy, followed Reno's men to the top of the bluffs. As Runs The Enemy was working his way up, he noticed two Lakotas waving their blankets. He rode over to them and they anxiously pointed to the north. Runs the Enemy looked to the north and saw the distant ridges covered with white soldiers. He thought there were "thousands" of them.[32]

Back in the valley, the Lakota warrior, Crazy Horse, arrived at the scene of the battle. He heard the opening shots of the attack, but it had taken him time to prepare his medicine for battle. He arrived shortly after the retreat of Reno's men to the hilltop. Short Bull, another Lakota, saw Crazy Horse and called out to him, "Too late! You've missed the battle!" Crazy Horse nodded his head and laughed, "Sorry to miss this fight! But there's a good fight coming over the hill!" Short Bull turned to look in the direction that Crazy Horse pointed, and saw soldiers coming over the ridges. He later said, "I thought there was a million of them."[33]

Tom and the main column moved down Cedar Coulee and entered the head of Medicine Tail Coulee. The cavalrymen rode up the opposite embankment, out of the coulee and onto the ground above the ravine. Tom looked down the hill, toward the head of the coulee and the Little Big Horn beyond. He saw Indians across the river, racing for the ford, at the base of the coulee. Armstrong ordered Captain Yates to take his battalion, move down the ridge, and make a demonstration against those Indians guarding the ford. This

---

[32]Michno, *Lakota Noon,* p. 96.
[33]Ibid., pp. 97–98.

action might pull enough Indians away from Reno and give him a bit of a respite. Unbeknownst to Custer, Reno's retreat from the valley liberated hundreds of warriors who were even now racing north, through the village, and over the ridges in the rear of the column.

Yates's battalion, companies E and F, moved down the ridge toward the Little Big Horn. Custer led the rest of the command onto a ridge top overlooking both Medicine Tail Coulee and Cedar Coulee. Boston Custer had arrived and Armstrong questioned him about the location of Captain Benteen's battalion. Boston reported he had seen Benteen watering his horses not twenty minutes earlier. Armstrong quizzed his brother about the numbers of Indians in their rear, and Boston assured him Benteen would have no difficulty moving forward. Satisfied with Boston's answers, Armstrong was certain that Benteen would arrive within the half hour and the main attack could begin. Armstrong positioned his men along the ridge so Benteen could see them.

At that moment, firing erupted from both the rear and from the head of Medicine Tail Coulee. Yates's battalion had moved a few hundred yards down the hill when dozens of Indians sprang up and fired at the soldiers. Yates halted his men and ordered a portion of the command to advance as skirmishers and dislodge the hidden warriors.[34] At that same moment, Cheyenne warriors under Wolf Tooth attacked Captain Keogh's battalion and the headquarter's staff from the ridges to the east.[35] Tom heard the bullets whizzing over his head and turned in his saddle to face the new threat. Armstrong shouted for the men to prepare for volley firing. Tom and the others leveled their rifles at the distant ridge, and aimed at the puffs of smoke that gave away the Indians' positions. Custer shouted out the command, "Fire!" The line

---

[34]Graham, *Custer myth*, p. 4.
[35]Stands In Timber, *Cheyenne Memories*, p. 198.

exploded in unison, and the small band of warriors slipped down behind the ridge line and fell back. Custer ordered the men to redirect their fire down the coulee and the line exploded again, and the sound reverberated across the hills.

During this time, Benteen's command saw Reno's men fighting on the bluffs, and moved to their assistance. Benteen arrived at Reno's defensive position at approximately 1630 hours. Reno's men were overjoyed to see their companions. Reno reported that his command had attacked the village, but due to overwhelmingly superior numbers, had been compelled to retreat to this position. Reno went on to say that perhaps as much as a third of his command were casualties. Lieutenant Luther Hare ran over to his friend, Lieutenant Godfrey, and clutched his hand tightly, "I am damned glad to see you, we've had a big fight in the bottom and got whipped like hell!"[36] A few minutes later, Godfrey distinctly heard volley firing coming from the north. Several other men also heard the firing and remarked that Custer was "really giving it to them." The firing escalated, and the men began to converse amongst themselves, theorizing about what it meant and what they should be doing.[37] Speculation or not, the combined commands busied themselves by digging in during the lull in fighting.

Tom and the troopers discharged another barrage at the Indians in the bottom. After firing, Armstrong ordered his battalion to move onto the next ridge line, closer to Yates's men, lower down on the ridge top. Yates ordered his men to move out, back up the hill to affect a rendezvous with the rest of the command. As soon as Yates's men began to move up hill, the Indians swarmed across the Little Big Horn, shooting into the rear of Yates's command, wounding several men,

---

[36]Nichols, *The Reno Court of Inquiry*, p. 482.
[37]Graham, *Custer's Last Battle 1876*, p. 26.

and killing two men, whose bodies were found in the coulee two days later.

Tom pivoted and saw a great dust cloud heading toward them from the ridge line to the south. In a few moments it became apparent that it was not Benteen, but hundreds of warriors. Tom rode over to Mitch Bouyer and ordered him to tell the scouts to take off and save themselves if possible. Bouyer looked at the young Crow scout, Curly, and told him the soldier chief said to ride away and save himself.[38]

The battalions reunited and continued northward under sporadic gunfire from the Indians who followed, albeit at a respectful distance. The command halted again atop a long narrow ridge. Tom looked down in the valley and saw hundreds of Indians; women, children, and the elderly, running across the flatland, heading for the hills opposite. Armstrong ordered Captain Keogh to hold this end of the ridge top, and await Captain Benteen's arrival. Armstrong directed Captain Yates's battalion to follow him. Tom continued riding along the ridge line, and down the slope of the hill onto an area of flatland, now known as Cemetery Ridge. Captain Keogh's battalion was approximately a mile to the south along the opposite end of the ridge line. Bouyer told Armstrong about another place to ford the river, at the base of this hill. A wide flat plain lay across the river, perfect for cavalry operations. Once on the flatland, the Seventh could make its power decisively felt. Armstrong halted the battalion on the flatland below the ridge line.[39]

Shots again rang out from behind the command. Wolf Tooth's band moved up the eastern side of the ridge, and began shooting down into Yates's battalion. The command also came under fire from the river bank. Warriors were crossing the river and moving into the brush and undergrowth

---

[38]Hammer, *Custer in '76,* p. 159.
[39]Stands in Timber, *Cheyenne Memories,* p. 199.

along the river bank, firing at the soldiers.[40] Custer dispatched
a small detachment to the upper ford, while he held the rest of
Yates's battalion on the flat ridge. A few of the soldiers, meanwhile, began to return fire at Wolf Tooth's band. Armstrong
continued to cast anxious glances toward Calhoun's command, hoping to see some sign of Benteen's arrival.

At the southern end of the ridge, now known as Calhoun
Hill, the Indian presence increased with every minute.
Keogh ordered Lieutenant Calhoun to dismount his company and move forward as skirmishers. Calhoun complied
with the directive and the men advanced in order taking up
positions along and slightly parallel to the ridge top. They
engaged the Indians moving up Medicine Tail Coulee and
occupying those ridges that the command had vacated only a
short time earlier. The Indians' rifles could not match the
range of the soldiers' single shot Springfield and so the warriors kept their distance and continued to snake their way
closer and closer, using the natural contours of the land.

Keogh ordered his own company I and Harrington's
Company C into position approximately fifty yards in the
rear of Calhoun's skirmish lines. Calhoun's men kept up a
slow, deliberate concentration of fire at the Indians. Scores of
warriors, though, were arriving every second on the ridges
and in the ravines around Keogh's battalion.[41] The Indian's
fire upon Calhoun's men from a ravine behind their position
began to increase. Keogh ordered Lieutenant Harrington to
dismount a portion of Company C, move down the ridge,
and engage the hostiles. Gunfire from the eastern slopes of
the ridge also increased. Keogh moved his command over the
ridge top in skirmish order and took up positions along the
eastern side of the slopes.

---

[40]Ibid.
[41]Fox, *Archeology, History, and Custer's Last Battle*, p. 147.

C Company sergeant's Jeremiah Finley and George Finckel took their positions behind the troopers and directed their fire at the warriors inching up the ravine. The warriors concealed themselves very well, exposing themselves only long enough to fire. This sporadic shooting continued for a few minutes without the soldiers suffering any casualties, but all the while more and more warriors crawled up the ravines to surround the soldiers. Lame White Man, a Cheyenne chief, rode up into the ravine and shouted to the warriors, "Come! We can kill them all!"[42] All at once, they stood and fired into the soldiers. The combined firepower of the warriors struck the soldiers from three sides, and more than a dozen men fell in the rain of bullets. The firing was so intense that the cohesive power of the company collapsed. Other warriors began waving blankets and shooting at the soldiers detailed to hold the horses. With many of the horse holders shot, the terrified horses ran from the ridge in all directions. Those soldiers still holding their horses found they could no longer manage the frightened steeds, and let them go. Soldiers abandoned their positions on the lower part of the ridge, and raced for the protection of Calhoun's company farther up on the ridge.[43] Several wounded men screamed for help from their retreating comrades, to no avail. Some men began to cry and held out their hands to the onrushing Indians while begging for mercy in a tongue the warriors could not understand. Other men, eyes filled with fear, raised their pistols to their heads and blew their brains out.[44] Those wounded men who could walk struggled to keep up with their retreating comrades but several were overtaken and killed. The warriors reached the dead and dying men, picked up their weapons, and turned them on the retreating soldiers.

---

[42]Marquis, *Wooden Leg*, p. 231.

[43]Fox, *Archeology, History and Custer's Last Battle*, p. 153.

[44]Marquis, *Wooden Leg*, p. 232.

At the other end of the ridge, Armstrong sent a squadron to check the area of the north ford. Reporter Mark Kellogg accompanied the men to the river. The men found the ford with no trouble and continued to move along the Little Big Horn when all at once the bushes exploded! Indians, concealed among the vegetation, opened fire with rifles and bows and arrows upon the soldiers. Chief trumpeter Henry Voss and reporter Kellogg fell from their saddles, their bodies filled with arrows.[45] The remainder of the detail retreated back to the command upon Cemetery Ridge.

Indian pressure began to increase upon Custer's battalion, and it was clear they had to move. Custer ordered the two companies to move south and east of Cemetery Ridge, into a basin just below the ridge line. One company moved toward the ridge top, to dislodge Wolf Tooth's band of forty to fifty warriors who had been firing on the command for some time.[46] At approximately this same time Company C fell apart on the south part of Calhoun Hill. All attention focused on the southern end of the field as the gunfire reached a deafening crescendo. Tom looked to the south and saw the bay horses of his command racing across the ridge top. It was clear that at least one section of the command had encountered massive resistance and met with momentary defeat. He saw soldiers running back up the ridge, toward brother-in-law Jimmi's positions.

The survivors of Company C reached Calhoun's troopers. They ran among the kneeling soldiers shouting and crying. Hard on their heels came dozens of warriors who had pursued the troopers up the ridge. Their shots struck several of Calhoun's men and the rest of the warriors, emboldened by their comrades joined in the rush. The infectious fear that permeated the survivors of Company C, coupled with the torrential

[45] Sandy Barnard, *I Go With Custer*, p. 144.
[46] Stands In Timber, *Cheyenne Memories*, p. 199.

onslaught of the Lakota and Cheyenne warriors, began the disintegration of Calhoun's company.

White Bull, a Lakota warrior among the Indians who rushed Calhoun's company, noticed a soldier who stood his ground, firing at the onrushing Indians. White Bull decided to kill the trooper and ran toward him. The soldier saw White Bull, but his Springfield was empty, and in desperation he threw the rifle at White Bull. White Bull knocked the rifle aside, grabbed the soldier, and pulled him to the ground. White Bull, armed with his pistol in one hand and a riding quirt in the other, lashed the soldier in the face with the leather. The soldier reached for the pistol in White Bull's hand, and tried to wrest it from the warrior. White Bull called out to his friends for help and several braves ran over and killed the soldier.[47] The entire rush occurred in a matter of just a few minutes.[48]

Jimmi Calhoun and his lieutenant, John Crittenden, had taken their places behind the skirmish line. The two officers moved up and down the line, shouting encouragement and pointing out targets to the men firing. Calhoun tried to stop the mad rush of C Company survivors, and hold his own men in check, but was unable to stem the tide. He and Crittenden fell in a maelstrom of bullets and arrows. A warrior knelt beside Calhoun's body and quickly scalped him.[49] Another warrior noticed Crittenden's glass eye and stood marveling at it for a few moments. Finally he shot an arrow into the eye and moved on to kill more soldiers.[50]

Hearing the roar of gunfire to the south, Tom and the command, under orders, moved toward the sound of the battle. Company E, the gray horse troop, moved off of Cemetery Ridge toward the crest of the hill. Company F moved

---

[47]Hardorff, *Lakota Recollections*, p. 116.
[48]Fox, *Archeology, History, and Custer's Last Battle*, pp. 153–154.
[49]Hardorff, *The Custer Battle Casualties*, p. 104.   [50]Taunton, *Custer's Field*, p. 40.

into the basin area below the ridge top, in support of Company E.[51] Warriors, again using the ridge top for protection, began shooting into the battalion. Custer ordered Company E to dismount and move up the slope as skirmishers to dislodge the hostiles. The warriors saw the soldiers' movement and attempted to break the troop. Mounted warriors lashed their horses over the ridge top and raced down toward the approaching soldiers. Tom and the soldiers fired point blank into the onrushing Indians who broke and scattered across the field.[52]

Captain Keogh's men were oblivious to the disintegrating situation on the western side of the ridge. Keogh's men had taken up positions a hundred yards below the ridge top, completely out of sight of the rest of the command, and themselves unable to see anything of the battle, except for the extreme left of Calhoun's skirmish line. They had been firing at warriors concealed along the bluffs several hundred yards to the east and southeast. They were under no real pressure and continued trading long range shots with the warriors. Suddenly, they became aware of the tremendous roar of gunfire from their rear, and a few moments later, saw troopers cascading down the slope toward them followed closely by hordes of warriors. Runs The Enemy said, "It looked like a stampede of buffalo."[53] The warriors rode alongside the panic-stricken soldiers and shot them down.

Keogh, still mounted upon his horse, Comanche, rode to the right of his line, and stared incredulously at the onslaught descending upon him. The warriors to the east saw the mad rush come over the hill and joined in the melee. Keogh tried to steady his men, but was struck just below the left knee by a bullet. The bullet passed through Keogh's leg and shattered

---

[51]Fox, *Archeology, History, and Custer's Last Battle*, p. 183.
[52]Ibid., p. 182.
[53]Michno, *Lakota Noon*, p. 233.

the bones of his lower leg.[54] He grimaced with pain as several of his men assisted him down from his saddle. At that moment the warriors charging the men from the south fired into the group of men surrounding Keogh wounding or killing them all.[55] The rest of the men fired a few shots at their attackers and began running uphill, toward Custer's battalion. A few troopers held their intervals and moved back in skirmish order, holding the Indians temporarily at bay. The panic, however, was contagious, and many men joined the remnants of companies C and L in a headlong race for Custer's positions on the other side of the ridge. One by one, the Lakota and Cheyenne warriors shot the soldiers and, in an instant, whatever cohesion remained, vanished. It was every man for himself.

Tom heard the roar of the battle coming closer. He reached the ridge top in time to see the disintegration of Keogh's command, and the flood of refugees scrambling up the ridge. Almost at that same moment, concealed Indian warriors in the gullies north and west of E troop jumped up and stampeded the gray horses.[56] F Company now also came under fire from Indians moving up the ravine in their front, and Armstrong motioned for them to come up the hill.

Custer's command had begun skirmishing with the warriors in Medicine Tail Coulee at approximately 1600 hours. For the greater part of an hour, the command experienced no appreciable pressure, maintaining a long range fire fight with the Indians. The situation, though, changed dramatically in the last few minutes as the final collapse of the command occurred in less than a quarter of an hour. Tom looked about and saw the landscape alive with hundreds of Indians. Several hundred more were in the distance, riding back and

---

[54]Hardorff, *The Custer Battle Casualties*, p. 102.
[55]Nichols, *The Reno Court of Inquiry*, pp. 453–454.
[56]Fox, *Archeology, History, and Custer's Last Battle*, p. 189.

forth, shouting encouragement to their comrades, and firing at the soldiers.

Armstrong shouted for the men to take up positions along and below the crest of the ridge. Tom rode up to the top of the ridge, a flat space not more than thirty feet across. From this vantage point, Tom recognized the completeness of the collapse of the command. He saw Indians riding over the soldiers' positions on Calhoun Hill, and below the summit at Keogh's positions. He observed the warriors moving from man to man, killing the wounded and mutilating their bodies.

In those last desperate moments several troopers on the hilltop circled their mounts and shot them in the head. The horses' bodies fell in a circle, and the men crouched behind them, all the while firing at the Indians moving toward them.[57] Approximately seventy soldiers, all that remained of Custer's five companies, banded together on the ridge top and the slope just below the summit.

The warriors nearest the soldiers on the hilltop continued their strategy of remaining hidden, using the terrain as a shield, exposing themselves only long enough to fire and drop down. Hundreds of Indians used their bows and arrows, raining death from above without ever exposing themselves to the soldiers. The intense gunfire from the encircled troopers filled the air with smoke from their rifles.[58]

The soldiers' position below the ridge offered little protection from the galling fire of the encroaching warriors. Man after man was shot. Those horses that had not been shot, bucked and pulled away from the soldiers. Bullets struck the ground all around the men, kicking up clouds of dust. The soldiers moved closer to their companions, seeking the illusionary safety of their comrades. This only succeeded in giving the warriors easier targets, and more men fell.

---

[57]Taunton, *Custer's Field,* p. 14.
[58]Michno, *Lakota Noon,* p. 252.

The evening before, a group of young Cheyenne warriors proudly announced they would take a suicide vow, and they declared in the next battle they would sacrifice their lives defeating their enemy. The suicide boys now began to shout that their time was coming. Other warriors heard them and shouted for everyone to be ready. As soon as the suicide boys entered the battle, everyone else would charge in and destroy the white soldiers.[59]

Tom and the other soldiers fired as fast as they could, vainly struggling to keep the warriors at bay. The Indian's gunfire intensified and more troopers fell with each passing minute. In those minutes before the final rush, Armstrong fell wounded with a gunshot wound in the left side of the chest.[60] The bullet entered the chest cavity and struck the left lung, and the thoracic cavity began to fill with blood and air escaping from the lung. Armstrong's breathing became more and more labored with each passing second.

The exact sequence of events surrounding Tom's death will never be known. What can be determined from Indian testimony and soldier observations concerning his body offer the only clues to his demise. Tom was probably alive during those last minutes before the final Indian onslaught. Most of the men were wounded or already dead, and their fire had slackened dramatically. During those last moments a bullet slammed into Tom's right arm.[61] He dropped his rifle to the ground, and reached over with his left hand to check his arm. He discovered his right arm was numb from the wound down to the fingers and he could not raise his arm at all. The bullet had shattered the humerus. Tom drew his revolver from its holster. His right arm hung uselessly at his side, throbbing with pain.

---

[59]Stands In Timber, *Cheyenne Memories,* pp. 200–201.

[60]Hardorff, *The Custer Battle Casualties,* p. 24.

[61]Windolph, *I Fought With Custer,* p. 30.

Lakota warriors began shouting it was time for the suicide boys. Firing from the soldiers' position continued to slacken, until only a few sporadic shots came from the hilltop. Warriors called out that all of the soldiers were dead. The suicide boys gave a shout and rushed the soldiers.[62] Tom heard the shouts of the warriors and leveled his pistol at the onrushing Indians. Other soldiers quickly dropped their rifles, pulled their pistols, and fired wildly at the tidal wave of Indians descending upon them. In an instant, the warriors were among the soldiers. Indians and soldiers filled the air with their whoops of victory and cries of defeat. The dust cloud created by the final charge made it nearly impossible to differentiate ally from enemy. Those horses still alive, bolted and ran in every direction, trampling both soldiers and Indians. The hilltop came alive, in a swirling mass of dust, and wrestling bodies.

As the warriors rushed among the soldiers those men not crippled by injuries bolted, running pell-mell downhill toward a deep ravine which emptied into the river beyond. Boston and Autie Reed were among those men racing against hope for their lives. They ran a few hundred feet when they and several others were cut down by a salvo of bullets.[63]

Approximately twenty-eight men jumped into the illusionary sanctuary of the ravine. Once inside, however, they discovered the head of the defile was so steep that they could not see out. In their panic they had entered a position that left them in just as much peril as the ridge top. Warriors slithered up to the edge of the ravine, and fired down into the mob of soldiers. A few soldiers tried to crawl up the steep sides of the gully in order to try and return fire. Those who made it fired only a few shots before they were hit and fell back into the ravine. In a few moments, all of them were dead.[64]

---

[62]Marquis, *Wooden Leg*, pp. 237–238.   [63]Taunton, *Custer's Field*, p. 27.
[64]Ibid., p. 14.

The battlefield fell into an ominous silence. A few shots still range out, but for the most part the battle was over. The warriors stood looking at each other, amazed that it was over so quickly, and that they had killed all of the soldiers. Warriors mounted their horses and rode back across the river to inform the village that the white soldiers were all dead. Other Indians helped the wounded back across the river, to their anxious families. Women and children crossed the Little Big Horn by the hundreds to scour the field for anything that might be of use. They especially wanted to look for wounded soldiers.

According to Indian tradition a soldier, who could have been Tom, had been knocked down by the charging warriors. Possibly the pain of his broken arm caused him to temporarily lose consciousness. He awoke to see the warriors killing the wounded, and stripping them of their clothes. He raised up and leveled his pistol at a warrior, but he could not find the strength to pull the trigger. In an instant the warrior was on top of him. He pulled the gun from Tom's left hand, placed the barrel against his head, and pulled the trigger. Tom's head exploded upon the impact of the bullet, and he fell backward on the ground. The warrior dropped the pistol, ripped open Tom's shirt, and pulled it off. Another warrior arrived and began tugging Tom's boots off, then his pants. One of the warriors pulled his knife and stabbed Tom in the chest, pulling the blade down the center of his body. Tom's intestines, freed from the constriction of the abdominal wall, spilled out onto the ground. The warrior then cut a deep gash into each of Tom's thighs. The warrior wanted all of Tom's scalp, so he grabbed Tom's left arm and pulled the body over, onto the stomach. The warrior straddled Tom's back and reached down with his hand and grabbed the front of Tom's hair. In a flash the warrior's knife began to cut away the scalp. The angle was a bit awkward, so the warrior pulled back on Tom's hair and dropped the blade to his throat. He cut deeply into the soft tissue, until he could feel the knife strike against Tom's spine. With Tom's head free, he continued cutting off the scalp.[65] The proud warrior held his bloody trophy in the air and let out a shout of victory. He picked the items that he wanted, and went in search of other wounded men. Later, the women came to Tom's body. One of the women had a mallet, and she beat Tom's skull until his cranium was crushed. A young boy tested his aim by shooting arrows into Tom's crushed skull.[66]

A warrior walked over to Armstrong's body. He could see the white man was dead, but to make sure he shot him in the temple with his pistol. The warriors began to strip Armstrong's body. According to Indian tradition, a warrior cut the tip from Armstrong's little finger while another warrior shoved an arrow up Armstrong's penis.[67] When the women came to Armstrong's body, some said they recognized him. According to their tradition, one of them took a bone used for sewing and shoved it into each of Armstrong's ears, to help him hear better in the next life. He had been warned about attacking the Cheyennes again many years ago; evidently he did not hear well.[68]

Wooden Leg walked among the dead and saw something he had never seen before. He saw a scalp that grew on the man's face. The white soldier's face whiskers grew very long, extending several inches below the dead man's chin. Wooden Leg looked at the man for a moment and decided he wanted this new kind of scalp. He pulled his knife and cut one side of the man's face, down below the chin.[69] Willie Cooke, the fleet-footed champion of the Seventh, was left to the women and boys.

---

[65]Hardorff, *The Custer Battle Casualties*, pp. 23–25.

[66]Graham, *The Custer Myth*, p. 345.

[67]Hardorff, *The Custer Battle Casualties*, pp. 19-21.

[68]Michno, *Lakota Noon*, p. 289.

[69]Marquis, *Wooden Leg*, p. 240.

The mutilation of the dead continued for several hours. Sometimes the women would begin cutting a man only to find that he was feigning death. Their struggle, though, was over in a few moments. Young boys came to the field and began using the soldiers' bodies for target practice. Some young men moved the soldiers into different positions and fired at them. Several men were propped so their buttocks were in the air. The Indian boys laughed as their arrows struck their targets again and again.

During this time, the combined commands of Reno and Benteen busied themselves by improving their defensive positions, and arguing amongst themselves over what they should do next. A few minutes after Benteen's battalion arrived, Lieutenant Varnum heard heavy gunfire from somewhere to the north of their position, in the direction of Custer's command. Varnum turned to Lieutenant Wallace and exclaimed, "Jesus Christ, Wallace, hear that? And that!"[70] It was evident to quite a few men that Custer was heavily engaged with the hostiles. Captain Thomas Weir, a Custer favorite, listened to the growing sound of gunfire. Finally, he could take no more and went to Reno and asked for permission to ride to the sound of the guns. Reno refused. The discussion between the two men grew heated, with Reno adamant that no move would be undertaken. Weir, angry and frustrated at his superior officer, stormed away, his mind made up. He approached his men and calmly mounted his horse. His troopers saw him, and assumed he had been ordered to move out, and without hesitation, the troopers mounted and followed their captain.[71]

Weir moved his command to the high place, immediately to the north of Reno's defensive position. Indian opposition

---

[70]Nichols, *The Reno Court of Inquiry,* p. 160.
[71]Willert, *Little Big Horn Diary,* p. 363.

was almost nil at this point, and the command accomplished
the move without molestation. Several of Benteen's captains
saw Weir's troop move out and assumed he had been ordered
to go. Benteen assumed the same and ordered his battalion to
saddle up and follow Weir. Eventually, Reno's men loaded up
their wounded and also followed the rest of the command
toward the high point, now known as Weir Point.

Weir continued to hear firing coming from the north as
his command hurried to the high point. At the base of the
hill, Weir ordered Lieutenant Edgerly to post the men in
skirmish order. Weir ascended to the top of the hill and, upon
reaching the summit, trained his eyes to the ridges to the
north. Great clouds of dust covered the ridge tops, obscuring
Weir's view. Lieutenant Edgerly arrived, and he too, strained
his eyes to the north. Others arrived and someone produced a
pair of field glasses. The men took turns, scanning the distant
ridges. Edgerly thought he saw, "A great many Indians, riding around and shooting at objects on the ground."[72]

Sometime later, Benteen and his command came up. The
officers ascended Weir Point and joined those already there.
Lieutenant Luther Hare arrived from Major Reno, with
orders to link up with Custer, if possible. Weir and the others
looked off to the north and saw the ridges filling with Indians. The Lakota and Cheyenne warriors saw the soldiers on
the hill top, and began moving to the south to engage them.
Reno arrived a few minutes later, as did the leading elements
of hundreds of victorious warriors. It was clear that the command could not stay where they were, and the decision was
made to retrace their steps and return to the defensive position on the bluffs. The move was affected with several casualties, and the soldiers spent the rest of the evening under siege.

Throughout the night men who had been abandoned earlier in the day by Reno in his retreat from the timber made

---

[72]Ibid., p. 369.

their way up the bluffs. The next morning, Lieutenant
Charles DeRudio tried to make his way out of the timber. He
crept through the underbrush until he came to the riverbank.
He cautiously looked for any Indians. At that moment he
heard horsemen downstream. The valley bottom was still
dark. The rising sun had not yet penetrated the river bottom.
In the half-light of the morning, DeRudio thought he saw
Tom Custer upstream. The man was dressed exactly as Tom,
and was even riding a sorrel colored horse. DeRudio was
convinced of the rider's identity and hollered, "Tom, send
your horse across here!" The man turned in the saddle and
looked around. Several Indian scouts appeared alongside
"Tom." DeRudio, frantic for help, stood up and shouted
again, "Here I am, don't you see me?" As soon as he shouted,
the Indian "scouts" and "Tom" opened fire on him. Indians!
DeRudio slipped back into the underbrush, and hid. He
made his way back to the command later.[73] The siege continued for the rest of the day, with the soldiers holding off any
attempts by the Indians to rush their lines.

The morning of the twenty-seventh dawned and showed
the soldiers an imposing sight. The great village had disman-
tled before daylight and was now moving down the valley
under the eyes of the embattled troopers. Far to the north the
soldiers saw a great dust cloud. The soldiers believed another
attack was forming and strengthened their defensive positions.
The soldiers watched the approaching mass for an hour before
it was determined that the men moving toward them were soldiers. The survivors of the Seventh scanned the oncoming
troops for signs of the gray horse troop, but no such unit could
be seen. The troops reasoned that it must be Crook's command. It could not be Terry or Gibbon because Custer would
be with them, and the gray horse troop could not be seen.[74]

[73]Nichols, *The Reno Court of Inquiry,* p. 324.
[74]Willert, *Little Big Horn Diary,* p. 420.

It was, infact, Gibbon's command that moved slowly up the valley and soon entered the area of the great camp. It was obvious to the soldiers that the Indians had departed in great haste, littering the ground with articles and utensils the Indians would not have abandoned. There were other objects, more ominous, such as articles of clothing belonging to members of the Seventh Cavalry. It became evident to Gibbon that a major battle had taken place. Several teepees were investigated, and found to be filled with dead warriors. The scouts reported seeing dozens of dead buffalos across the river, on the hills opposite the campsite and Gibbon dispatched an officer to investigate. A few moments later troopers observed figures on the bluffs a couple miles to the south, and several scouts were sent to investigate.[75]

Terry and Gibbon passed a few anxious minutes when the officer who had been sent across the river returned. The officer, visibly pale, saluted and with a voice filled with emotion said, "I have a very sad report to make. I have counted one hundred and ninety-seven dead bodies lying in the hills!" Terry and Gibbon, the blood draining from their faces, looked at each other and asked, "White men?" "Yes, white men," came the reply.[76]

A few minutes later a messenger from Major Reno galloped up, overjoyed at seeing the relief column. The command hurried down the valley toward Reno's positions while more of Reno's men crossed the river to intercept the relief column. They all asked the same question, "Have you seen Custer?" Reno and Benteen told Terry and Gibbon of their two-day ordeal. Gradually, as the officers compared their information, the reality of the situation dawned on them. Custer and most, if not all, the men of his battalion were dead.

At daylight on the twenty-eighth, Major Reno moved his

---

[75]Gibbon, *Adventures On The Western Frontier*, p. 137.
[76]Ibid., pp. 137–138.

command down the bluffs to Custer battlefield to bury their fallen comrades. Godfrey went to Custer Hill and counted forty-two bodies and thirty-nine dead horses.[77] There on the hilltop lay General Custer, Cooke, Algernon Smith, George Yates, Lieutenant Reilly, and the color guard.[78]

A heated argument began to brew over one mutilated body lying about twenty feet from General Custer's body. Godfrey and Dr. Porter debated back and forth over the identity of the dead man. Finally, the argument was settled when they turned the body over and discovered the initials "TWC" tattooed on the right arm.[79] Charles Windolph came up to the hill top, and he recognized Tom's body by the tattoos. He later wrote, "There was in the army no more popular man than Tom Custer. He was young, handsome, a prince of good fellows and full of that bravery that ever characterized the Custers."[80]

First Sergeant John Ryan assisted in burying the two brothers. He later wrote:

> At the foot of the knoll we dug a grave about 18 inches deep, and laid the body of the general in it. We then took the body of Tom and laid him beside the general. Then we wrapped the two bodies in canvas and blankets, and laid them side by side in the shallow grave, and then covered them with earth. We took a basket from an Indian travois, turned it upside down, and put it over the grave, and laid a row of stones around the edge to keep the wolves from digging them up. This was the best burial of any of the bodies on the field.[81]

Nothing could separate the Custer boys. Neither time, nor distance, war, or peace—not even death. Tom was now, as his father once hoped, a soldier of the Lord.

---

[77]Taunton, *Custer's Field*, p. 8.
[78]Ibid., p. 11.
[79]Ibid., p. 29.
[80]Windolph, *I Fought With Custer*, p. 171.
[81]Barnard, *Custer's First Sergeant John Ryan*, p. 198.

Custer Ridge–Little Bighorn Battlefield. *Carl F. Day Collection.*

CHAPTER FOURTEEN

At Rest

The Great Sioux War continued throughout the summer, fall, and winter. The Sioux and Cheyenne were harried across the Plains by an army of "Custer Avengers." In the spring of 1877, those left alive either surrendered or escaped into Canada. The Treaty of 1868 was declared null and void by the federal government and the Native American tribes found themselves stripped of their reservation lands, especially the Black Hills. A few hundred acres scattered between the Pine Ridge Reservation and the Standing Rock Reservation, both located in South Dakota, became the permanent home of the Lakota and Cheyenne.

The battlefield of the Little Big Horn lay silent under the summer sun. The first storms washed away the clods of dirt that covered the bodies of the slain soldiers. Wolves and coyotes visited the field, attracted by the overpowering stench of death that flew heavily on the winds. Flies and birds of carrion attacked the exposed portions of the decaying bodies. Four legged carnivores dug up the dead and pulled their mangled bodies apart, feasting on the rotting flesh. The animals made no distinction between officer or enlisted man, hero or coward.

While the bones of the Seventh lay bleaching in the Montana sun, life went on for the living. On 9 August 1876, Margaret Calhoun, acting as the executor of Tom's will, filed a petition in the probate court of Monroe County asking that her brother's estate be given to their mother, Maria.[1] Persuant to

---

[1] The Estate of Thomas Ward Custer, Probate Court of Monroe County, Monroe, Michigan.

the law, notification of the petition for probate was published for three consecutive weeks in the Monroe newspaper. The notice stated the petition hearing was to take place on 1 September 1876, and all persons having an interest in the estate should be present.[2] Margaret provided the court with an inventory list of Tom's estate which contained eight hundred-seven dollars and ninety-eight cents, one spring wagon valued at sixty dollars, one double harness set valued at twenty-five dollars, and one double seated sleigh worth twenty-five dollars.[3] No one contested the will or placed a lien against the estate and on 5 October, Margaret remitted to Maria the sum of nine hundred—two dollars and seventy eight cents. The balance of the cash in Tom's account was paid to Margaret for expenses.[4] The disposition of the wagon, sleigh, and harness is unknown.

More legal maneuvering surrounding Tom followed the next year. On 31 March 1877, Monroe attorney J.K. Rauch filed a motion with the federal government on behalf of Maria Custer. Tom's elderly parents were dependent upon the money Tom sent home to them to augment their own meager resources. Now, without Tom's generosity, they found themselves strapped financially. The lawyer applied to the government on Maria's behalf for the pension she deserved as Tom's mother. When Maria died five years later on 13 January 1882, Attorney Rauch petitioned the government on Emmanuel's behalf when he applied for Tom's pension.[5]

The notoriety of the battle, coupled with the popularity of General Custer, ensured the public would find their way to the hills overlooking the Little Big Horn. Reports began to circulate that the battlefield was being ravaged by more than wild animals. General Sheridan wrote that:

> I am half inclined to think, strange as it may appear, that nearly all the desecration of graves at the Custer battlefield has been done by curiosity hunters in the shape of human coyotes. I have myself

[2]Ibid.   [3]Ibid.
[4]Ibid.   [5]Office of the Circuit Clerk, Monroe County, Monroe, Michigan.

Battlefield markers for Tom Custer (fore-ground) and George Armstrong Custer, Little Bighorn National Monument. *Carl F. Day Collection.*

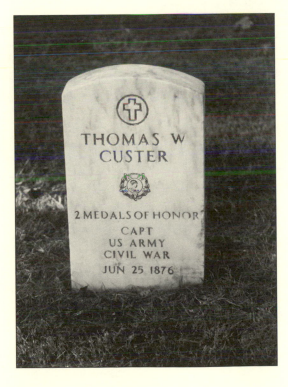

Tom Custer's final resting place-Fort Leavenworth National Cemetery. *Carl F. Day Collection.*

heard of one or two cases where bones were exhibited as relics from
the Custer battlefield.[6]

Libbie Custer desired to see her husband buried at West
Point. She and Armstrong had often spoken of his love for the
academy and his desire to be buried there. Emanuel Custer also
wanted to bring his son, Boston, home to rest with his family.
Tom's brother-in-law, David Reed also desired to bring home
the remains of his son, Harry. Other families also expressed
desires to have their loved ones brought back to civilization.
Philip Sheridan, aware of the wishes of the various family
members, and of the morbid fact that the battlefield was being
picked over by ghouls, gave the necessary orders to facilitate the
requests of the families and take the precautions to stop the dis-
turbance of the fallen troopers' final resting places. He ordered
his brother, Lieutenant Colonel Michael V. Sheridan, his aide
de camp, to go to the battlefield, recover the bodies of the officers, and attend to the reburial of the enlisted men.[7]

Colonel Sheridan left Chicago and arrived at the mouth of
the Tongue River on 20 June. Here he was met by Captain
Henry Nowlan and a detachment of troopers from the Seventh
Cavalry. Sheridan explained to the men their mission and gave
them instructions to proceed over land to the headwaters of the
Little Big Horn River. Sheridan continued by boat to the rendezvous point where he found Captain Nowlan already in camp
and waiting for him. The command continued overland to
their destination. They arrived on 2 July and made camp on the
site of the Indian encampment. Sheridan and a few other officers crossed the Little Big Horn to visit the battlefield. Curly,
one of the Crow scouts with Custer who survived the battle,
accompanied the troopers. He pointed out to Sheridan the different points of the battlefield and tried to explain what happened and what he saw. Sheridan listened to Curly's account
with a growing suspicion. Later, he dismissed the scout by say-

---

[6]Graham, *The Custer Myth*, pp. 370–371.   [7]Ibid., p. 373.

ing he believed Curly abandoned the column well before the battle began and so he discounted the Indian's tale.[8]

The map drawn by Lieutenant Edward Maguire, an engineer with Terry's relief column, showed the men where the officers were buried. The map was plainly marked with numbers assigned to the graves of the individual officers. According to Sheridan, the remains of General Custer, Tom, Yates, Calhoun and the other officers were located without difficulty and removed from the earth. They carefully removed the remains of each man from their shallow grave and placed them in pine boxes. Lieutenant Crittenden was identified, his remains placed in a coffin, and reburied where he fell at the request of his father. With the officers' remains in custody, the soldiers began to attempt to rebury the rest of the fallen troopers. Two days later, the men left the battlefield and returned with their precious cargo to post number two, later renamed Fort Custer. They placed the coffins in the only building of the post, where they remained until 7 July. The coffins were transferred onto the steamer *Fletcher* and began their journey to Fort Lincoln. The remains arrived at Fort Lincoln where they were temporarily interred at the post cemetery until the proper coffins arrived from Chicago. With the remains transferred to the coffins, they began their trip by rail to Chicago and their various destinations.[9]

There is a problem with the proceedings as documented by Michael Sheridan. His report on the expedition may contain more wishful thinking than actual fact. According to other members of Sheridan's party, events did not quite move as Colonel Sheridan reported to his commander brother. When Sheridan reached the battlefield, he referred to Maguire's map to assist him in locating the graves of the officers. Marker number one on Maguire's map marked the final resting place of Tom and Armstrong. As stated earlier this grave was the most elaborate of the soldiers' graves. It was some eighteen inches deep, covered by

[8]Ibid., pp. 373–374.   [9]Ibid., p. 375.

dirt and canvas, weighted down by stones to deter the wolves and coyotes from disturbing the grave. The stake at the head of the grave bore the name of George Custer. When they opened the grave they uncovered skeletal remains, lying on a blue soldier blouse. They removed the bones from the grave and carefully laid them in the pine box. The soldiers then picked up the blouse, which bore the name of an enlisted man. The soldiers found themselves with a dilemma. They decided they had the wrong remains and returned them to the grave. "They found another body and placed it in the coffin. I think we got the right body the second time," wrote Sergeant Michael Caddle.[10]

Scout George Herendeen observed the proceedings and later stated,". . . out of the grave where George Custer was buried not more than a handful of bones were picked up. The body had been dragged out and torn to pieces by coyotes and bones scattered about."[11] Herendeen went on to say it was he who pointed out the soldiers had made an error in the removal of the first body. He was quite adamant that he identified the correct spot and the remains of Armstrong and Tom Custer.[12] The uncertainty of the soldiers about the graves particularly bothered Sergeant Caddle who later wrote to a friend, "It was a disconcerting discovery to find that even the general could not be satisfactorily identified."[13]

It is apparent the graves of the Custers had been disturbed, whether by wolves or from relic seekers who identified the Custer name on the stake and rifled the grave. In any event, the grave was sufficiently disturbed to cause the members of the detail to be confused. There should have been no doubt in their minds about the gravesite. The map plainly marked the location of the grave, the only prominent grave on the hill side to contain two corpses. It is clear no such grave was found, which led to the confusion. Sergeant Caddle reported the battlefield

[10]King, *Tombstones For Bluecoats*, p. 10.   [11]Ibid., p. 11.
[12]Ibid.   [13]King, *TombstonesFor Bluecoats, Vol. 11.*

was littered with the skeletal remains of Custer's command. Sheridan, under the guidance of Herendeen, apparently gathered bones from the area where Custer had been buried.

There is every possibility he did not gather the bones of Tom and Armstrong Custer. He could not find them. Their grave was open and its contents scattered across the hillside, mingling with the remains of the other men buried in the area. Herendeen was right in his assessment of the scene; the grave had been opened and robbed. Sheridan had no desire to report to his brother, or to the families and civilization in general, that the remains of their loved ones were scattered across the Montana hills. He made every effort to locate the graves, and when he had done so, removed the remains either in the grave or nearest the grave. He reported to his brother that his mission had been successful, both in the removal of the remains of the officers and the re-interment of the enlisted men. With his mission "completed" the command left the battlefield.

A few weeks later the battlefield received more visitors. Dr. William Allen and some friends visited the battlefield on 18 August. He later wrote:

> When our party gained the other side, a horrible sight met our eyes. Each soldier yet lay where he had fallen on that fated day . . . each with a small amount of dirt thrown over him, with his head protruding from one end of the grave and his feet from the other . . . their skulls in many instances had been crushed.[14]

Later, a detachment of the Seventh Cavalry visited the field. Private Frank Mulford revealed his shock as he wrote, "The bodies of our dead had never been properly buried . . . Their bones, divested of clothing by the heartless and brutal savages and of flesh by wolves and other animals, lie bleaching on the ground where they fell.[15] These words, written less than a month after Sheridan's visit to the battlefield plainly state Sheridan's mission accomplished very little.

---

[14]Graham, *Custer Myth*, p. 371.   [15]Ibid., pp. 378–379

That same month the commander of Fort Custer dispatched a sergeant to the home of a local rancher for the purpose of retrieving artifacts taken from the battlefield. The official order read as follows:

> The commanding officer has been informed that you have in your possession a human skull taken from the battlefield, labeled a "trophy," and belonging to, or intended for, Mr. Patrick, one of the proprietors of the stage line—you will hand it to the bearer, Sergeant Barnaby, who has verbal instructions concerning it.[16]

A reporter from Massachusetts visited the battlefield and later described it for his readers: "The work of the burial was so carelessly and hastily done . . . shortly after the battle, that the first heavy rains laid bare the bodies and ravenous wolves devoured the flesh of the victims of this massacre and scattered their bones about the field." These words were written a few weeks after the Sheridan detail had been to the battlefield and supposedly reburied the dead. It is abundantly clear that their efforts were half-hearted at best.

Meanwhile, preparations proceeded to give a proper burial to the honored dead. General Custer's remains proceeded to West Point, New York, for burial. Tom, Jimmi Calhoun, George Yates, Donald McIntosh, and Algernon Smith arrived at Fort Leavenworth, Kansas, on 2 August. Captain S.C. Ilsley, designated by the department commander to officiate over the proceedings, met the Chicago, Rock Island and Pacific train at the station and escorted the coffins to the post chapel where, surrounded by a guard of honor, they lay in state all night. Visitors quietly entered the chapel to pay their last respects to the fallen officers. The memorial service followed on the next day, 3 August at 5 P.M.[17]

The flag-draped caskets rested on biers in the chapel in front of the alter. From left to right lay Captain Yates, Tom, Lieutenant Smith, Jimmi Calhoun, and Lieutenant Donald

---

[16]King, *Tombstones For Bluecoats*, p. 12.   [17]*Leavenworth Daily Times*, 4 August 1877.

McIntosh. The small chapel filled to overflowing. Margaret Custer Calhoun, representing the Custer family, accompanied by her brother-in-law Lieutenant Fred Calhoun occupied a prominent place in the chapel. Mrs. Algernon Smith and Mrs. George Yates sat nearby, as well as General William T. Sherman's wife. General John Pope, the district commander and his entire staff sat near them in their dress uniforms. The service began with the burial service of the Episcopal Church, read by post chaplain Reverend John Woart. Reverend W. N. Page of Leavenworth and Reverend Mr. Anthony of San Francisco also took part in the service.[18]

At the conclusion of the service, the procession slowly filed out of the chapel. The Guard of Honor removed the remains of the officers, and placed them on caissons drawn up outside the chapel doors. The band of the Twenty-third Infantry led the procession to the place of interment. Captain Ilsley, marshall of the day, followed the band. Behind him marched two companies of the Twenty-third Infantry with reversed arms under the command of Captain Joseph T. Haskell. The caisson carrying the remains of Jimmi Calhoun followed. The pall bearers placed Tom's coffin on the second caisson. Major J. P. Wright and Colonel D. G. Swaim flanked the caisson, followed by a sergeant with a detail of four men. A horse draped in black, led by a cavalryman, followed each caisson. The remains of Captains Yates, Smith, and Lieutenant McIntosh followed in succession.[19]

A great crowd lined the streets of the post, all hoping to glimpse the coffins and pay their last respects. Soldiers placed along the route had difficulties keeping the roadway clear from the throngs of onlookers. The procession moved eastward from the chapel to Arsenal Road, then south to the avenue leading to the garrison. After reaching the parade ground, the procession was saluted by the post artillery who fired their guns in honor of

[18]Ibid.   [19]Ibid.

the dead. The mourners followed the road around the parade ground and moved toward the post cemetery. All the while the band played a somber dirge. At last, they reached the cemetery, filled with over two thousand mourners and the morbidly curious. The pall bearers removed the coffins from the caissons and moved them into place over their final resting places. A final service was read by the ministers. With the service ended, the caskets were lowered into the earth. As a final honor, Captain Ilsley showered the coffins with flowers and wreaths.[20]

In 1916, President Woodrow Wilson signed a law which established new criteria for winning the Medal of Honor. The medal was established during the Civil War, and at the time was the only official recognition of bravery. Men earned the medal for a variety of reasons. Many men, however, received the medal for actions which contained no element of danger whatsoever. The twenty-nine men comprising the honor guard of President Lincoln's coffin all received the award. The entire Twenty-Ninth Maine received medals as an inducement for their re-enlistment. The new legislation required that a review board be established to reevaluate the files of past winners, eliminating those citations that did not really earn the medal under the new guidelines. In June 1916, a review board of five generals, headed by Tom's old friend, Lieutenant General Nelson Miles, began their work. They evaluated 2,625 files and, when finished in February 1917, removed 911 citations from the official roster. The board reviewed Tom's citations and determined that his efforts merited the awards under the new guidelines.[21]

Tom, however, had long since entered into his eternal sleep. He is, as his father once wished, a soldier of the Lord. World without end, Amen.

---

[20]Ibid.
[21]Editors of Boston Publishing Company, *Above and Beyond*, pp. 122–123.

Bibliography
and Index

Bibliography

ARCHIVAL SOURCES.

Appomattox Court House National Battlefield
Fort Abraham Lincoln Historical Foundation
Harrison County Historical Society
Little Big Horn National Battlefield, E.B.C.
Michigan State Archives
Monroe County Courthouse
Monroe County Historical Society
Monroe County Library
Museum of the Confederacy
National Archives, T.W.C. Collecton.
North Dakota Historical Society
New York Public Library, Merington Collection.
Ohio State Historical Society

PUBLISHED SOURCES.

Above and Beyond. Editors of Boston Publishing Company. Boston, Massachusetts: Boston Publishing Company, 1985.

Adams, Jacob. *The Diary of Jacob Adams.* Columbus, Ohio: Ohio State Historical Society, 1930.

Alexander, Edward P. *Fighting for the Confederacy.* Edited by Gary Gallagher. Chapel Hill, North Carolina: Chapel Hill Press, 1989.

Ambrose, Stephen. *Crazy Horse and Custer.* Garden City, New Jersey: Doubleday and Company, 1975.

Athearn, Robert G. *William Tecumseh Sherman and the Settlement of the West.* Norman, Oklahoma: University of Oklahoma Press, 1995.

Barnard, Sandy. *Custer's First Sergeant John Ryan.* Terre Haute, Indiana: AST Press, 1996.

_____. *I Go With Custer. The Life and Death of Reporter Mark Kellogg.* Bismarck, North Dakota: Bismarck Tribune Press, 1996.

Barnitz, Albert. *Life In Custer's Cavalry: Diaries and Letters of Jeannie and Albert Barnitz.* Edited by Robert Utley. Lincoln, Nebraska: University of Nebraska Press, 1977.

Bearss, Ed and Christopher Calkins. *The Battle of Five Forks.* Lynchburg, Virginia: H.E. Howard Inc., 1985.

Bell, Raymond Martin. *The Ancestry of Maria Ward Kirkpatrick Custer, 1807-1882.* Washington, Pennsylvania: Privately printed, 1992.

The Black Hills Engineer. November, 1929.

Brininstool, E. A. *Troopers With Custer.* Lincoln, Nebraska: University of Nebraska Press, 1989.

Burkey, Blaine. *"Custer Come At Once!" The Fort Hays Years of George and Elizabeth Custer.* Privately Published, 1976.

Calkins, Christopher. "With Shouts of Triumph and Trumpets Blaring.' George Custer versus Rufus Barringer At Namozine Church, April 3, 1865." *Blue and Gray.* August, 1990.

_____. "We Had A Spirited Fight At Namozine Presbyterian Church, April 3, 1865." *Blue and Gray Magazine.* August 1990.

Canfield, Captain S.S. *History of the 21st Regiment Ohio Volunteer Infantry in the War of the Rebellion.* Toledo, Ohio: 1893

Carroll, John, Editor. *Custer's Chief of Scouts: The Reminiscences of Charles K. Varnum.* Lincoln, Nebraska: University of Nebraska Press, 1987.

_____. *The Benteen-Goldin Letters On Custer and His Last Battle.* Lincoln, Nebraska: University of Nebraska Press, 1974

_____. *The Teepee Book.* New York: Sol Lewis Company, 1974.

_____. *They Rode With Custer.* Mattituck, New York: John M. Carroll and Company, 1993.

Carroll, John and Lawrence Frost, editors. *Private Theodore Ewert's Diary of the Black Hills Expedition of 1874.* Piscataway, New Jersey: CRI Books, 1976.

Charles, Allen D. *Narrative History of Union County, South Carolina.* Spartanburg, South Carolina: The Reprint Co. Press, 1960.

Chandler, Melbourne. *Of Garryowen In Glory: The History of the Seventh Cavalry Regiment.* Annadale, Virginia: Turnpike Press, 1960.

Chester, Captain H. W. *Recollections of the War of the Rebellion.* Wheaton, Illinois: Wheaton History Center, 1986.

Clark, Charles M. *Scalp Dance: The Edgerly Papers on the Battle of the Little Big Horn.* Oswego, New York: Heritage Press, 1985.

Clark, Walter, editor. *Histories of the Several Regiments and Battalions From North Carolina in the Great War, 1861-1865.* Raliegh, North Carolina: 1901.

Crawford, Samuel. *Kansas in the Sixties.* Ottawa, Kansas: 1994

Custer, Chester. "The Kusters and Doors of Kaldenkirchen, Germany" *Pennsylvania Mennonite Heritage,* Vol. 9, No. 3 (July, 1986).

Custer, Elizabeth B. *Tenting On the Plains.* Norman, Oklahoma: University of Oklahoma Press, 1971.

_____. "A Beau Sabreur." In *Uncle Sam's Medal of Honor: Some of the Noble' Deeds for Which the Medal Has Been Awarded. Described by Those Who Have Won It.* Edited by Theodore F. Rodenbaugh. New York, 1886

_____. *Boots and Saddles or Life In the Dakotas with General Custer.* Norman, Oklahoma: University of Oklahoma Press, 1977.

_____. *Following the Guidon.* Norman, Oklahoma: University of Oklahoma Press, 1966.

_____. *The Civil War Memories of Elizabeth Bacon Custer.* Edited by Arlene Reynolds. Austin, Texas: University of Texas Press, 1994.

_____. *The Custer Family So United.* Edited by Arlene Reynolds Killian. Privately printed, 1993.

Custer, George Armstrong. *My Life On the Plains.* Norman, Oklahoma: University of Oklahoma Press, 1976.

Custer, Milo. *Custer Genealogies.* Bryan, Texas, 1974

Custer, Nevin. "General Custer As His Brother Remembers Him." *Detroit Michigan News Tribune.* 10 May 1910.

Custer, Thomas Ward. Military Service Records. National Archives, Washington D.C..

Early, Jubal. *Jubal Early's Memoirs.* Baltimore, Maryland: THe Nautical & Aviation Publishing Company of America, 1989.

Evening Post. Grand Rapids, Michigan. 12 February 1892.

Foner, Eric. *Reconstruction.* New York: Harper and Row, 1988.

Fougera, Katherine Gibson. *With Custer's Cavalry.* Lincoln, Nebraska: University of Nebraska Press, 1986

Fox, Richard Allen. *Archeology, History, and Custer's Last Battle.* Norman, Oklahoma: University of Oklahoma Press, 1993.

Freeman, Douglas Southall. *Lee's Lieutenants*. New York: Charles Scribners Sons, 1943.

The Freeman's Journal. Cooperstown, New York. February 25, 1875.

Frost, Lawrence A. *With Custer's Cavalry in '74. James Calhoun's Diary of the Black Hills Expedition*. Provo, Utah: Brigham Young University Press, 1979.

_____. *Custer's 7th Cav and the Campaign of '73*. El Segundo, California: Upton and Sons, 1986.

_____. *The Custer Album*. Seattle, Washington: Bonanza Press, 1964.

_____. *The Court Martial of General George Armstrong Custer*. Norman, Oklahoma: University of Oklahoma Press, 1968.

_____. *General Custer's Libbie*. Seattle, Washington: Bonanza Press, 1976.

Gibbon, John. *Adventures On The Western Frontier*. Bloomington, Indiana: Indiana University Press, 1994.

Godfrey, Edward Settle. *The Field Diary of Lt. Edward Settle Godfrey*. Portland, Oregon: The Champoeg Press, 1957.

_____. *Custer's Last Battle*. Olympic Valley, California: Outbooks Press, 1976.

Goplen, Arnold O. *The Historical Significance of Fort Lincoln State Park*. Bismarck, North Dakota: North Dakota Parks and Recreation Dept., 1988.

Graham, William A. *The Custer Myth*. New York: Bonanza Books, 1953.

Grant, Ulysses S. *Personal Memoirs of U.S. Grant*. New York: Dacapo Press, 1982.

Gray, John. *Centennial Campaign*. Norman, Oklahoma: University of Oklahoma Press, 1976.

Greene, Jerome A. *Lakota and Cheyenne Indian Views On the Great Sioux War 1876–1877*. Norman, Oklahoma: University of Oklahoma Press, 1994.

_____. *Evidence and The Custer Enigma*. Golden, Colorado: Outbooks Press, 1986.

Hammer, Kenneth, Editor. *Custer In '76. Walter Camp's Notes on the Custer Fight*. Norman, Oklahoma: University of Oklahoma Press, 1990.

_____. *Men With Custer: Biographies of the 7th Cavalry*. Edited by Ron Nichols. Hardin, Montana: Custer Battlefield and Museum Association Inc., 1995.

Hardorff, Richard. *Lakota Recollections of the Custer Fight.* Lincoln, Nebraska: University of Nebraska Press, 1997.

_____. *Hokahey! A Good Day To Die!* Spokane, Washington: The Arthur H. Clark, Company, 1991.

_____. *The Custer Battlefield Casualties.* El Segundo, California: Upton and Sons Publishers, 1989.

Harrison, Joseph T. *The Story of the Dining Fork.* Cincinnati, Ohio: The C.J. Krehbebiel Company, 1927.

Hedren, Paul, editor. *The Great Sioux War.* Helena, Montana: Montana Historical Society Press, 1991.

Hoig, Stan. *The Battle of the Washita.* Garden City, New York: Doubleday and Company, 1976.

Humphreys, Andrew H. *The Virginia Campaigns of 1864–1865.* Wilmington, North Carolina: Broadfoot Publishing, 1989.

Hutton, Paul A. *The Custer Reader.* Lincoln, Nebraska: University of Nebraska Press, 1992.

_____. *Phil Sheridan and His Army.* Lincoln, Nebraska: University of Nebraska Press, 1985.

Keim, De Benneville Randolf. *Sheridan's Troopers On the Borders.* Glorietta, New Mexico: Rio Grande Press, 1977.

Kidd, James Harvey. *Personal Recollections of a Cavalryman.* Ionia, Michigan: The Sentinel Press, 1908.

King, William Kent. *Tombstones For Bluecoats.* Privately Printed, 1980.

_____. *Tombstones For Bluecoats. Vol. II.* Privately Printed, 1980.

Korn, Jerry. *Pursuit to Appomattox.* Alexandria, Virginia: Time-Life Books, 1987.

Leckie, Shirley. *Elizabeth Bacon Custer and the Making of a Myth.* Norman, Oklahoma: University of Oklahoma Press, 1993.

Libby, O.G. *The Arikara Narrative of the Campaign Against the Hostile Dakotas.* Glorietta, New Mexico: Rio Grande Press, 1976.

Liddic, Bruce and Paul Harbaugh. *Camp On Custer.* Spokane, Washington: The Arthur H. Clark Company, 1995.

Linderman, Gerald. *Embattled Courage.* New York: Free Press, 1987.

McDonough, James Lee. *Stones River—Bloody Winter In Tennessee.* Knoxville, Tennessee: University of Tennessee Press, 1980.

McPherson, James. *Ordeal By Fire: The Civil War and Reconstruction.* New York: Alfred A. Knopf Company, 1982.

Marquis, Thomas B. *Wooden Leg, A Warrior Who Fought Custer*. Lincoln, Nebraska: University of Nebraska Press, 1931.

Merington, Marguerite. *The Custer Story*. New York: Adair Publishing Co., 1950.

Michno, Gregory F. *Lakota Noon*. Missoula, Montana: Mountain Press Publishing Company, 1997.

Millbrook, Minnie Dubbs. *Michigan Medal of Honor Winners*. Lansing, Michigan: State of Michigan Publishing Office, 1966.

Miller, David Humphreys. *Custer's Fall*. Lincoln, Nebraska: University of Nebraska Press, 1957.

Monaghan, Jay. *Custer—The Life of General George Armstrong Custer*. Lincoln, Nebraska: University of Nebraska Press, 1959.

Nichols, Ron, editor. *The Reno Court of Inquiry*. Crow Agency, Montana: Custer Battlefield Historical and Museum Association, 1992.

Porter, Horace. *Campaigning With Grant*. Secaucus, New York: Blue and Gray Press, 1984.

Richmond, Rebecca. *Life In Kansas With The Custers*. Edited by Alice T. O'Neill. Privately printed, 1995.

Robertson, James. *Tenting Tonight—The Soldier's Life*. Alexandria, Virginia: Time-Life Books, 1984.

Robinson, Charles M. *A Good Year To Die*. New York: Random House, 1995.

Ronsheim, Milton. *Life of General Custer*. Monroe, Michigan: Monroe County Library System, 1991.

Sarf, Wayne. *The Little Bighorn Campaign*. Conshohocken, Pennsylvania: Combined Books, 1993.

Sheridan, P. H. *Personal Memoirs of P.H. Sheridan*. New York: Charles M. Webster, and Company, 1888.

Stampp, Kenneth. *The Era of Reconstruction*. New York: Vantage Books, 1965.

Stands-In-Timber, John and Margot Liberty. *Cheyenne Memories*. New Haven, Connecticut: Yale University Press, 1967.

Street, James Jr. *The Struggle For Tennessee*. Alexandria, Virginia: Time-Life Books, 1985.

Taunton, Francis B. *Custer's Field: "A Scene of Sickening Ghastly Horror."* London, England: The Johnson-Taunton Military Press, 1986.

Taylor, William O. *With Custer on the Little Bighorn.* New York: Viking Press, 1996.

Trelease, Allen W. *White Terror: The Ku Klux Klan Conspiracy and Southern Reconstruction.* Baton Rouge, Louisiana: Louisiana State University Press, 1971.

Tremain, Henry Edwin. *The Last Hours of Sheridan's Cavalry.* New York: Bonnell, Silver and Bowers, 1904.

Urwin, Gregory J.W. *Custer Victorious.* Rutherford, New Jersey: Associated University Press, 1983.

U.S. War Department. *The War of The Rebellion: A Compilation of the Official Records of the Union and Confederate Armies.* Washington D.C.: U.S. Government Printing Office, 1880-1901. *Confederate*

Utley, Robert. *The Lance and Shield: The Life and Times of Sitting Bull.* New York: Henry Holt and Company, 1993.

_____. *Cavalier In Buckskin.* Norman, Oklahoma: University of Oklahoma Press, 1988.

Wallace, Charles B. *Custer's Ohio Boyhood.* Freeport, Ohio: Freeport Ohio Press, 1993.

Warner, Liberty. *Liberty Warner Collection.* Bowling Green University, Bowling Green, Ohio.

Wemett, W.M. "Custer's Expedition to The Black Hills In 1874." *North Dakota Historical Quarterly.* Vol VI, no. 4 (July 1932).

Wert, Jeffrey D. *Custer: The Controversial Life of George Armstrong Custer.* New York: Simon and Schuster, 1996.

Whittaker, Frederick. *A Popular Life of General George Armstrong Custer.* New York: Sheldon and Company, 1876.

Willert, James. *Little Big Horn Diary.* La Mirada, California: Upton and Sons, 1977.

Windolph, Charles. *I Fought With Custer.* Lincoln, Nebraska: University of Nebraska Press, 1987.

Index